Americas

Telecourse
Faculty Guide

BY BERNADETTE M. ORR

with Bárbara Cruz

Americas is a coproduction of WGBH Boston
and Central Television Enterprises for Channel 4, U.K.,
in association with the School for International and
Public Affairs at Columbia University, the Latin American
and Caribbean Center at Florida International University,
and Tufts University.

The *Americas Study Guide* is part of a college credit course from

 From
The Annenberg/CPB Collection

New York   Oxford
OXFORD UNIVERSITY PRESS, 1993

Cover Image: Peter Martinez

Cover Design: WGBH Design

Printed in the United States of America

ISBN: 0-19-507796-2

This book was developed for use by faculty teaching the *Americas* telecourse. The telecourse consists of 10 one-hour public television programs; a study guide; this faculty guide; a reader, *Americas: An Anthology*, edited by Mark B. Rosenberg, A. Douglas Kincaid, and Kathleen Logan; a textbook, *Modern Latin America*, by Peter H. Smith and Thomas E. Skidmore; and an optional book entitled *Americas: New Interpretive Essays*. All of the publications are available from Oxford University Press.

Americas was produced for PBS by WGBH Boston and by Central Television Enterprises for Channel 4, U.K., in association with the School of International and Public Affairs at Columbia University, the Latin American and Caribbean Center at Florida International University, and Tufts University.

Major funding was provided by the Annenberg/CPB Project, with additional funding from the Carnegie Corporation of New York,* the John D. and Catherine T. MacArthur Foundation, the Rockefeller Foundation, the Corporation for Public Broadcasting, and public television viewers.

The series is closed-captioned for the hearing-impaired.

For further information about the print components of the *Americas* television course, contact:
Americas
Oxford University Press
Attention: College Sales Coordinator
198 Madison Avenue
New York, New York 10016-4314

*The Carnegie Corporation of New York is not responsible for any statements or views expressed in the *Americas* programs or materials.

For more information about television course licenses and off-air taping, contact:
Americas
PBS Adult Learning Service
1320 Braddock Place
Alexandria, VA 22314-1698
1-800-ALS-ALS8

For more information about *Americas* videocassettes and print materials, off-air taping and duplication licenses, and other video and audio series from the Annenberg/CPB Collection, contact:
Americas
The Annenberg/CPB Collection
P.O. Box 2345
South Burlington, VT 05407-2345
1–800–LEARNER

Acknowledgments

We would like to thank the Annenberg/CPB Project, whose support made this telecourse possible. We would also like to thank the Carnegie Corporation of New York, the John D. and Catherine T. MacArthur Foundation, the Rockefeller Foundation, and the Corporation for Public Broadcasting, as well as Channel 4, U.K.

We also wish to acknowledge the direction and guidance of Mark B. Rosenberg of the Latin American and Caribbean Center at Florida International University, the Project Education Director, who began thinking about creating a television course on Latin America and the Caribbean in late 1982; Alfred C. Stepan, former Dean of the School of International and Public Affairs at Columbia University, who joined the endeavor as Chair of the Academic Advisory Board in 1984; and Peter Winn of Tufts University, who became Project Academic Director in 1985.

In addition, our distinguished board of academic advisers, listed below, provided invaluable assistance in developing both the television programs and the print materials for the telecourse. Margaret E. Crahan provided valuable guidance on three of the units: Unit 2, "Legacies of Empire: From Conquest to Independence"; Unit 8, "Miracles Are Not Enough: Continuity and Change in Religion"; and Unit 11, "Fire in the Mind: Revolutions and Revolutionaries." Peter H. Smith provided direction on two of the units: Unit 3, "The Garden of Forking Paths: Dilemmas of National Development"; and Unit 10, "Get Up, Stand Up: The Problems of Sovereignty." Albert Fishlow assisted with Unit 4, "Capital Sins: Authoritarianism and Democratization." M. Patricia Fernández Kelly and Alejandro Portes reviewed Unit 5, "Continent on the Move: Migration and Urbanization." Kay Barbara Warren and Anthony Maingot provided guidance on Unit 6, "Mirrors of the Heart: Color, Class, and Identity." Cornelia Butler Flora, Helen Safa, and Marysa Navarro-Aranguren helped create Unit 7, "In Women's Hands: The Changing Roles of Women." Jean Franco advised on Unit 9, "Builders of Images: Writers, Artists, and Popular Culture." Franklin Knight greatly assisted with Unit 10, "Get Up, Stand Up: The Problems of Sovereignty," and also reviewed the print materials for Unit 6. Cynthia Arnson assisted with Unit 11, "Fire in the Mind: Revolutions and Revolutionaries"; and Rubén Rumbaut helped create Unit 12, "The Americans: Latin American and Caribbean Peoples in the United States."

The development of the educational print materials was a long process involving the input of many people in addition to those on the academic advisory board. Members of our utilization advisory board, listed below, helped create the structure for the television course materials and reviewed the materials for level and curriculum fit. Special thanks go to Pam Quinn, Chief Utilization Adviser.

Bárbara Cruz, formerly of the Latin American and Caribbean Center at Florida International University, wrote the pilot lesson plan, which was reviewed and tested before the rest of the materials were developed. She also participated in the development of the structure and focus for both the study guide and the faculty guide, and contributed to some chapters. Nancy Lane, Eddie Harcourt, and David Roll of Oxford University Press assisted in the publication of the books.

A special note of thanks goes to the producers, especially to senior editor Adriana Bosch Lemus, WGBH staff, and others whose cooperation helped us create these materials: David Ash, Marc de Beaufort, Pam Benson, Javier Betancourt, Peter Bull, Elizabeth Buxton, Yezid Campos, Margaret Carsley, Tania Cypriano, Ann Downer, Orna Feldman, Rachel Field, Andrew Gersh, Karen Jersild, Kevin Keogan, Gaye Korbet, Julia Mallozzi, Juan Mandelbaum, Rebecca Marvil, Elizabeth Nash, Marisol Navas, Debbie Paddock, Lourdes Portillo, Christina Ragazzi, Jane Regan, João Resende-Santos, Margo Shearman, Virginia Sietz, Roderick Steel, Ann Strunk, Fay Sutherland, Andrés di Tella, Raymond Telles, Joseph Tovares, Mauricio Vélez, Ann Weinstock, Sonia Walrond, Vernonica Young, and Jeanne Zimmerman.

Bernadette M. Orr
Author

Patricia Crotty
Project Director, Educational Print and Outreach

Beth Kirsch
Director, Educational Print and Outreach

Judith Vecchione
Executive Producer

WGBH Educational Foundation
Boston, MA

The Americas Project

CONTENTS

Preface: The Americas Telecourse

COURSE OVERVIEW

Before the end of the century, people of Latin American and Caribbean origin will constitute the largest minority in the United States.

The 33 sovereign states that make up Latin America and the Caribbean represent the United States' most important trade partners in the developing world and most reliable source of many strategic resources, including oil. And, in the next century, our relationship with this vital region will take on even greater significance. Yet much about the history, politics, economics, social structures, and complex relationships between this important region and other world powers eludes us. Too often, our perspective is colored by stereotypes, broad generalizations, and incomplete or inaccurate information.

Americas, an innovative 10-part television series and 13-unit complete television course, brings to life a startlingly diverse region that encompasses great wealth and desperate poverty, countries as tiny as Jamaica and as enormous as Brazil, with democratic and authoritarian governments and a complex, multicultural heritage. The series provokes a re-examination of U.S. relations with its hemispheric neighbors and with people of Latin American and Caribbean origin living in the United States by highlighting key issues and events of the twentieth century, providing a new per-

spective that extends far beyond the limited images and crisis-driven headlines of the nightly news.

Americas presents the human face of important issues from representative countries. Its stories range from personal or family issues, to pivotal moments in history, to aspects of local and international culture. In each case, individual community and country examples illuminate the larger processes affecting the region as a whole.

The challenges facing the countries of Latin America and the Caribbean are daunting, but the responses of the peoples of the region have often been positive and innovative. Many of their strategies, crafted in response to local conditions, offer instructive lessons applicable far beyond the boundaries of their particular situation. Some have had international impact in widely diverse areas: witness the new social and political roles of the Catholic Church in Latin America, the development of unique popular music that enhances cultural identity in the Caribbean states, and the multiclass coalitions forged by women in the countries of the Americas.

In its explorations of the forces underlying the contemporary problems and achievements of Latin America and the Caribbean, *Americas* examines these and other questions:

- What is the meaning of sovereignty in the Americas? Why are sovereignty and nationalism so important throughout the region?

- Has foreign intervention in the region's political and economic affairs helped or hindered the goals of democracy and stability?

- What forces contributed to the heavy international debt burdens confronting many countries in the region?

- Why do rural people continue to migrate to urban areas even as the cities become increasingly unlivable? How does domestic and international migration affect families and countries?

- How have women reconciled their traditional places in family, church, and community with the expression and exercise of political and economic power?

- What are some of the possible future trends for U.S. relations with Latin America and the Caribbean, and for the region's political, economic, and social development?

COURSE OBJECTIVES

The *Americas* telecourse is designed to help students:

- increase knowledge and understanding of the nations of Latin America and the Caribbean.

- see the people of the Americas as creative and productive, actively confronting their problems, and becoming a force on the global scene.

- become aware of the long-standing economic, political, social, and cultural ties that link the United States with the other nations of the Americas.

- gain insight into the future of the nations of the Americas and the impact they will have on this country in coming years.

COURSE COMPONENTS

The 13-unit *Americas* telecourse consists of the following components:

- 10 one-hour video programs

- a study guide

- this faculty guide

- the reader, *Americas: An Anthology*, by Mark B. Rosenberg, A. Douglas Kincaid, and Kathleen Logan, published by Oxford University Press

- the textbook, *Modern Latin America* (3d edition, 1992), by Thomas E. Skidmore and Peter H. Smith, published by Oxford University Press

A book of essays written by members of the *Americas* academic advisory board entitled *Americas: New Interpretive Essays*, edited by Alfred Stepan, published by Oxford University Press, is available as an optional component of the television course.

THE STUDY UNITS

Unit 1

Introduction and Overview (a print-only unit) lays out the structure of the course, including the key themes and issues to be studied. It also surveys the geography and peoples of the region.

Unit 2

Legacies of Empire: From Conquest to Independence (a print-only unit) provides a brief history of the region. The readings outline the precolonial period and trace the history of the Spanish and Portuguese conquest, the years of empire, and the early independence period of the 1800s.

Unit 3

The Garden of Forking Paths: Dilemmas of National Development (program 1) examines the twentieth-century development of the nations and national economies of the Americas. The program focuses on Argentina and includes the Perón years, the military dictatorship of the 1970s, the Malvinas/Falklands War, and the return to civilian government.

Unit 4

Capital Sins: Authoritarianism and Democratization (program 2) begins in the 1960s, when many nations' economic and political systems were in disarray and a move toward authoritarian government swept the region. The film focuses on Brazil, a major and influential nation in the region, whose experience of military rule, economic growth, and redemocratization was echoed elsewhere in the Americas. The program also considers the legacy of the military period and the prospects for future economic and political development in Brazil.

Unit 5

Continent on the Move: Migration and Urbanization (program 3) explores the causes and effects of one of the most important forces transforming the Americas: the migration of vast numbers of people within the region. Set in Mexico, the unit focuses on the steady flow of rural migrants to congested cities, in search of jobs, education, and a better future for their children. Following the fortunes of a migrant family, the film looks at the reality of migrants' lives and the difficult choices that must be made.

Unit 6

Mirrors of the Heart: Color, Class, and Identity (program 4) is set on the island of Hispaniola, shared by the countries of Haiti and the Dominican Republic—nations with very different languages, histories, and cultural identities—and in Bolivia, a country with a large indigenous population. It examines the issues of race, class, and ethnic identities in the region and considers how they continue to be redefined by individuals, communities, and nations.

Unit 7

In Women's Hands: The Changing Roles of Women (program 5) looks at how women in the region are adopting, by choice or necessity, new economic and political roles that break traditional stereotypes about gender and family. The spotlight is on Chile, where the social and political turmoil of the 1970s and 1980s challenged women of every social class and pushed many women into political activism and a new understanding of feminism.

Unit 8

Miracles Are Not Enough: Continuity and Change in Religion (program 6) travels to Brazil to observe the explosion of theological debate, social activism, and spiritual revival that is changing a region where religion has long been important in society and politics. The program explores the diversity of religious beliefs and practices in the Americas, where institutional churches coexist with indigenous and African religions and with newer Pentecostal movements.

Unit 9

Builders of Images: Writers, Artists, and Popular Culture (program 7) reflects on the extraordinary creative ferment that has given the region a prominent place on the global artistic map, tracing the evolution of the visual arts, music, and literature in Latin America and the Caribbean. The challenges of artists in the region to define an authentically American voice and their effectiveness in raising important social and political issues are highlighted in this program, which is set in Puerto Rico, Brazil, Mexico, and Argentina.

Unit 10

Get Up, Stand Up: The Problems of Sovereignty (program 8) examines the ways in which nations in the Americas struggle to maintain economic and cultural sovereignty in the face of strong pressures, both foreign and domestic. Set in Colombia, Jamaica, and Panama, the program explores a wide range of threats to sovereignty, from domestic guerrilla movements and the power of the drug lords, to economic dependency and foreign intervention.

Unit 11

Fire in the Mind: Revolutions and Revolutionaries (program 9) looks at the reasons for and composition of revolutionary movements in the region. Set in El Salvador and Peru, the program compares and contrasts the two countries' revolutionary struggles and links these movements to earlier twentieth-century revolutions in Mexico, Cuba, and Nicaragua.

Unit 12

The Americans: Latin American and Caribbean Peoples in the United States (program 10) returns to the United States to explore how communities of Latin American and Caribbean origin are challenging and redefining the U.S. sense of national identity. Using the examples of the long-established Mexican-American community in southern California, Cuban-Americans in Miami, and the Puerto Rican and non-Hispanic Caribbean communities of New York City, the program considers the issues of assimilation and cultural identity, and looks at the growing impact of these communities on the local and national political and cultural scenes.

Unit 13

Course Review (a print-only unit) summarizes the themes and materials of the course and suggests applications of what students have learned in the course to issues of vital importance in the Americas today.

THE ANALYTIC FRAMEWORK

The *Americas* television course provides an analytic framework to define the special character of the region and to guide students through a large body of information. This four-part framework underlies every unit of the course.

International Relations

The region's distinct relationship to the world order results from its experience of conquest, colonization, and settlement, and from the manner in which it was integrated into global economic, political, and cultural systems. The dynamic tension among these elements defines the region as much as its language, culture, and religion, and shapes its key ideals and values.

The region's relatively late incorporation into the world economy has produced complex and often problematic relationships with the major industrial powers. Particularly important is the region's paradoxical stance toward the United States, which is perceived as both benefactor and aggressor, a success story and a cautionary tale, the home of liberal democratic ideals and the source of Yankee imperialism.

Tension

The history of the region's relationship with the rest of the world helps to explain the Americas' high levels of internal tension and social and political instability. The strain shows in a history of authoritarian governments, glaring inequalities of income, and economic policies that have led to some of the highest national debts in the world. These problems are not solely the products of colonial legacies and external constraints, though; they also stem from such internal factors as the concentration of land ownership, the weakness of key democratic political institutions, and the conscious decisions of particular political leaders and social groups to maintain a monopoly on power.

Innovation

The social and political realities of the Americas have spawned innovative cultural, economic, political, and religious responses. New movements that empower women, peasants, and other marginalized groups have arisen, and new literary, musical, and theatrical forms are dissolving national and international cultural barriers. Common to these innovations is the push toward social participation, which is on the rise throughout the region.

Transformation

Ever since the idea of the New World captured the imagination of the European conquerors, a complex process of reciprocal transformation has characterized Latin America's relationship to the world. Transformation born of tension and innovation is still evident today, as the new forms pioneered in the Americas are altering the world's intellectual and imaginative landscape.

Latin American and Caribbean literature and the theology of liberation claim worldwide attention. Multiclass coalitions in which women have set forth new political agendas serve as models for organizing women in other parts of the world. In response to the region's crisis, Latin American social scientists have produced some of the field's most original thinking on the economic and political problems of developing countries. And, paradoxically, the size of the region's foreign debt has given it enormous leverage in the world economy while its importance in international trade continues to expand.

In geopolitical terms, the countries of the Americas have emerged as key actors. For example, Brazil's resources and economic strength promise to make it a growing global force in the coming decades; Cuba has exercised an influential role in the region and throughout the developing world; and Mexico has become increasingly important as a potential member of a North American Free Trade Zone.

THE TELEVISION PROGRAMS

The 10 one-hour television programs, corresponding to Units 3 through 12 of the telecourse, examine the contemporary history, politics, culture, economics, religion, and social structures of this important region, as well as past, present, and future influences on change in the area. Moving personal stories from representative countries illustrate larger themes.

THE STUDY GUIDE

Ten of the 13 study guide units correspond directly to the 10 television programs, two print-only units precede the television programs, and a final print-only unit concludes the course. The study guide is designed to prepare students to view each television program critically, and to help them evaluate their understanding of what they have seen. It also integrates the program material with assigned readings in the textbook and anthology, and reinforces the themes of the telecourse.

Each unit of the study guide includes the following sections:

- **Unit Summary**: provides an outline of the material presented in the textbook and anthology readings for the unit, as well as a description of the television program.

- **Key Issues**: lists critical questions that address the learning objectives for each unit.

- **Glossary**: defines key terms, individuals, and concepts presented in the unit, with pronunciation guides for any non-English words.

- **Overview**: summarizes the information covered in the unit, integrating the program with the material included in the reading assignment.

- **Reading Assignment**: indicates required readings from the textbook and anthology.

- **Unit Review**: states the learning objectives of the unit.

- **Self-Test Questions**: includes multiple choice, true or false, and identification/short answer questions to prepare students for examinations. Correct answers with sources are provided at the back of the book.

- **Questions to Consider**: poses open-ended questions that encourage critical thinking about the issues presented in the unit.

- **Resources**: lists nonfiction, fiction, films, recordings, and other materials to encourage students to pursue questions or interests that may develop as they complete the unit.

THE FACULTY GUIDE

The faculty guide corresponds to the study guide, with two print-only units preceding broadcast of the 10 television programs, and a final print-only unit concluding the course. The faculty guide includes background information on important concepts addressed in each program, integrates the programs with the textbook and supplementary readings, and includes a test bank and supplemental resources.

Each unit of the faculty guide includes the following components:

- **Unit Summary**: provides a brief outline of the material presented in the textbook and anthology readings for the unit, as well as a description of the television program, if there is one.

- **Learning Objectives**: lists 6–10 objectives that highlight concepts your students should master.

- **Overview**: summarizes the content of the unit, emphasizing major themes and concepts and relating the program to the unit's assigned textbook and anthology readings.

- **Student Reading Assignment**: lists sections from the textbook, *Modern Latin America*, and the relevant chapter from *Americas: An Anthology*.

- **Writing Assignments/Discussion Questions**: includes two to six questions to foster critical

thinking and provide a basis for class discussion or written assignments. These questions are deliberately open-ended, encouraging students to distill lessons from material in the unit rather than simply to recapitulate facts and concepts.

- **Suggested Activities**: suggestions for short-term projects, most designed to engage students in research or in observing and relating what they are learning about Latin America and the Caribbean to their own lives.

- **Resources**: provides annotated listings of non-fiction, fiction, film, curriculum materials, and recordings relevent to each unit. In most units, the list includes both academic references and numerous publications aimed at a general audience, which are also included in the study guide. You may wish to consult these to deepen your own understanding of the course concepts, refer students to them, or photocopy sections or articles for distribution to distant learners enrolled in your class. The film listings include information on format and distribution. If your institution has an audio-visual department that can purchase or rent supplementary materials for faculty, you may be able to arrange to use one or more of the suggested videos in a regular or special meeting of your class.

- **Test Bank**: includes multiple choice, identification/short answer, and essay questions based on concepts introduced in the anthology, textbook, study guide, and accompanying television programs. These questions may be reproduced directly from the faculty guide units to be used as quizzes or compiled in a final examination, or excerpted or modified as appropriate to your situation. Correct answers to the questions are listed at the end of each unit.

THE ANTHOLOGY

Americas: An Anthology
Edited by Mark B. Rosenberg, A. Douglas Kincaid, and Kathleen Logan
380 pages

Oxford University Press, 1992
ISBN 0-19-507792-X

Key source materials tailored to fit the structure of the television course make this anthology a valuable resource. *Americas: An Anthology* brings together vivid accounts of places and events, speeches, profiles, interviews from national newspapers and magazines, oral histories, excerpts from a wide range of literature, policy papers, and other readings. Many of the readings are translations from Spanish, Portuguese, and French sources.

Each chapter contains an introduction that sets the stage for the readings and links them to the film and the other print components of the course.

THE TEXTBOOK

Modern Latin America
Third Edition
Thomas E. Skidmore and Peter H. Smith
approximately 450 pages
Oxford University Press, 1992
ISBN 0–19–507648–6 (hardcover)
ISBN 0–19–507649–4 (paperback)

Modern Latin America, the textbook for this course, is a critically acclaimed text already widely used in colleges and universities. The authors, one of whom is a member of the *Americas* academic advisory board, have updated the book to coincide with the television course premiere. The textbook is an important companion to the television pro-grams, setting each film in historical context. Its in-depth, case-study approach guides students through the major countries and the region as a whole in a straightforward, clear, and readable style.

THE BOOK OF ESSAYS

Americas: New Interpretive Essays
Edited by Alfred Stepan
approximately 320 pages
Oxford University Press, 1992
ISBN 0-19-507794-6 (hardcover)
ISBN 0-19-507795-4 (paperback)

Americas: New Interpretive Essays is an optional addition to the television course for upper-level students and is a supplement to traditional courses on Latin American and Caribbean studies. The book is composed of original essays written as a companion to the series by leading scholars, who are members of the *Americas* academic advisory board. Each essay expands on the themes and materials presented in the program and other print materials of the course, with the goal of presenting the most current and innovative interpretations in each issue area. The authors are prominent social scientists and humanists in Latin American and Caribbean studies. The editor, Alfred Stepan, is Burgess Professor of Political Science at Columbia University and is an internationally recognized Latin American scholar.

Teaching a Telecourse

Higher education has been adapting and changing in response to a growing demand for more flexibility and convenience, especially from part-time students. A reflection of these changes is seen in the expanding role of television as an instructional methodology. Today, television-based courses offered in all fifty states enroll more than 500,000 students yearly through the cooperative efforts of public television stations, cable systems, and more than nine hundred participating colleges and universities.

THE FACULTY ROLE

The role of the telecourse instructor is just as crucial and requires just as much preparation and dedication as in traditional courses. Because a telecourse is a self-contained instructional unit, it is possible for learning to occur with less personal contact between students and the faculty member assigned to a course. As a result, your role and involvement as an instructor will vary depending on:

- how your institution coordinates the course and defines your responsibilities.

- the level (lower or upper division, amount of credit) at which the course is being offered.

- the extent to which you want to shape the course to reflect your own area of specialization and interests.

- the limitations and restrictions under which your students will be functioning (distance, schedule conflicts, other physical restrictions).

Within the parameters just described and within the guidelines established by your institution, you may perform a variety of roles. In its most narrow definition, your role could be that of a course manager who is responsible for organizing a syllabus, sending materials to students, receiving and evaluating assignments, grading examinations, and responding to students' questions. However, research indicates that most students, even though they are self-motivated, prefer some level of instructor-initiated interaction, as well as the opportunity to meet occasionally with fellow students. Students' needs and preferences may expand the role of a telecourse instructor to encompass the

Note: This section was adapted from telecourse materials for *The Africans*, produced by WETA-TV, Washington, D.C.

functions of tutor, discussion leader, research director, and mentor.

Although some students are truly homebound or prefer to be independent learners, studies have revealed that students benefit from review sessions and group discussions or occasional seminars. However, since one of the unique features of the telecourse concept is that it allows students to do their work at home, on-campus visits and attendance at special events can be less frequent than in traditional instructional formats. Despite the departure from tradition allowed by the use of television as an instructional medium, it is important that a mechanism be provided to allow regular student-faculty and student-student contact. In fact, evaluators of college instruction have emphasized the importance of regular contact between students and the faculty member. ("Learning technologies should be designed to increase, and not reduce, the amount of personal contact between students and faculty on intellectual issues," according to *Involvement in Learning*, Final Report of the Study Group on the Conditions of Excellence in American Higher Education, sponsored by the National Institute of Education, October 1984.) Probably the best way to accomplish this is to arrange regular on- or off-campus meetings between the faculty member and the class. Attendance at such meetings can be optional, but attendance should be encouraged so that students can derive maximum benefit from the learning experience. Circumstances may require that you adopt nontraditional methods of contact with your students, such as by telephone or computer (see below under "Conducting the Telecourse").

Likewise, research indicates that students benefit from tests, quizzes, and writing assignments scheduled at regular intervals throughout the course. These activities encourage students to keep up with their assignments and provide feedback on their performance in the course. To assist you in planning and preparing writing assignments and examinations, each unit of this faculty guide includes suggestions for writing assignments, along with multiple choice, short answer/identification, and essay questions that can be used for writing assignments or as aids for student review.

Planning and organizing a telecourse is not unlike preparing a traditional course, except that much of the energy normally exerted in the classroom is instead concentrated in planning and prep-

aration. A telecourse requires that you carefully design the week-by-week activities and that you clearly articulate course expectations. The ultimate success of the course will still depend to a large extent on how adept you are at dealing with the students, even though your relationship is somewhat different. The course components provide a solid foundation for learning; your adaptability, imagination, and creativity can enhance the experience.

Preparing the Course

The key to successful course presentation is planning. You need to institutionalize the course within the administrative and academic processes of your school. The following tasks are proposed as preparation activities for teaching *Americas*.

1. Become familiar with the concept of telecourse learning and successful implementation strategies.
2. Identify administrative or academic policies and procedures that will govern the offering of the course, and make note of any special exceptions.
3. Identify the type and level of services that will be available to you as the course instructor and to your students.
4. Identify the public television station or stations offering the course and establish contact with the station or with your institutional liaison to the station. Obtain information about the broadcast schedule of the course. Establish procedures for dealing with changes in the station's broadcast schedule.
5. Establish contact with your public relations office, and become familiar with the promotional materials developed to publicize the course.
6. Obtain desk copies of the course materials, and review the faculty guide; the study guide; the reader, *Americas: An Anthology*; the textbook, *Modern Latin America*; the optional book of essays, *Americas: New Interpretive Essays*; and any other books you plan to use. Change, omit, or add assignments and readings as you see fit to ensure that the course meets your

institution's requirements for academic credit.

7. Develop a detailed syllabus that correlates the television broadcasts and reading assignments with activities, writing assignments, examinations, on-campus sessions, and other activities related to the course.

8. Prepare a letter of orientation that can be mailed to enrolled students after they register or upon request before they register. Also, try to arrange an initial meeting with enrolled students so that they can become acquainted with you and with each other and can learn about the material to be covered, your plans for the course, library and audio-visual services available to them, and your expectations (see suggestions below for an orientation session).

9. If possible, preview the television programs; otherwise, view them as they are broadcast.

10. Verify that your bookstore has ordered sufficient copies of the book(s) that you have selected for the course.

CONDUCTING THE TELECOURSE

In general, telecourse students are highly motivated individuals; however, some students will express a certain amount of insecurity with the process. Keep in mind that these courses attract new students who are unfamiliar with college learning; and even those who have completed college-level work will probably be unfamiliar with the processes of distant learning and independent study. You can reduce their anxiety by providing clear directions and support materials.

LETTER OF ORIENTATION

Your most important communication with students taking the *Americas* telecourse will be the letter of orientation, the first contact after registration. This letter should confirm the student's registration and extend a welcome to the course. The letter should contain all the crucial information the student needs to participate in the course and to complete the course requirements successfully. More specifically, your letter should:

1. Reassure the student and express wishes for a rewarding experience.

2. Introduce you, the instructor, and describe your background, experience, and interest in the subject. Also provide phone numbers, office location, office hours, telephone conference hours, and any other essential information on how to reach you for assistance.

3. Provide specific information about the content of the course and your expectations concerning work assignments, participation in seminars, examinations, and deadlines. Also establish a grading policy and provide sufficient details to avoid subsequent misinterpretations.

4. Identify required print materials by name and list costs. Also provide information on the location and operating hours of the bookstore.

5. Include information on the week-by-week activities of the course and correlate this information with the television broadcast of the programs.

6. Identify the support services available to telecourse students and provide information on how to use these services.

7. Indicate when and where on-campus seminars or group discussions are to be held; specify whether they are optional. Also enclose a campus map and provide directions.

8. Indicate clearly where and when examinations will be held, as well as your policy on make-up examinations.

9. Include a special section identifying provisions for the homebound student.

ORIENTATION SESSION

Your first and possibly only opportunity to meet with all of your students is the orientation session. Ideally, the session should be scheduled for a day and time that will minimize possible conflicts with other activities or commitments. A number of institutions schedule the orientation session on a Saturday afternoon. Some programs schedule two separate sessions on different days and at different times to give their students an option. The purpose of the orientation session is to meet your students in person, to introduce them to the campus, and to have them meet their fellow students.

You should use every resource possible to make this a meaningful session and to create an environment that facilitates interpersonal communication. More specifically, you should aim to accomplish the following:

1. Welcome the students to your institution and the course.
2. Introduce yourself, with the purpose of establishing rapport with the students, conveying your interest in the subject matter, and making clear your availability as a tutor, mentor, or problem solver.
3. Have the students meet and exchange telephone numbers and addresses in order to establish a learning support system and to encourage the exchange of ideas outside of scheduled class meetings.
4. If possible, match up experienced television course students with first-time students of telecourses. The ratio does not have to be one-to-one.
5. Describe the course expectations, your standards of scholarship, academic and administrative policies governing the course, and the evaluation methods you will use to judge students' performance.
6. Review with students the broadcast schedule and the correspondence between television programs and print materials, and recommend study patterns appropriate for learning the subject matter.
7. Discuss support services and explain how and where they can be used.
8. Explain what you plan to accomplish during optional on-campus sessions held during the term.
9. Devote time to individual sessions with students who have expressed concerns or with students who need special attention.

ADDITIONAL CONTACT WITH STUDENTS

As you conduct the *Americas* telecourse, you will need to initiate and maintain additional contacts with students to ensure that they are making satisfactory progress and to provide interaction and feedback. You may want to consider the following activities:

1. Shortly after the start of the course, call your students to ask how they are managing.
2. At various intervals throughout the course, call your students just to keep in touch.
3. Encourage students to call you during prearranged telephone conference hours.
4. Develop four to five newsletters and mail them on pre-established dates. Use the newsletters to remind students of important assignments, events, or activities.
5. Encourage students to submit written materials on time, and *promptly* return their work with useful comments. Schedule the first written assignment to be due no later than three weeks into the course to encourage students to start out on the right foot.
6. Schedule on-campus seminars or group discussions to provide students with an opportunity to exchange views, debate issues, and ask questions.
7. Hold review sessions before midterm and final examinations.

Remember that students who are involved in some form of interaction with the college and have personal contact with the faculty member generally tend to complete the course and achieve at a higher level.

EVALUATING STUDENTS

To help students prepare for tests, multiple choice, true or false, and identification/short answer questions can be found in the study guide for each unit of the course. They can be used as core material for assignments, review sessions, or seminars. Questions and activities in the faculty guide can also be used to prepare students for exams, or they can be modified or used as is for quizzes or examinations.

As you plan for testing or examinations, keep in mind that many students chose this learning mode for its flexibility or convenience. Examinations organized under a rigid schedule will certainly cause conflicts. If your institution does not have a proctored testing center where students can take examinations during a pre-established testing period, you may want to consider scheduling an examination on two separate days at different times, or developing an evaluation process that is not totally dependent on a proctored environment. As with on-campus courses, you may wish to offer alternatives to formal examinations: field projects, term papers, or directed research. These options may be suited to the varied learning styles of your students.

PROFILE OF THE TELECOURSE STUDENT

Although enrollment in telecourses varies greatly, in many of the courses 60–65 percent of the students are women. Students find that the courses provide a structure for the efficient use of time, allowing them to keep up regular commitments in the workplace as well as at home. When surveyed, many say that they would not have enrolled in a standard class on that subject if the telecourse option had not been offered.

Students tend to be busy, working adults who choose telecourses because they reduce travel cost and time and permit a heavier course load without a proportionate increase in commuting or class time. This profile of the student was confirmed through a comprehensive survey coordinated by the Instructional Telecommunications Consortium of the American Association of Community and Junior Colleges (AACJC), with funding from the Annenberg/CPB Project. Some 8,000 junior and community college students who were enrolled in 42 telecourses participated in the survey, which was conducted in the spring of 1984 by member institutions in Arizona, California, Florida, Illinois, Maryland, North Carolina, Oklahoma, and Texas.

The survey showed that more than half of the students had enrolled in telecourses because on-campus classes conflicted with their work or other schedules. The majority of students were married, and more than 50 percent had at least one dependent at home. The percentage of women students enrolled increased with age: 65 percent of the students in the 18–21 age category were women, while nearly 74 percent of those aged 50–59 were women. About 80 percent of the students reported having part-time or full-time jobs, with more males employed full-time than females. More than 4,000 respondents had full-time jobs.

The survey supports previous research, which credits these courses with attracting new students to higher education. As reported, 20 percent of the students were enrolled for the first time in the college where they were taking the course, and about the same number were enrolled only in the telecourse. Almost two-thirds of the students were enrolled in on-campus courses, with 40 percent enrolled for 10 or more credit hours.

Although the AACJC survey focused on students at junior and community colleges, there is a vast amount of documentation from colleges and universities with successful telecourse programs which supports a similar profile of students at four-year institutions. Research commissioned by the Annenberg/CPB Project on student uses of Annenberg/CPB telecourses offered in the fall of 1984, updated in 1988, yielded results that support previous research and also provide new insight on course use.

The national study, conducted by Research Communications, Ltd., was designed to determine factors that influenced students' decisions to take or drop the telecourses, how students used the materials available to them, how effective they found these materials to be, and how this course experience compared to other college course experiences. In this national study, half of the institutions participating were two-year and half were four-year.

The new study reports the following findings:

- The Annenberg/CPB telecourse student is a distant learner but not an isolated one. These students often are enrolled concurrently in on-campus courses, and most have prior experience with on-campus courses. Most live within a half-hour drive of the campus. Although they take telecourses to minimize travel to the campus, this is more a function of scheduling conflicts that would prevent them from taking the course on campus than total inaccessibility to the campus.

- Most students reported that they first learned of the Annenberg/CPB telecourse from the college course catalogue. Students indicated that institutions should expand their promotional efforts to inform students about the availability of telecourses. Mailed brochures were received by more than a third of the students, but the mass media were infrequently cited as sources for hearing about course offerings.

- A key ingredient for a successful telecourse is that the instructor be available to students, either by phone or during office hours. Telecourse students often wanted more optional on-campus class meetings. This finding contradicts the misconception held by some faculty that a telecourse eliminates the need for an instructor.

- The telecourse students found scheduling proper viewing and study time the greatest challenges to their coursework, since they carry heavy job and family responsibilities along with their courseload. Institutions need to recognize the demand on these students' time and facilitate the learning process by scheduling multiple broadcasts of programs in the telecourse and by making backup videotapes available when programs are missed.

The findings from this national study also reveal that nearly half of the students surveyed hope to achieve a master's degree, and almost 4 out of 10 reported that the course in which they were enrolled was in their academic major. When polled on viewing preferences, students selected a variety of time slots, but 7:00–11:00 p.m. was most frequently cited as the best viewing time. Weekends were preferred for viewing by more than 4 out of 10 students. The results also suggest that students are predisposed to one-hour viewing sessions.

The Annenberg/CPB courses were perceived to be as difficult, interesting, and challenging as on-campus courses. Grades for these courses were comparable to those obtained for prior courses students had taken. First-time users of the courses tended to be surprised by the amount of work required, while students who had previously taken telecourses acknowledged the self-discipline demanded in comparison with on-campus courses. Learning patterns and study habits varied considerably among students. About half the students reported that they took notes on the programs while viewing. Those who did not take notes reported that it interrupted the flow of the program or that it was not necessary because the print materials covered the subject matter. Interaction with print materials also varied. Although the print materials were designed to be read before students viewed the programs, the study reports that this did not always happen. Six out of 10 students read the study guide and 4 out of 10 read the textbook prior to viewing the program. Students also varied their patterns of use across the semester, with some starting out reading before viewing and changing this pattern during the semester. The study further reports that, on average, students studied three and a half hours a week in addition to television viewing. They indicated spending a comparable amount of time studying for on-campus courses.

PROGRAM COORDINATION

Although launching a telecourse program is a matter of institutional processes, the basis for a successful program is the development of a team approach that involves administrators, faculty, and support personnel. The number of individuals involved in the enterprise will vary depending upon the institutional structure and the projected size of the telecourse program. If the program encompasses a number of telecourses, or if courses are offered by different academic departments or divisions, it may be advantageous to create a coordinating office within the institution. Otherwise, much of the coordination can be accomplished by the designated faculty member or administrator in whose department the course is to be offered.

If your institution is new to telecourse learning, the following broad recommendations will be useful:

- Formalize a liaison with your public television station and/or the cable system in order to develop a working relationship on issues such as course selection, broadcast schedule, preview materials, on-air promotion, licensing arrangements, enrollment reporting requirements, and, if appropriate, shared print advertising.

- Coordinate academic review and approval of the program and/or individual courses by obtaining and circulating preview materials, initiating course review and approval throughout the academic process of the institution, developing policies and procedures for the program, and clarifying faculty roles and expectations about the course or program.

- Coordinate academic support for faculty and students by arranging for off-air recording of televised lessons, maintaining a copy of the televised lessons for student and faculty viewing, and arranging for flexible registration, testing, and counseling of students.

- Coordinate support for the program with other administrative units, especially in the area of student services and promotion/publicity. Be certain that information about the course is available for the appropriate college catalogues, since students often base their decisions on that resource.

As your institution examines the process of program implementation and its promotional strategies, it needs to identify target populations that will benefit from the program. Telecourses can successfully meet the needs of:

- Current part-time students who normally take one or two courses but, given the opportunity, will carry a telecourse to increase their course load and accelerate progress in completing their program.

- Employees in the workplace who will participate in telecourses as part of an employee development program sponsored or facilitated by the employer.

- Homebound students who, for various reasons, do not have access to the campus or its extension centers as a result of a physical disability, lack of transportation, prolonged illness, or parenting responsibilities. This category can include the incarcerated and the hospital-bound.

- High school students who are academically advanced and interested in being concurrently enrolled in college courses but are unable to attend traditional college classes.

- Undecided prospective students who enroll in telecourses before taking traditional classes because they perceive telecourses as a nonthreatening way of testing their ability to perform college-level work.

Success in the initial telecourse is important because a number of the students will be experiencing their first college course and their first contact with your institution. Frequently, the telecourse provides their first opportunity to meet faculty, observe facilities, learn about other courses, and make decisions about further studies through your institution.

SUPPORT SERVICES

Convenient access to information, facilities, staff, student services, and faculty is of paramount importance to prospective students. Therefore it is crucial that the existence of the telecourse program be clearly explained within the institution and that the necessary level of support for its faculty and students be planned. The support services listed below are proposed as key elements of a successful program. They will also be useful tools for promoting *Americas*.

PROMOTION AND PUBLICITY

Eventually, your most effective promotion will be the testimonials of successful former telecourse students, who will attract new students to your program. Initially, however, you need to recognize that you are introducing a new concept and you need personnel, time, and funds to develop a well-planned promotional effort. To the extent possible, you should involve the professionals within your institution and work closely with your public television station. Consider these ideas:

- Send out to local press the generic public service announcements (PSAs) developed by PBS for use in conjunction with telecourses.

- Ask your local PBS station to broadcast previews of the courses.

- Feature the telecourse program in the schedule of classes and the catalogue.

- Market to your own part-time students.

- Ask your public relations office to prepare radio spots, flyers, and brochures.

- Use direct-mail announcements to selected zip codes in your area.

- Develop newspaper press releases and consider placing ads in your local newspaper.

TELECOURSE INFORMATION

Because you are advancing a new learning concept, you should develop comprehensive information about the program or the individual course. And since prospective students are very likely to be adults, the materials should be presented from a consumer-oriented perspective. As you develop your information, consider these items:

- Provide a general conceptual statement on telecourses as an instructional mode.

- Incorporate a profile of students who are expected to benefit most from the program.

- Provide key admissions and registration information.

- Describe support services and how they can be used.

- Provide a description and explanation of course activities, a schedule of events, course objectives, and grading policies.

- Provide cost information, including tuition and all applicable fees.

- Develop a detailed syllabus for the course and release it upon request.

COUNSELING

A well-informed and readily accessible counseling staff is crucial to a smooth operation. Ideally, the counseling staff should have an opportunity to preview sample lessons, review course materials, and be informed about the mechanics of the program. Counselors and academic advisers should also be made aware of characteristic student profiles for the purpose of guiding potential students to suitable course sections.

REGISTRATION

The registration process should be flexible and structured to meet the needs of working adults. If your current registration system is an open-ended process with convenient hours and multiple locations, further enhanced by telephone or mail registration options, you will meet the needs of prospective telecourse students. If, on the other hand, your existing system is focused on an in-person registration process held over a somewhat limited period of time at a central location, you may want to consider developing more flexible options. You should be aware that the registration staff can play a key role in attracting students. The staff will need to be briefed and to be sufficiently well informed to answer basic questions or to know where to refer students who need additional assistance.

TESTING FACILITY

Access to a testing center can provide flexibility and convenience consistent with the rest of the program. If your institution already operates such a center, you may want to expand its uses to meet the needs of the program. If a center needs to be established, there may be advantages in cooperating with other departments or prospective users. Ideally, a testing center is staffed by paraprofessionals and has accessible daytime, evening, and even weekend hours. Course instructors are encouraged to place each of their examinations on file for a period of one week, during which students must take the examination. The student may choose the most convenient hour and day within that week to be tested at the center. Thus the center offers convenience for both the students and the instructors.

THE TELECOURSE LICENSE

When your institution elects to use a telecourse, it executes a license that governs the appropriate uses of the course and identifies institutional responsibilities. Without presuming to substitute the legal language of the license, here is a broad outline of the institutional responsibilities and the contractual parameters of course uses and applications.

Rights of the Institution

The telecourse license normally conveys to the institution the right:

- to use the specified telecourse for an identified period, usually an academic term.

- to record the television programs by means of videotape, which usually includes the right to record off-air.

- to retain the cassettes only for the term of the license and to use the television program only with students enrolled in the course for whom the institution remits an enrollment fee.

- to make additional copies of the cassettes for use on- or off-campus, provided that the use is limited to students enrolled in the course and that all copies are erased when the term of the license

expires unless other arrangements are made with the PBS Adult Learning Service.

Obligations of the Institution

These are the responsibilities of the institution:

- Return a signed license to the PBS Adult Learning Service.

- Remit payment for the licensing fee.

- Report enrollment in the telecourse.

- Pay the required enrollment fee.

- Maintain accurate records documenting enrollments.

- Erase the television programs or communicate in writing the intent to renew the license agreement.

- Do not physically alter the content of the videocassettes of a course.

Instructors who do not wish to license a complete telecourse but would like to use individual programs in their classrooms may obtain cassettes by calling the Annenberg/CPB Collection, 1-800-LEARNER.

A FURTHER NOTE TO THE INSTRUCTOR

This guide is not a prescription for a course based on the television series. Instead, it is meant as an *aid* to instructors of such a course. Each instructor is free to use all, some, or none of the teaching points, supplementary readings, suggested video resources, or activities. We envision that a course based on the television series will be offered in a variety of formats: the traditional college format, with the class meeting the instructor at least once weekly; open seminar, with minimum but regular face-to-face contact between the instructor and students; or distance delivery, with limited opportunity for direct contact between instructor and students. Wherever possible, we have sought to suggest activities, additional readings and video resources, and teacher-provided materials that would be usable in any course delivery format.

We also envision that faculty members who teach courses based on the television series will come from a variety of disciplines. Accordingly, we have sought to construct this faculty guide in such a way that it will be useful for many different academic areas: geography, political science, history, and literature, as well as Latin American and Caribbean studies.

If your college or university library has a video media section, you may wish to ask the library to acquire additional video resources for this telecourse. We have suggested available video resources for nearly every unit of the telecourse, and all can be rented or purchased from major commercial suppliers.

Unit 1

Introduction and Overview

UNIT SUMMARY

This introductory unit provides background on the physical geography and demographic characteristics of the region and explains the four primary themes of the course. It also introduces the student to two major interpretive theories of political and economic development in the Americas, modernization theory and dependency theory, and provides a few important criticisms of those theories. Unit 1 consists only of print materials, as does Unit 2. Together, these two units provide a background and context for the 10 units that accompany the television series.

LEARNING OBJECTIVES

After completing this unit, students should be able to:

- Identify the major groups of people whose presence in Latin America and the Caribbean has contributed to the complexity and diversity of today's societies in the region.

- Explain the different motivations and methods that characterized the arrival of non-indigenous groups to the region.

- Recognize the most important features of Latin America's physical geography and the impact those features have had on the region's economic development.

- Understand two major theories that scholars have used to explain the unique patterns of social, economic, and political development in Latin America and the Caribbean, and identify some important criticisms of those theories.

- Describe the four basic themes of the course.

OVERVIEW

North America shares many cultural, political, and economic features with Latin America and the Caribbean. The two halves of the Western Hemisphere are connected by both historical and modern ties. But, despite all we have in common with our southern neighbors, many of our current impressions of the region are based on misleading stereotypes and sweeping generalizations. The nations of Latin America and the Caribbean defy precise categorization. The region exhibits great geographic and cultural diversity and a variety of national historical legacies.

The textbook introductory chapter "Why Latin America?" discusses some of the most striking paradoxes of the region in terms of its history, politics, and economic development. The chapter also critiques some of the most common stereotypes of Latin America and the Caribbean and explains the two interpretive theories of modernization and dependency.

The anthology introduction provides the reader with a geographic, economic, political, and cultural overview of the region. Particular attention is given to describing the four themes of the course.

STUDENT READING ASSIGNMENT

Modern Latin America, 3d ed.
Prologue, "Why Latin America?" pp. 3–13.

Americas: An Anthology, chapter 1, pp. 3–16.

WRITING ASSIGNMENTS/ DISCUSSION QUESTIONS

1. Have students consider the table on page 4 of *Modern Latin America*. Note that the poll was taken in 1940. Ask students whether they believe that these stereotypes are still held today. Are there any not listed that they think should be included as commonly held views?

2. Why is it important for U.S. citizens to study and learn more about Latin America and the Caribbean?

SUGGESTED ACTIVITIES

1. Provide students with two copies of an outline map of the region at the beginning of the course. On one copy, have them identify as many countries, bodies of water, and other important points of reference as they can. Then have students label and annotate the second copy as the course proceeds and their familiarity with the region increases. At the end of the course, have them compare their initial and final maps.

2. Have students informally poll their family and friends for opinions and thoughts about Latin America and the Caribbean. Students should ask subjects to provide five descriptive words that come to mind when they think of Latin America and the Caribbean. Have students tally the results and draw some general conclusions about the findings. Have a class discussion about the findings, or distribute the results through a student newsletter if your class does not meet often as a group.

3. Have students identify a range of influences from Latin America and the Caribbean in their communities. They can look in the phone book and local newspapers for community, cultural, religious, political, and educational organizations, as well as restaurants, clubs, food and clothing stores. Draw up a list of the findings to share with the class as a whole.

RESOURCES

Nonfiction

Athey, Lois. *Latin America: History, Culture, and Geography* (Regional Studies Series). New York: Globe Book Company, 1987. This overview of the region includes case studies that encourage students to use primary and secondary resources. Includes self-tests.

Beezley, William H., and Judith Ewell, eds. *The Human Tradition in Latin America: The Nineteenth Century*, and *The Twentieth Century*. 2 vols. Wilmington, Del.: Scholarly Resources, 1987. This two-volume set is a collection of 23 biographies of "ordinary" people in independent Latin America.

Collier, Simon, Harold Blakemore, and Thomas E. Skidmore, eds. *The Cambridge Encyclopedia of Latin America and the Caribbean*. New York: Cambridge University Press, 1985. This essential reference offers a very thorough overview of the physical and human geography of the region.

Global Studies: Latin America. Edited by Paul Goodwin. Guilford, Conn.: Dushkin, 1990. A convenient source for short histories and summaries of important historical data on all the Latin American and Caribbean states. The regional introduction and extracts from press publications provide extremely useful information on current themes.

Keen, B., ed. *Latin American Civilization: History and Society, 1492 to the Present.* Boulder, Colo.: Westview Press, 1986. Anthology of primary sources that provides various perspectives on Latin America from the time of the Aztecs to the present.

Kidron, Michael, and Ronald Segal. *The New State of the World Atlas.* New York: Simon and Schuster, 1987. Comparative maps show the distribution of natural resources, money, population, weapons, industries, and more.

Knight, Franklin W., and Colin A. Palmer, eds. *The Modern Caribbean.* Chapel Hill: University of North Carolina Press, 1989. A compilation of studies that approach the Caribbean from different disciplines and perspectives, examining the region's colonial past, its diverse racial heritage, and its complex relationship with the United States.

Oxford Analytica. *Latin America in Perspective.* Boston: Houghton Mifflin, 1991. Overview of society, economics, politics, and international relations.

Other Resources

Bermudez, Pedro R., and Bárbara C. Cruz. *Latin America from a Global Perspective: A Resource Guide for Teachers.* Miami: Latin American and Caribbean Center, Florida International University, 1991. Provides an overview of some of the global concerns in the region. Available from the Latin American and Caribbean Center, Florida International University, PC 237, Miami, FL 33199; (305) 348-2894.

Contreras, Gloria. *Latin American Culture Studies: Information and Materials for Teaching About Latin America.* 2d ed. This 310-page curriculum volume includes introductory papers on Latin American culture from the colonial era to the present, as well as lesson plans, writing assignments, games, activities, and an annotated bibliography. Available for $21.45 from the Institute of Latin American Studies, Richardson Hall, Unit 1, Austin, TX 78712.

Cornbleth, C., and C. Gill. *Key Ideas and Concepts in Teaching About Latin America.* Austin: Institute of Latin American Studies, University of Texas, 1977. This 41-page monograph for teachers presents important concepts about Latin American society, culture, history, and geography.

Curcio-Nagy, Linda, ed. *Latin America: Land of Diversity.* New Orleans: Center for Latin American Studies, Tulane University, 1990. Each of the 19 units in this course on Latin America covers a range of subjects, such as geography, history, and contemporary issues, and includes color slides. Available for $100, including shipping, from the Center for Latin American Studies, Tulane University, New Orleans, LA 70118-5698; (504) 865-5164.

Fenton, Thomas P., and Mary J. Heffron, eds. *Latin America and the Caribbean: A Directory of Resources.* Maryknoll, N.Y.: Orbis Books, 1986. Audio-visual catalog that includes bibliographies and indexes for teaching resources on Latin America and the Caribbean.

Latin American Studies Association. *It's the Image That Counts: Cartoon Masters for Latin American Study.* Gainesville, Fla.: Latin American Studies Association, 1976. These full-page cartoons stimulate class discussion on common stereotypes that North Americans have about Latin Americans and vice versa. Available from: Outreach Lending Library, Center for Latin American Studies, University of Florida, 319 Grinter Hall, Gainesville, FL 32611; (904) 392-0375.

Lombardi, Cathryn L., and John V. Lombardi. *Latin American History: A Teaching Atlas.* Madison: University of Wisconsin Press, 1983. Covers history of the region from 24,000 B.C. to the present with information on topography, ancient civilizations, climate, and trade. More than 50 reproducible maps (ideal for transparencies) show each country in the region and illustrate social and economic conditions.

TEST BANK

Questions reflect content from the textbook, study guide, and anthology.

Multiple Choice

*Mark the letter of the response that **best** answers the question or completes the statement.*

_____ 1. The American Rockies are part of a mountain chain that continues into South America and forms:

   a. the Sierra Nevada.
   b. the Urals.
   c. the Serra do Mar.
   d. the Andes.

_____ 2. The conquest and colonization of Latin America that began in 1492 was carried out by:

   a. African powers.
   b. Asian powers.
   c. North American powers.
   d. European powers.

_____ 3. Which of the following languages are widely spoken in the Caribbean? *(Mark all that apply.)*

   a. German
   b. Creole
   c. French
   d. Spanish

_____ 4. The *altiplano* is:

   a. one of the longest rivers in Latin America.
   b. home to many descendants of the original inhabitants of Latin America.
   c. the location of the capital city of Mexico.
   d. a lowland area of rice, sugar, and other agricultural production.

_____ 5. *Quechua* is:

   a. a language that contains elements of Spanish and French as well as words from various African dialects.
   b. a language spoken by indigenous people in Guatemala and Mexico.
   c. one of the official languages of Peru.
   d. a language no longer spoken in Latin America.

_____ 6. Dependency theory states that:

   a. economic development is dependent on the location of physical features such as mountain ranges and river systems.
   b. economic development in Latin America is dependent on external factors such as the demand for and prices of its exports.
   c. economic growth depends on the existence and stability of democratic political systems.
   d. North America depends on raw materials from Latin America for its industrial production.

_____ 7. Modernization theory:

   a. was developed by Latin American scholars in response to the rise of military governments in the 1960s and 1970s.
   b. was a generally pessimistic view of the prospects for democracy in Latin America.
   c. held that colonial societies such as those in Latin America could never become modernized.
   d. associated economic growth and industrialization with political democracy.

_____ 8. Which of the following groups of people had a significant presence in Latin America and the Caribbean during the colonial period? *(Mark all that apply.)*

   a. Africans
   b. Eastern Europeans

c. Western Europeans

d. Indigenous peoples

_____ 9. Latin America has been referred to as a "living museum" because:

a. it has a rich past dating to precolonial times.

b. traditional cultures and ways coexist with modern cities and means of production.

c. it has experienced little change over the centuries and appears today almost as it did during the colonial period.

d. it still has many indigenous groups who have had little contact with modern society.

_____ 10. Which of the following are themes of this course? *(Mark all that apply.)*

a. Events in the Americas have little direct impact on the United States or on other countries outside the Western Hemisphere.

b. Latin America and the Caribbean have a unique historical relationship to the rest of the world.

c. International and domestic political and economic choices have created internal tensions in the nations of the Americas.

d. The peoples of Latin America and the Caribbean developed many innovative responses to their social and political reality.

_____ 11. Poverty and inequitable distribution of income in the Americas:

a. have been largely eliminated.

b. are restricted to the rural areas.

c. are still widespread both within and among nations of the region.

d. are relatively new to the region.

_____ 12. Population in the Americas: *(Mark all that apply.)*

a. has remained stable for centuries.

b. had the world's highest growth rates in the early 1960s.

c. is characterized today by large numbers of women in their childbearing years.

d. has become increasingly urban in recent decades.

_____ 13. One of the most important criticisms of modernization theory is that:

a. it did not predict or explain the rise of military governments in the mid–twentieth century.

b. it argued that only military governments could bring about rapid economic growth.

c. it was based on the belief that the colonial legacy in Latin America had been completely eliminated by the mid–twentieth century.

d. it assumed that Latin America's upper classes would use their wealth to transform the socioeconomic situations in their countries.

_____ 14. Which of the following statements are true of dependency theory? *(Mark all that apply.)*

a. It explained the advent of authoritarian regimes in South America during the 1960s and 1970s.

b. It accurately predicted the fall of military governments and the turn toward civilian, electoral democracies in the 1980s.

c. It viewed Latin America's economic development as constrained by events outside the region.

d. It argued that the consequence of dependent development was a society with elites tied to external markets and masses of workers left out of the benefits of economic growth.

_____ 15. The physical geography and features of Latin America and the Caribbean: *(Mark all that apply.)*

   a. influenced the location of human settlements, which were concentrated in the lowlands and coastal areas.
   b. affected economic development in several different ways, such as the reliance on hydroelectric power and the exploitation of natural resources for export markets.
   c. make Latin America a very inhospitable region for modern industrial production.
   d. exhibit enormous variety, including mountains, fertile grasslands and plains, and tropical forests.

Identification/Short Answer

Define and/or describe the following terms, concepts, or persons, or answer the following questions. Answers should be no longer than a few sentences.

16. Río de la Plata:

17. Creole:

18. The people of Latin America and the Caribbean today are descendants of three major population groups that first came into contact in the Western Hemisphere during the colonial period of conquest and domination. The three groups are:

19. What are some of the forces that have been suggested as causes of internal political and cultural tensions in the Americas?

20. What features of Latin American society are described by the phrase "Latin America is a beggar atop a mountain of gold"?

ESSAY QUESTIONS

1. What are some of the contrasts within Latin America and the Caribbean that are the basis for the textbook comment that the region is "rich in paradox"? Consider historic, economic, geographic, and political factors in your answer.

2. Compare and contrast dependency theory and modernization theory. What contributions has each made to our understanding of the region?

3. What do you see as a rationale for studying Latin America and the Caribbean? In your answer, be sure to consider some of the major factors—physical, cultural, and political—that link North and South America.

ANSWER KEY

Test Bank

Answers indicate sources.
 1. d (anthology)
 2. d (anthology, textbook)
 3. b, c, d (anthology)
 4. b (anthology, study guide)
 5. c (anthology, study guide)
 6. b (textbook, study guide)
 7. d (textbook, study guide)
 8. a, c, d (textbook, study guide)
 9. b (anthology)
10. b, c, d (anthology, study guide)
11. c (anthology)
12. b, c, d (anthology)
13. a (textbook, study guide)
14. a, c, d (textbook, study guide)
15. a, b, d (anthology, textbook)
16. A major river system in Argentina, Uruguay, and Paraguay. (anthology)
17. Creole is one of the official languages in Haiti. It is a language with African roots that is widely spoken throughout the Caribbean, especially by those with little formal education. (anthology, study guide)
18. Indigenous groups, Europeans, and Africans. (anthology, study guide, textbook)
19. The pressures caused by Latin America's unique history of conquest, colonization, and economic relationship with the rest of the world, combined with key internal decisions, have affected the area. Social tensions have resulted as elites strive to maintain their privileged position, peasants and working classes push for a greater share of economic benefits in the form of increased wages and lower prices; middle-class professionals, students, and others try to increase their share of economic and political power. Military regimes throughout the region have often reacted to social tensions by imposing strict controls over political and civil liberties. (anthology, study guide)
20. Latin America is both prosperous and poor in terms of income levels and standards of living; as a region, it is also tremendously rich in natural resources but has continuing high levels of poverty and delayed or partial industrialization. (textbook)

Essay Questions

1. Students' answers should be a synthesis of the textbook and anthology assignments. According to the textbook, Latin America is "rich in paradox" because as a region it is both young and old, tumultuous and stable, independent and dependent, prosperous and poor. Latin American countries are the oldest independent nations among those that were former European colonies, yet their societies are still undergoing transformation. Similarly, though their independence is nearly 200 years old, they continue to be limited in their economic and political decisions by dependency on the United States and Europe. The conquest began a tradition of political violence and social upheaval that has frequently marked Latin America's history, yet traditions and norms persist that are rooted in the colonial and precolonial past. Finally, despite having enormous natural wealth, and several countries that have experienced periods of remarkable economic growth, the region also has large numbers of citizens living in dire poverty. The diversity of the region in terms of the size of its nations, their topography and culture, should also be mentioned.

2. Subscribers to modernization theory believe that economic growth can generate the social change that is necessary for "developed" politics—that is, stable democracy. This theory was revealed as inadequate by the history of Latin America in the 1960s and 1970s, which saw a rise of military regimes, not political democracy. Dependency theory asserts that economic dependency leads to political authoritarianism and that economic development in Latin America and the Caribbean has been qualitatively different from that of North America and Western Europe. This theory appears to be too rigid, since it did not predict the social changes that swept the military from power during the period of economic downturn in the mid to late 1980s. In terms of each theory's

contribution, modernization theory has provided the useful notion that socioeconomic factors are linked to political outcomes; dependency theory underscores the idea that Latin America's economic relationship with the world affected and limited its development, including its social and political options.

3. Students' rationale should be developed along but not limited to the following points:
   - North American economic interests;
   - political links: crises in the area that challenge U.S. foreign policy;
   - immigration to the United States from Latin America and the Caribbean;
   - the role of Latin American and Caribbean culture within the United States and around the world; and
   - the historical connections between North and South America.

Unit 2

Legacies of Empire:
From Conquest to Independence

UNIT SUMMARY

Unit 2 summarizes the key features of the colonial experience in Latin America and the Caribbean. It illustrates the political, economic, social, religious, and cultural heritage of the new nations that achieved independence from European imperial powers in the nineteenth and twentieth centuries. The textbook chapter provides a history of the period from 1492 to the 1880s, relating developments in Europe to the different phases of conquest and consolidation of the Spanish and Portuguese empires, the rise of a powerful creole class in the Spanish colonies, and the emergence and eventual triumph of national independence movements and their aftermath. The text also illustrates some of the most important distinctions between Spanish and Portuguese America. The anthology readings convey the harsh reality of the conquest and the colonial period for the indigenous and African peoples and convey the turmoil that accompanied the period immediately after independence.

LEARNING OBJECTIVES

After completing the unit, students should be able to:

- Describe the intermingling of indigenous peoples, Africans, and Europeans which created new groups, such as *mestizos* and *mulattos*, and resulted over time in the complex, multicultural societies of modern Latin America and the Caribbean.

- Understand that colonial society in both Spanish and Portuguese America was characterized by hierarchies based on race and class: at the top was a small group of white elites; in the middle a somewhat larger group of whites, *mestizos*, and *mulattos;* and, at the bottom, the vast majority, mainly indigenous and African populations.

- Realize that colonial economic systems were based on the production and export of raw materials—especially silver and cacao in Spanish America and sugar and gold in Brazil—and that these systems relied on the forced labor of indigenous populations and enslaved Africans.

- Recognize that the inability of Spain and Portugal to maintain tight control over their colonies allowed important administrative and legal matters to fall into the hands of powerful local elites.

- Understand the important role played by the Catholic Church in the establishment and maintenance of the Spanish and Portuguese empires.

- Describe the different means by which the former colonies in Spanish and Portuguese America and the Caribbean obtained their independence, and understand why the various independence movements generally did not seek the total transformation of political, economic, and social structures.

OVERVIEW

The brutality of the European conquest, and the experience of more than three centuries of domination by imperial powers, left an indelible mark on Latin America and the Caribbean which is still evident throughout the region. The specifics of the colonial period and its legacy vary from country to country, depending on the numbers of original indigenous inhabitants, the degree of control exerted by the imperial powers, each area's natural resources, and other factors. The most important aspects of the colonial heritage can be summarized as:

- Strong tendencies toward regionalism, local autonomy, and authoritarian governments, including a reliance on military leaders and local bosses, or *caudillos*, to provide stability;

- The persistence of social hierarchies based on race, class, and ethnicity;

- Unequal socioeconomic systems that concentrated wealth in the hands of a few while leaving the majority in a persistent state of poverty; and

- Economic systems focused on the production of raw materials and commodities for export to the world market, limiting domestic economic development.

The political, economic, social, cultural, and religious structures developed during the colonial period have had an enduring impact on the region's development that is still visible today. Students should recognize that the colonial experience is linked to present-day conditions throughout the region, and that two of the four themes of this course focus on the colonial heritage: Latin America's unique historical relationship with the rest of the world; and the internal tensions that have led to social and political turmoil in the postindependence period.

STUDENT READING ASSIGNMENT

Modern Latin America, 3d ed.
Chapter 1, "The Colonial Foundations, 1492–1880s," pp. 14–42.

Americas: An Anthology, chapter 2, pp. 17–47.

WRITING ASSIGNMENTS/ DISCUSSION QUESTIONS

1. Ask students to consider as many points of view about the age of European exploration and expansion as possible, using some of the resources cited in the guides as well as the anthology selections. What do they think of the way Columbus and the "discovery" of the Americas have been portrayed and celebrated in our society? On balance, do they view the Europeans as having had a positive or negative impact on the development of Latin America and the Caribbean?

2. What are some of the major differences in the colonial experiences of the United States, Latin America, and the Caribbean? How might those differences have affected the later course of social, political, and economic development in those regions?

SUGGESTED ACTIVITIES

1. Have students create five timelines covering events that occurred in Europe, Africa, Asia, and North and South America from the late 1400s to the early 1800s. Students should divide their timelines into periods that indicate

the major changes occurring in culture, religion, society, government, and economy in each of the five regions. The timelines should be used to compare the events taking place in the different parts of the world, and to show the impact that historic change in one area had on people living in another area (for example, the impact of the expulsion of the Moors from the Iberian peninsula on the Age of Conquest; the impact of European wars on the associated colonies; the global reach of the European imperial powers).

2. Have students research, individually or in groups, how the 500th anniversary of Columbus's arrival in the Western Hemisphere was marked in some or all of the following places. In the United States: your local area; Miami, Florida; Los Angeles, California; and one or more American Indian reservations. Internationally: Argentina; Brazil; the Dominican Republic; Ecuador; Guatemala; Italy; Jamaica; Mexico; and Spain. Students should examine newpaper clippings and write to the following organizations or educational groups to obtain their information, and should answer the following questions: Was Columbus's arrival celebrated? Commemorated? Condemned? Why? If there were celebrations, were there also demonstrations against them?

Organizations to contact:
American Indian Community House
404 Lafayette Street
New York, NY 10003
(212) 598-0100

Committee for American Indian History
6802 S.W. 13th Street
Gainesville, FL 32608
(904) 378-3246

National Hispanic Quincentennial Commission
810 First Street, N.E.
Washington, DC 20002-4205

Quincentenary Programs
S. Dillon Ripley Center
Room 2123

Smithsonian Institution
Washington, DC 20560
(202) 357-1300

Quinto Centenario/Quincentennial
Organization of American States
1889 F Street N.W.
Washington, DC 20006
(202) 458-3908

Spain '92 Foundation
1821 Jefferson Place N.W.
Washington, DC 20036
(202) 775-1992

1992 Alliance
P.O. Box 2007
Santa Fe, NM 87504

RESOURCES

Nonfiction

Bedini, Silvio A., ed. *The Christopher Columbus Encyclopedia.* New York: Simon and Schuster, 1991. This two-volume reference encyclopedia contains more than 350 original articles by nearly 150 contributors from around the world.

Bowser, Frederick P. *The African Slave in Colonial Peru, 1524–1650.* Stanford, Calif.: Stanford University Press, 1974. A very well-written account of the impact of slavery on colonial society and individuals.

Bray, Warwick. "How Old Are the Americans?" *Américas* (May–June 1988). Explores the debate over when humans first reached the New World. Although most archaeologists once accepted the theory that America was first inhabited 12,000 years ago, artifacts recently discovered indicate that humans may have reached the area as long as 34,000 years ago.

Buarque, Cristobal. "A Lingering Legacy," *Américas.* (May–June 1988). Examines the adverse impact of slavery on Brazilian society.

Burkholder, Mark, and Lyman Johnson. *Colonial Latin America*. New York: Oxford University Press, 1990. An up-to-date college text that provides an overview of Latin America in colonial times.

Clendinnen, Inga. *Ambivalent Conquests: Maya and Spaniards in the Yucatan, 1517–70*. New York: Cambridge University Press, 1987. Illuminating account of the religious role in the conquest and its ambiguities.

Columbus, Christopher. *The Log of Christopher Columbus*. Translated by Robert Fuson. Camden, Maine: International Maritime Publishing, 1987. The explorer's own account of his epochal journey and first encounters with the indigenous people of the New World.

Díaz del Castillo, Bernal. *The Conquest of New Spain*. Translated by J.M. Cohen. Baltimore: Penguin Books, 1963. A vivid, personal account by one of Cortés's soldiers of the conquest of the Aztec Empire. Good to contrast with *Broken Spears* in the anthology (reading 2.2).

Gutierrez, A. *When Jesus Came, the Corn Mothers Went Away*. Stanford, Calif.: Stanford University Press, 1990. This social history uses marriage as a case study to show the lasting impact of the Spanish conquest on the Pueblo Indians of New Mexico.

Hart, Richard. *Slaves Who Abolished Slavery: Blacks in Bondage*, vol. 1. University of the West Indies, Jamaica: Institute of Social and Economic Research, 1980. This volume deals with the origins of the slave trade and slavery in the West Indies. The conclusion focuses on the abolitionist movement in Britain and the successful revolt that ended slavery in Haiti.

Hemming, John. *Red Gold: The Conquest of the Brazilian Indians, 1500–1700*. Cambridge: Harvard University Press, 1978. Historical overview of the relations among the Portuguese monarchy, the Catholic Church, and the colonists and indigenous peoples of Brazil.

Hoetink, H. *Slavery and Race Relations in the Americas*. New York: Harper and Row, 1973. An insightful analysis of the realities and texture of slave societies and their consequences.

Knight, Franklin W. *The African Dimension in Latin American Societies*. New York: Macmillan, 1974. An excellent introduction to the topic.

Knight, Franklin W. *Slave Society in Cuba during the Nineteenth Century*. Madison: University of Wisconsin Press, 1970. A socioeconomic analysis of the role of slavery in Cuban historical development.

Lavrín, Asuncion, ed. *Sexuality and Marriage in Colonial Latin America*. Lincoln: University of Nebraska Press, 1989. A pioneering collection of essays on the subject.

León-Portillo, Miguel, ed. *Broken Spears: The Aztec Account of the Conquest of Mexico*. Boston: Beacon Press, 1962. Excellent compilation of surviving Aztec views of the conquest. Excerpted in *Americas: An Anthology*.

Lynch, John. *The Spanish-American Revolutions, 1808–1826*. New York: Norton, 1973. Classic study of the origins and course of the wars of independence.

Milanich, J., and S. Milbrath, eds. *First Encounters: Spanish Explorations in the Caribbean and the United States, 1492–1570*. Gainesville: University of Florida Press, 1989. Using recent research, the period of early Spanish contact with the peoples of the New World is explored.

Padden, R. S. *The Hummingbird and the Hawk*. New York: Harper & Row, 1970. Classic account of the rise and fall of the Aztec Empire.

Poma de Ayala, Huamán. *Letter to a King: A Peruvian Chief's Account of Life Under the Incas and Under Spanish Rule*. Edited by Christopher Dilke. New York: Dutton, 1978. First-person account with drawings by the author depicting indigenous life before and after the conquest.

Queirós Mattoso, D. Katia. *To Be a Slave in Brazil, 1550–1888*. Translated by Arthur Goldhammer. New Brunswick, N.J.: Rutgers University Press, 1986. Illuminating and readable exploration of the topic.

Sale, Kirkpatrick. *Conquest of Paradise: Christopher Columbus and the Columbian Legacy*. New York:

Knopf, 1990. Examines the impact of the conquest, with special emphasis on ecological and environmental consequences.

Todorov, Tzvetan. *The Conquest of America: The Question of the Other*. New York: Harper & Row, 1984. Fascinating exploration of the role of language and mentalities in the conquest.

Fiction and Poetry

Benitez-Rojo, Antonio. *Sea of Lentils*. Amherst: University of Massachusetts Press, 1990. This novel combines fact and fiction in portraying sixteenth-century Cuba, Puerto Rico, and the Dominican Republic. The novel's title comes from the misidentification of French cartographer Guillaume de Testu, who mistook the word *antilles* for *lentilles* (French for "lentils").

Galeano, Eduardo. *Memory of Fire*. New York: Pantheon, 1985. Loosely based on historical accounts of the conquest and colonization, this trilogy of vignettes ("Genesis," "Faces and Masks," and "Century of the Wind") offers a Latin American view of the New World in the making. The first and second volumes are most relevant to this unit.

Manzano, Juan Francisco. *The Life and Poems of a Cuban Slave*. Edited by Edward J. Mullen. Hamden, Conn.: Archon Books, 1981. Collection of creative writing by a Cuban slave (1797–1854). The reader has the opportunity to reflect on the effects of the transportation of enslaved Africans to the New World.

Rhys, Jean. *Wide Sargasso Sea*. New York: Norton, 1982. Written in a stream-of-consciousness manner, this novel tells the tale of women in early nineteenth-century Jamaica and Dominica. The concepts of race, gender, and class under slavery are dealt with from a woman's point of view.

Schwartz-Bart, Simone. *The Bridge of Beyond*. Translated by Barbara Bray. London: Heinemann, 1982. In this historical novel, a Guadeloupan woman recounts her life's story and reflects on her great-grandmother's life as a slave.

Zobel, Joseph. *Black Shack Alley*. Translated by Keith Q. Warner. Washington, D.C.: Three Continents Press, 1980. This novel, set in French Colonial Martinique, tells the story of José, a young boy being raised by his grandmother in a community of sugar-cane workers. (Filmed as "Sugar Cane Alley"; see "Films," below.)

Films

Unless otherwise indicated, all films listed are available in VHS video format.

Cimarrones. 24 minutes, 1983 (Spanish, with English subtitles). This docudrama takes its name from the term for runaway slaves in Spanish-speaking America. The film portrays everyday life in a typical slave village during the nineteenth century and an attack by *cimarrones* on a Spanish caravan. The film is available for purchase (film, $400; video, $295) or rental ($50) from the Cinema Guild, 1697 Broadway, New York, NY 10019; (212) 246-5522.

Columbus and the Age of Discovery. Seven hours, 1991. Originally broadcast on public television, this documentary series is a balanced exploration of Columbus and the European conquest of America and its consequences. Available for purchase ($29.95 for each 60-minute program) from The WGBH Collection, P.O. Box 2053, Princeton, NJ 08543; (800) 828-WGBH.

Creation of the World: A Samba-Opera. 56 minutes, 1978. Performed by the Beija Flor Samba school, this samba-opera recounts the creation of the world according to myths of the Nago people of Africa. This film shows an eclectic mix of African, Latin, and Brazilian song and dance. It is available for purchase ($395) or rental ($95) from The Cinema Guild, 1697 Broadway, New York, NY 10019; (212) 246-5522.

History through Art and Archaeology. This series of programs on ancient civilizations includes three in particular that are of use in describing the precolonial civilizations of the Americas. *The Pre-Inca Civilization of the Central Andes, The Incas and Their Empire,* and *The Civilization of the Ancient Maya and Its Collapse* are a collection of filmstrips, cassettes, instructor's manual, and wall poster. Each provides an overview of the civilization in question, as well as the people's relationship to their environment. Available for $49 each from Alarion Press, P.O. Box 1882, Boulder, CO 80306; (800) 523-9177.

Simón Bolívar: The Great Liberator. 58 minutes, 1984. This portrait of the revolutionary explores the forces that shaped Latin America in Bolívar's time as well as today. Available for rental ($75) from Films for the Humanities and the Sciences, 743 Alexander Road, P.O. Box 2053, Princeton, NY 08540; (800) 257-5126.

Sugar Cane Alley. 107 minutes, 1984 (French, with English subtitles). Examines plantation life in colonial Martinique from the vantage point of José, an Afro-Caribbean boy whose grandmother is determined to free at least one of her grandchildren from the drudgery of life on a sugar cane plantation. Available for rental ($20) from Facets, 1517 West Fullerton, Chicago, IL 60614; (800) 331-6197.

Other Resources

Bower, B., G. O. Martin, and B. Uhrmacher. *Two Visions of the Conquest.* Stanford, Calif.: SPICE, 1988. This set of 23 slides uses primary sources to teach two perspectives on the conquest of Mexico.

Bryce-Laporte, R. *African Americans: The Coming of Blacks to America, a Historical Perspective.* Washington, D.C.: Portfolio Project, 1989. The first section of this project deals with the "discovery" of America and describes the African presence in the New World before slavery.

Curcio-Nagy, Linda. *Colonial Mexican Society.* New Orleans: Latin American Curriculum Resource Center (CRC), Tulane University, 1989. This 27-slide media packet describes life in Mexico's colonial period (1519–1824) and places particular emphasis on the trans-Atlantic trade, the rise of large landed estates, and labor systems. Available for $10 from the Center for Latin American Studies, Tulane University, New Orleans, LA 70118-5698; (504) 865-5164.

Guyatt, J. *Ancient America.* St. Paul, Minn.: Greenhaven Press, 1980. This 32-page curriculum packet compares the Mayan, Aztec, and Incan empires in the Americas.

Painter, D. *Columbus.* St. Paul, Minn.: Greenhaven Press, 1980. Columbus's voyages to the Americas are discussed, including his navigation techniques and the Spanish conquest.

TEST BANK

Questions reflect content from the textbook, study guide, and anthology.

Multiple Choice

*Mark the letter of the response that **best** answers the question or completes the statement.*

_____ 1. Which empire stretched for 3,000 miles along the Andes mountains?

    a. Inca
    b. Maya
    c. Aztec
    d. Toltec

_____ 2. At the time of the Spaniards' arrival, the Maya:

    a. were a warlike people whose empire was at its height in the late fifteenth century.
    b. were nomads whose numbers had dwindled to fewer than 5,000.
    c. were exterminated by the Spanish.
    d. had a complex society with many accomplishments but were already in decline at the time of the conquest.

_____ 3. The conquest and colonization of the Americas: (*Mark all that apply.*)

    a. took place in the seventeenth century.
    b. only slightly reduced the numbers of indigenous peoples in the region.
    c. was motivated by complex factors, including the search for wealth and the desire to spread Christianity.
    d. was devastating for the ancient indigenous civilizations.

_____ 4. Enslaved Africans:

    a. were brought mostly to the Andean region.
    b. were an important part of colonial society by the end of the seventeenth century.
    c. did not play a large role in the colonial economic system.
    d. were never brought in large numbers to Latin America, as they were to the cotton plantations of North America.

_____ 5. The 1494 Treaty of Tordesillas:

    a. was negotiated between Spain and the Inca Empire of Peru.
    b. ended European exploration in Latin America.
    c. granted Portugal the eastern half of South America.
    d. granted the English and French rights to colonize the Caribbean.

_____ 6. The indigenous peoples of Central America:

    a. had certain religious beliefs, such as the concept of an afterlife, that made their conversion to Christianity easier.
    b. did not have formal religious beliefs or practices.
    c. rejected Christianity despite the strenuous efforts of missionaries to convert them.
    d. were unaffected by the religious aspects of the conquest.

_____ 7. According to the textbook, the conquest caused the indigenous population of central Mexico to decline by approximately:

    a. 50 percent.
    b. 75 percent.
    c. 80 percent.
    d. 95 percent.

_____ 8. Women in colonial societies in the Americas:

    a. had many more options than women in Europe during the same period.

b. were particularly active in commerce and trade, although some also owned large estates or *haciendas*.

c. should not be viewed as a homogenous group since their experiences varied a great deal depending on their class and race.

d. only had children with men from their own class and race, a practice that helped maintain the distinct lines between different social groups.

_____ 9. Under the colonial economic systems, most indigenous groups:

a. benefited from their inclusion in mining and export agriculture since they gained a permanent source of income.

b. moved and migrated voluntarily throughout the region in search of the best jobs.

c. were forcibly uprooted from their communities and brought as laborers to work in the mining and *hacienda* systems.

d. worked mostly in the production of copper and tin.

_____ 10. Europeans or *peninsulares* who came from Spain and Portugal to the Americas:

a. were typically from the nobility in their home countries.

b. dominated society and maintained their privileges with legal regulations.

c. attempted to create new societies in the colonies based on Enlightenment principles of equality and reason.

d. typically did not support the monarchies' right to govern the colonies.

_____ 11. Colonial administrative patterns:

a. helped to foster later tendencies toward regionalism because many important matters were left to local elites.

b. gave rise to traditions of pan-Americanism because of the many important political and economic bonds among the colonies.

c. were highly effective at enforcing royal decrees throughout the colonial territories.

d. relied on native-born *mestizos* working in a network of small town councils throughout the region.

_____ 12. Which of the statements below are true of the plantation system in northeastern Brazil? (*Mark all that apply.*)

a. It was Europe's single most important source of cane sugar by the early 1600s.

b. It relied on the exploitation of African slave labor in the *engenho* system.

c. Its legacy is visible today in the form of large-scale commercial agriculture for export.

d. It relied largely on a combination of African, Indian, and *mestizo* labor.

_____ 13. The Catholic Church in colonial Latin America: (*Mark all that apply.*)

a. reinforced European control over the Indians while also playing an important social role for the colonizers.

b. had a vested interest in the success and maintenance of the colonial empires.

c. remained insulated from African and indigenous beliefs and retained its purely European character.

d. was not accepted by the indigenous populations of the Americas.

_____ 14. Which of the following statements contrasting the Spanish and Portuguese colonies are true? (*Mark all that apply.*)

a. Portuguese colonies tended to concentrate on agriculture, especially the production of cane sugar.
b. Portugal was able to exert greater control over its own colonies than was Spain.
c. The areas colonized by Portugal had smaller concentrations of indigenous peoples; this led to the importation of large numbers of enslaved Africans to work as laborers.
d. Spanish America had more silver.

_____ 15. The first nation to achieve independence in Latin America and the Caribbean was:

a. Brazil.
b. Mexico.
c. Haiti.
d. Cuba.

_____ 16. Independence from the imperial powers: (*Mark all that apply.*)

a. was achieved at about the same time for nations throughout the Americas.
b. led to prolonged periods of political instability marked by coups, rebellions, and regional conflicts.
c. ushered in new social patterns that rejected the rigid hierarchies of the colonial past and replaced them with egalitarian societies based on Enlightenment thought.
d. did not come to many of the Caribbean island nations until the 1960s or later.

_____ 17. One of the important economic legacies of the colonial period was:

a. the growth of domestic industries and large internal markets.
b. trade patterns that emphasized linkages among the former colonies rather than with Europe.

c. a system focused on export to Europe of raw materials and natural resources.
d. well-developed internal transportation systems, especially railroads, which distributed goods to local markets.

_____ 18. The societies that emerged in the newly independent countries of Latin America:

a. were able to increase socioeconomic equality markedly once they were free of the constraints of the colonial period.
b. suffered from prolonged political instability, coups, civil wars, and general upheaval in the postindependence years.
c. continued to be characterized by the hierarchies of class and race which were developed during the colonial period.
d. threw off the yoke of the past, especially the forced labor of slaves and indigenous peoples, once they were sure of their independence.

Identification/Short Answer

Define and/or describe the following terms, concepts, or persons, or answer the following questions. Answers should be no longer than a few sentences.

19. Bartolomé de las Casas:

20. What was the viceroyalty system? Was it an effective administrative tool?

21. *Mestizos*:

22. *Engenho*:

23. Toussaint L'Ouverture:

24. Simón Bolívar:

25. *Caudillo*:

ESSAY QUESTIONS

1. Compare and contrast the movements for independence in Spanish America, Portuguese America, and the Caribbean.

2. What were the most enduring social legacies of the colonial period? Why didn't the move to republican governments bring about significant socioeconomic change in Latin America?

3. Describe the impact of the *mita, encomienda,* and *hacienda* systems on the indigenous people of the Americas who were affected by them.

ANSWER KEY

Test Bank

Answers indicate sources.

1. a (textbook, study guide)
2. d (anthology, textbook)
3. c, d (anthology, textbook, study guide)
4. b (anthology, textbook, study guide)
5. c (anthology, textbook, study guide)
6. a (anthology)
7. d (textbook)
8. c (anthology, textbook, study guide)
9. c (anthology)
10. b (textbook)
11. a (textbook, study guide)
12. a, b, c (anthology, textbook)
13. a, b (anthology, study guide)
14. a, c, d (anthology, textbook, study guide)
15. c (anthology)
16. b, d (anthology, textbook, study guide)
17. c (textbook, study guide)
18. b, c (anthology, textbook, study guide)
19. Former conquistador turned friar who criticized the brutal conquest of the indigenous peoples in the Americas. (anthology, study guide)
20. Viceroyalty was the name assigned to the principal administrative divisions of the Spanish Empire in the New World. One viceroyalty had its seat in Peru, another in Mexico. In the eighteenth century, Peru was subdivided into three viceroyalties. The viceregal administrators had only limited ability to communicate with and control the enormous territory assigned to them, leaving important matters in the hands of local authorities. This contributed over time to the growth of regionalism and a tradition of local, not centralized, seats of power. (textbook, study guide)
21. Persons of mixed European and indigenous ancestry. (textbook, study guide)
22. From the Portuguese for "engine"; the enormous sugarcane plantations with on-site mills that dominated northeastern Brazil during the colonial period. (anthology, study guide)
23. Educated son of enslaved Africans who led more than 100,000 Haitian slaves in a 1791 rebellion. (anthology)

24. Venezuelan political and military leader who led the independence movements against Spain throughout most of Northern and Central America. He dreamed of a unified Spanish America once independence was achieved. (anthology, textbook)
25. Term applied to a "strong man" or dictator, often a military officer or ex-military officer, who dominated local struggles for political power. The postindependence period was an era of *caudillos* throughout Spanish America. (anthology, textbook, study guide)

Essay Questions

1. Independence did not come at the same time or in the same way to the Spanish and Portuguese colonies in Latin America and the Caribbean. Spain resisted the loss of its empire, and in many cases the rebels had to fight long and hard wars before achieving independence. Brazil was quite different; because of conflict with Napoleon in Europe, the Portuguese monarchy transferred to Brazil in 1808. Brazil became an independent monarchy in 1822, and did not become a republic until 1889. The transition, however, was a peaceful one. In the Caribbean, most nations did not become independent until the 1960s, and some are still colonies. Haiti was an exception; slaves led the second uprising in the hemisphere (the first outside of North America) in a true revolt against the social order, resulting in an independent republic in 1804.
2. The most enduring social legacy of colonial Latin America was a hierarchical system based on race and class and characterized by great socioeconomic inequality. Independence movements in the colonies were led by local elites who wanted to retain power, not to democratize society. Therefore, independence did little to change the social reality of Latin America.
3. With the destruction of their societies during the conquest, the descendants of the Aztec, Inca, Maya, and other indigenous groups generally experienced a drastic decline in their standard of living and were reduced to poverty. In several areas, indigenous peoples were up-

rooted from their homes and transported long distances where they were forced to labor for the Spanish in mines and on agricultural estates. Conditions were extremely harsh, especially in the mines, and most of those taken were not expected to survive for long. In most cases, those working as agricultural laborers did not suffer from as cruel treatment although they did endure the loss of their dignity and the right to ownership of their ancestral lands.

Unit 3

The Garden of Forking Paths: Dilemmas of National Development

UNIT SUMMARY

Unit 3 traces the transition from the immediate postcolonial period to the challenges of economic and political development in the late nineteenth and early- to midtwentieth centuries. The unit uses the example of Argentina to illustrate the policy choices facing political leaders in the Americas, their decisions, and the consequences of those actions. Students may need guidance in understanding how Latin America's position in the world economy affected domestic decisions, and in explaining the importance of ideologies such as nationalism and populism, which formed Peronism in Argentina. The most difficult aspects of the unit are likely to be the introduction to national economic policies (export-import growth and import-substituting industrialization) and international economic concepts such as *foreign exchange*, *balance of payments*, and *trade surplus/deficit*. The question of bureaucratic-authoritarianism, although part of the material for this unit, is considered in greater depth in Unit 4, "Capital Sins: Authoritarianism and Democratization."

LEARNING OBJECTIVES

After completing this unit, students should be able to:

- Understand why, in the first century after independence, most Latin American countries pursued the export-import economic model.

- Recognize that the export-import economy brought prosperity (although mostly to a small elite), vulnerability to external conditions, and overreliance on only a few products for export.

- Explain why many of the larger Latin American governments chose to move toward a policy of import-substituting industrialization (ISI) during the 1930s and 1940s, and describe the social and political trends that accompanied ISI.

- Name the factors that make Argentina different from the rest of Latin America, while also recognizing that Argentina faced the same constraints as other nations in the region in seeking to pursue independent economic development.

- Analyze Argentina's social and political history in the twentieth century, especially the importance of nationalism and its role in supporting the leadership of Juan Perón and other political and military figures.

- List the reasons for the Argentine military's increasing involvement in politics in the second half of the twentieth century.

- Explain how the Argentine military lost its domestic legitimacy and describe the challenges facing Argentina's democratically elected governments in the postmilitary period.

OVERVIEW

This unit has two objectives: to introduce students to important concepts of economic and political development in twentieth-century Latin America, and to provide a historical perspective on the experience of Argentina. Among the economic concepts covered in the unit are the export-import economic model, economic and political liberalism, import-substituting industrialization, foreign exchange, balance of payments, trade surplus and deficits, stabilization packages, and austerity measures.

Political trends accompanying the increased economic and social diversification of the early- to mid-twentieth century include liberal "reformist" policies, various efforts to mobilize labor, co-optative democracy, populism, political polarization, and bureaucratic-authoritarianism (which will be covered in more depth in Unit 4). The television program focuses especially on the concept of nation building and on the use and misuse of nationalism by a wide variety of political leaders.

Argentina is presented as a case study for interpreting the effects of these historical trends and understanding how they have shaped today's society. Students should recognize the major distinctions between Argentina and other nations of the region—most importantly, that it is a nation of immigrants, without a large indigenous population or peasantry, and lacking a history of both European conquest and significant domestic conflict over land. Argentina has tended to see itself as a European nation, different from and essentially superior to the other countries of the region.

The textbook selections include an overview of economic and political development throughout the region in the period from 1880 to the 1960s, along with a chapter devoted exclusively to Argentina's political and economic history. Argentina's early domestic prosperity was shattered in the mid-twentieth century by a series of cyclical economic declines coupled with repeated repudiation of electoral politics by the armed forces, which intervened five times between 1930 and 1976. The textbook and program highlight the fact that Argentina has been unable to achieve industrialization and development with social equity, despite numerous efforts and experimentation with a variety of domestic political formulas.

In 1983, after seven years in power, the Argentine military was forced to leave government because of the economic instability of the country, its conduct of the "dirty war," and its loss to Great Britain in the Falklands/Malvinas War. The country's civilian leaders were left to confront the same economic dilemmas as their military predecessors. Over the last decade they have had to balance the desire for justice for the thousands of *desaparecidos* ("the disappeared") with the need to unite the nation and create a stable, resilient political system. The program presents the social realities of Argentina today, and looks at the interaction of the different social groups that make up the nation.

The anthology readings give a sense of the commonalities among the countries of the Americas as they attempted to craft a successful development strategy. Students should recognize that the experiences of the nations of Latin America, whether economic (export-import growth, the reliance on foreign capital, import-substituting industrialization) or political (liberalism, nationalism, populism), were not convoluted, misguided, or "backward." In fact, the policy choices made were logical, conditioned primarily by the realities of Latin America's relationship with the rest of the world, especially with the industrialized powers of Europe and North America.

STUDENT READING ASSIGNMENT

Modern Latin America, 3d ed.
In chapter 2: "The Transformation of Modern Latin America, 1880s–1980s," pp. 43–56.

Chapter 3: "Argentina: From Prosperity to Deadlock," pp. 68–111.

Americas: An Anthology, chapter 3, pp. 48–71.

WRITING ASSIGNMENTS/ DISCUSSION QUESTIONS

1. Discuss in class, or have students write an essay about the concept of nationalism. Have students give examples from the programs and readings of events that were motivated by nationalism, or cases in which governments capitalized on nationalist feelings to create support for their programs. Have them discuss how nationalism is expressed in the United States and other parts of the world, and who benefits and who loses when nationalism is used as a justification for political actions.

2. Have students discuss or write about the main aspects of the economic history of the Americas in order to appreciate the reasons why nationalism has become associated with and nearly synonymous with anti-imperialism. What kind of dilemmas does this pose for governments in the region at the end of the twentieth century, when the dominant economic model appears to be one of growth based on full integration into the world market and a reliance on export-led development?

3. The United States has been partially shielded from some of the worst effects of balance of payments deficits and foreign exchange crises because its currency is universally accepted. Discuss or have students write about the concepts of foreign exchange, devaluation, and balance of payments, in order to understand the very different and difficult position faced by countries that do *not* have the dollar as their currency.

SUGGESTED ACTIVITIES

1. Have students research newspaper articles, looking for examples of nationalism in the world today. They should look at the major national and international dailies, local newspapers, and any foreign newspapers or news magazines accessible to them. Students should photocopy any articles showing how nationalism has played an overt or covert role in a political event. Discuss the articles in class, or have students write a few lines about each event, and about how they perceive nationalism to have played a role.

2. Show the film *The Official Story* (listed in the Resources section), and have students discuss the following questions: What is the effect on society of a government's use of terror against its own citizens? What are some of the internal divisions within Argentina that the film helps illuminate? In addition to the demands for justice for military offenders, what are other aspects of the legacy of the "dirty war" in Argentina?

RESOURCES

Nonfiction

Bergquist, Charles. *Labor in Latin America: Comparative Essays on Chile, Argentina, Venezuela, and Colombia.* Stanford: Stanford University Press, 1986. Comparative review of the labor movement in Latin America which explores the implications of the labor movement for raw material export.

Brading, D. A. *The First America: The Spanish Monarchy, Creole Patriots, and the Liberal State, 1492–1867.* Cambridge: Cambridge University Press, 1991. Traces the origins of nation-states in Spanish America to the colonial period, and the liberal ideology of the nineteenth century.

Díaz-Alejandro, Carlos F. *Essays on the Economic History of the Argentine Republic.* New Haven: Yale University Press, 1970. Follows the economic development of Argentina from the midnineteenth to midtwentieth century and challenges conventional thought about the agricultural economy and the origins of industrialization in contemporary Argentina.

Fraser, Nicolas, and Marysa Navarro. *Eva Perón*. New York: Norton, 1980. The life of Juan Perón's controversial second wife, who rose from obscurity to a position of power second only to that of her husband.

Hartz, Louis, ed. *The Founding of New Societies*. New York: Harcourt, Brace & World, 1964. Interpretation of cultural factors in societies created by European expansion in Latin America, Australia, and Africa.

Jacobsen, Nils, and Joseph L. Love, eds. *Guiding the Invisible Hand: Economic Liberalism and the State in Latin American History*. New York: Praeger, 1988. These essays explore the role of strong states in creating and guiding liberal economies. Especially relevant are "Argentina: Liberalism in a Country Born Liberal," by Tulio Halperín Donghi; "Structural Change and Conceptual Response in Latin America and Romania, 1860–1950," by Joseph L. Love, and "The Economic Role of the State in Liberal Regimes: Brazil and Mexico Compared, 1888–1910," by Steven Topik.

Love, Joseph L. "Raúl Prebisch and the Origins of the Doctrine of Unequal Exchange." *Latin American Research Review* 15:3 (1980): 45–72. Reveals the European origins of doctrines underlying strategies for import-substituting industrialization in Latin America.

Martínez Estrada, Ezequill. *X-Ray of the Pampas*. Translated by Alain Swietlicki. Austin: University of Texas Press, 1971. A survey of the social conditions and national characteristics of Argentina.

Page, Joseph. *Perón: A Biography*. New York: Random House, 1983. This biography of Juan Perón also studies the enduring impact of his extraordinary political career on Argentina.

Partnoy, Alicia. *The Little School: Tales of Disappearance and Survival in Argentina*. San Francisco: Cleis Press, 1986. A nonfiction, autobiographical account of the author's experience of being one of the thousands of political detainees during the 1976–83 military regime in Argentina.

Rock, David. *Argentina 1516–1987: From Spanish Colonization to Alfonsín*. 2d ed. Berkeley: University of California Press, 1987. Historical survey of Argentina.

Rock, David, ed. *Argentina in the Twentieth Century*. Pittsburgh: University of Pittsburgh Press, 1975. Examines Argentina's politics and economy from the nineteenth century to the 1970s, with attention to the durability of the Peronist movement.

Shumway, Nicolas. *The Invention of Argentina*. Berkeley: University of California Press, 1991. An analysis of nineteenth century Latin American politics, exploring the problems of national ideology and nation-building.

Smith, Peter H. "Crisis and Democracy in Latin America." *World Politics* 43:4 (July 1991): 608–34. Explores the paradox of how several Latin American countries became democracies during the economic crises of the 1980s.

Smith, Peter H. "The Failure of Democracy in Argentina, 1916–1930." In *The Breakdown of Democratic Regimes*, edited by Juan Linz and Alfred Stepan. Baltimore: Johns Hopkins University Press, 1978. Interpretation of factors that led to the overthrow of one of the first and apparently well-developed democracies in twentieth century Latin America.

Smith, Peter H. "The State and Development in Historical Perspective." In *Americas: New Interpretive Essays*, edited by Alfred Stepan. New York: Oxford University Press, 1992. A revisionist reinterpretation of the history of Latin American states and their development projects, written by a member of the *Americas* academic advisory board as an optional addition to this unit.

Smith, Peter H. *Politics and Beef in Argentina: Patterns of Conflict and Change*. New York: Columbia University Press, 1969. A study of the political economy of a major export industry in Argentina and Latin America, from the midnineteenth century to the rise of Juan Perón.

Timerman, Jacobo. *Prisoner Without a Name, Cell Without a Number.* New York: Knopf, 1981. Testimony of a Jewish Argentine journalist imprisoned by the military regime of the 1970s.

Waisman, Carlos H. *Reversal of Development in Argentina: Postwar Counterrevolutionary Policies and Their Structural Consequences.* Princeton: Princeton University Press, 1987. Interpretation of why Argentina plunged from 1930s prosperity into 1980s economic crisis. The author argues that economic policy was flawed because it was designed to prevent Communism from coming to Argentina.

Whitehead, Laurence. "Tigers in Latin America?" *Annals of the American Academy of Political and Social Sciences* 505 (September 1989). Examines strategies of newly industrializing economies in Asia, and explains why they cannot be blindly applied in Latin America.

Fiction

Borges, Jorge Luis. *Labyrinths.* New York: New Directions, 1964. A collection of essays and fiction by Argentina's foremost literary figure, including the story "The Garden of Forking Paths," from which the program title was taken.

Cortázar, Julio. *Hopscotch.* New York: Pantheon, 1987. A complex and sometimes whimsical novel heavily influenced by the French surrealists. Explores the dilemma of the "overeducated" and the bankruptcy of the Western cultural tradition.

Hernandez, José. *The Gaucho Martin Fierro.* Binghamton: State University of New York Press, 1974. An epic poem depicting gaucho life in its twilight hours in the late nineteenth century.

Puig, Manuel. *Betrayed by Rita Hayworth.* New York: Random House, 1981. Puig's first novel portrays a sensitive middle-class boy growing up in provincial Argentina in the 1930s and 1940s. As in all of Puig's books, themes and techniques are borrowed from popular culture, especially film.

Sábato, Ernesto. *The Tunnel.* New York: Random House, 1988. An artist murders his mistress and is tormented by his own isolation and inability to communicate.

Films

Unless otherwise indicated, all films listed are available in VHS video format.

Camila. 105 minutes, 1984. (Spanish, with English subtitles.) True story of a young socialist in Buenos Aires who runs away with a priest. They marry and live happily until they are discovered and condemned to death without a trial. Available in most video-rental outlets.

Hour of the Furnaces. 240 minutes, 1968, 16-mm. (French and Spanish, with English subtitles.) This landmark Fernando Solanas film, an open call for armed insurrection, was shown clandestinely for many years. Available for rental ($325) from New Yorker Films, 16 West 61st Street, New York, NY 10023; (212) 247-6110.

The Official Story. 112 minutes, 1985. A film about a woman's political awakening and the legacy of the *desaparecidos* in Argentina. Winner of the 1985 Academy Award for best foreign film. Directed by Luis Puenzo. Available in most video-rental outlets.

A World of Ideas, with Bill Moyers: Carlos Fuentes. 30 minutes, 1988. In this interview, Fuentes offers his perspective on current Latin American economics and on the prospects for the political independence of South American countries. Available for purchase ($39.95) from PBS Video; phone: (800) 424-7963; fax: (703) 739-5269.

TEST BANK

Questions reflect content from the programs, textbook, study guide, and anthology.

Multiple Choice

*Mark the letter of the response that **best** answers the question or completes the statement.*

_____ 1. The decision to pursue export-import growth strategies in Latin America and the Caribbean was logical because:

   a. the export of manufactured goods from the Americas was likely to bring the greatest profits.
   b. government control over agriculture throughout the region meant high revenues for state treasuries.
   c. export-import growth was seen as most likely to build strong and diverse economies in Latin America and the Caribbean.
   d. the Americas had a comparative advantage in the export of raw materials and agricultural products.

_____ 2. The export-import economic model had which of the following weaknesses? (*Mark all that apply.*)

   a. Export prices were volatile and unreliable, while the prices of imported goods did not fluctuate to the same degree.
   b. The markets for Latin American exports diminished over time due to slow growth in the trading partners' economies.
   c. Decisions with important impact on Latin America's economies were made outside the region.
   d. The reliance on exports did little to develop domestic manufacturing capability in Latin America.

_____ 3. Which of the following is a political change that accompanied export-import growth?

   a. The decline in influence of land-owning elites.
   b. The growth in power of an urban working class.
   c. The increase in political influence of landowning elites.
   d. The rise of populism.

_____ 4. Argentina's prosperity at the turn of the twentieth century was linked to which product(s)? (*Mark all that apply.*)

   a. Silver
   b. Oil
   c. Beef
   d. Wheat

_____ 5. According to the theory of economic liberalism popular in Latin America at the end of the nineteenth century:

   a. only military governments could promote economic growth.
   b. governments should nationalize foreign companies.
   c. government should protect domestic industries.
   d. economic growth would result from laissez-faire policies and free trade.

_____ 6. Immigrants to Argentina in the late nineteenth and early twentieth centuries came *primarily* from:

   a. England and Ireland.
   b. the United States.
   c. Germany and Austria.
   d. Italy and Spain.

_____ 7. Immigration to Argentina from the 1860s to the 1930s:

   a. undermined the strong pre-Colombian culture of Argentina's indigenous population.

b. led to the growth of *gauchos* as a distinct political group.

c. encouraged Argentines to see themselves as inherently different from the rest of Latin America.

d. reduced long-standing differences between the urban center and the rural interior.

_____ 8. Which of the following was a deliberate appeal to nationalism by Argentine political and/or military leaders? (*Mark all that apply*.)

a. The signing of the Roca-Runciman Pact in 1933.

b. The expropriation of Argentina's railways in 1948.

c. The coup against Isabel Perón in 1976.

d. The invasion of the Falkland/Malvinas Islands in 1982.

_____ 9. What did the Great Depression reveal about the export-import economic model?

a. Latin American manufactured goods were competitive on the world market.

b. Latin American economies were vulnerable to foreign economic cycles.

c. European governments were restricting the availability of needed capital.

d. The developing regions of Africa and Asia were stable markets for Latin American exports.

_____ 10. Industrialization in Argentina had which of the following social consequences? (*Mark all that apply*.)

a. A rise in numbers and political activism of organized labor.

b. A rise in political activism of landowning elites.

c. Increased polarization between two competing social groups, peasants and workers.

d. Emergence of new elites to contest the landowners' influence.

_____ 11. To be successful, import-substitution industrialization (ISI) strategies relied on:

a. government promotion of agro-export industries.

b. an influx of foreign capital to build needed infrastructure.

c. trade barriers and subsidies to protect new industries.

d. government appeals to patriotism to reduce purchases of imports.

_____ 12. Latin American populism: (*Mark all that apply*.)

a. was a phenomenon restricted to Argentina and Brazil.

b. resulted from the need to craft more broad-based political movements.

c. relied on nationalization of key industries to solidify domestic support.

d. was characterized by government hostility toward the armed forces.

_____ 13. According to the anthology, Getúlio Vargas, Lázaro Cárdenas, and Victor Haya de la Torre shared:

a. a pro-Communist political stance.

b. an export-led development strategy.

c. nationalist and anti-imperialist rhetoric.

d. a strong base of support among landowning elites.

_____ 14. Argentina's Juan Perón ultimately moved from a multiclass coalition to a nearly exclusive political alliance with which group?

a. The military
b. Middle-class entrepreneurs
c. Organized labor
d. Elite industrialists

_____ 15. One of Peronism's lasting effects on Argentine politics has been:

a. a history of political compromise.
b. increased influence for middle-class parties, such as the Radicals.
c. the importance of organized labor as a key political and social force.
d. a weak and politically apathetic working class.

_____ 16. One of the legacies of import-substituting industrialization in Argentina was:

a. rapid industrial growth that helped eliminate the gap between the rich and the poor.
b. repeated cycles of growth and contraction marked by rising problems with inflation.
c. ever increasing dependence on imported capital, especially from England, to build infrastructure.
d. protection from balance of payments problems due to increased self-sufficiency in the world economy.

_____ 17. Perón's exile from 1955 to 1973 resulted in:

a. the near elimination of Peronism as a political force.
b. an improvement in the ability of political rivals to compromise.
c. a decrease in the propensity of the armed forces to intervene in politics.
d. the increased polarization of Argentina's social and political systems.

_____ 18. Which of the following is true of the military in Argentina?

a. They tended to remain out of politics until the increasing level of civil violence in the 1970s necessitated military intervention.
b. They took power in 1976 with the intention of restoring Argentina's democratic institutions within one year.
c. They intervened repeatedly after 1930 and developed a high degree of hostility toward electoral politics.
d. They left power in 1984 after becoming convinced that democracy was essential to economic progress.

_____ 19. What was one of the most surprising consequences of the Argentine military's decision to invade the Malvinas?

a. The United States dropped its criticism of the military government to come out in favor of Argentina's right to the islands.
b. The Argentine public refused to rally around a government that had been so abusive of civil and human rights.
c. The nationalistic response within Argentina led even long-standing military opponents to support the government's action.
d. The British government was able to gain the support of most of the rest of Latin America for its swift retaliation.

_____ 20. Which of the following remains an important challenge for Argentina's civilian governments?

a. Ongoing agitation by Peronists who refuse to participate in the electoral system.
b. Continued attacks on infrastructure and military installations by a resurgent revolutionary left.
c. Renewed calls for a military-led government to restore economic growth.
d. Evidence of some military dissatisfaction with the democratic system.

Identification/Short Answer

Define or describe the following terms, concepts, or persons or answer the following questions. Answers should be no longer than a few sentences.

21. What was the major investment for which Latin American countries turned to Great Britain in the late 1800s and early 1900s? Why was this reliance necessary?

22. Name three errors the Argentine armed forces made when they invaded the Malvinas.

23. Import-substituting industrialization:

24. The tango:

25. What is nationalism and how has it been used by Latin American political and military leaders?

26. Evita:

27. Name two important political and/or economic ideologies that were imported from Europe and affected Latin American development.

28. What is a country's balance of payments, and how was the balance of payments of many Latin American countries affected by the Great Depression?

29. Name an important similarity and an important difference between Peru and Argentina at the turn of the twentieth century.

30. *Desaparecidos*:

ESSAY QUESTIONS

1. Argentina's history since independence has been marked by a continual search for national identity. Is Argentina justified in considering itself "different" from the rest of Latin America? Why or why not? How important is nationalism in modern Argentina?

2. What are some of the social changes that accompanied the shift from the export-import economy to import-substituting industrialization? How did these changes affect politics in Latin America?

3. Why did the level of political violence in Argentina escalate so dramatically after the 1950s? What were some of the factors that contributed to the military's determination to eradicate subversives, even if that meant the use of terror, torture, and disappearances?

ANSWER KEY

Test Bank

Answers indicate sources.

1. d (anthology, textbook, study guide)
2. a, c, d (anthology, textbook, study guide)
3. c (textbook)
4. c, d (program, textbook, study guide)
5. d (textbook, study guide)
6. d (anthology, textbook)
7. c (program, textbook, study guide)
8. b, c, d (program, anthology, textbook, study guide)
9. b (anthology, textbook, study guide)
10. a, d (anthology, textbook)
11. c (textbook, study guide)
12. b, c (anthology, textbook, study guide)
13. c (anthology)
14. c (program, anthology, textbook, study guide)
15. c (program, textbook, study guide)
16. b (program, textbook, study guide)
17. d (program, textbook)
18. c (program, textbook, study guide)
19. c (program, anthology, textbook)
20. d (program, textbook, study guide)
21. The railroad was the major investment; it was necessary because of the need for improved infrastructure to move agricultural goods and raw materials out of the country, and because Latin America lacked the capital and technology to make the investment itself. (program, anthology, textbook, study guide)
22. Students could cite the military's belief that Britain would not respond in any significant way; their expectation that the United States would remain neutral; their belief that they could win if the action resulted in war; their belief that the appeal to nationalism could restore their credibility with the public. (program, textbook)
23. Economic strategy to reduce economic dependence and vulnerability. The strategy, which sought to substitute locally produced manufactured goods for formerly imported goods, was adopted by countries throughout the region in the 1930s, 1940s, and 1950s. (anthology, textbook, study guide)
24. Argentine dance, with immigrant and working-class roots, that originated in Buenos Aires in the 1880s and became enormously popular in Europe in the 1910s. The tango eventually became accepted in the upper circles of Argentine society and has become an important symbol of national culture and pride. (program, anthology, textbook, study guide)
25. Ideology of devotion to one's nation, especially its freedom and independence. Nationalism has been an important theme in Latin American political history, and has been used repeatedly by leaders of every political persuasion to enhance their legitimacy and popular appeal. In Argentina, at different times, various leaders have attempted to link nationalism with Juan Perón's anti-imperialist economic policies, and with the military government's doctrine of national security. The invasion of the Falklands/Malvinas Islands is another example of how nationalism was used successfully by the generals to increase (for a limited time) their popular support. (program, study guide)
26. Second wife of Juan Perón; charismatic and influential political leader in her own right who earned the fanatic loyalty of hundreds of thousands of Argentines with her personal compassion and state-financed handouts to the *descamisados*, the "shirtless ones." Evita's death in 1952 brought an outpouring of national grief as she had come to symbolize the essence of Peronism. (program, anthology, textbook, study guide)
27. Students could cite any of the following: economic liberalism, Marxism, syndicalism, corporatism, fascism. (anthology, textbook)
28. The balance of payments is a record of all economic transactions between one country's residents and the residents of foreign countries, including trade of goods, services, and capital. The Great Depression had a serious impact on Latin American countries' balance of payments because the demand and prices for their exports went down dramatically, while the prices and demand for imported goods remained about the same. (anthology, textbook, study guide)
29. Students should draw on the anthology for their information on Peru, as well as on their general knowledge of Argentina. Similarities: both countries were pursuing an export-led growth strategy (guano in Peru, and beef and

wheat in Argentina); both relied on foreign investment; both saw an increasing disparity in incomes due to the limited distribution of the benefits of growth. Differences: the government of Peru was much more involved in the financial aspects of the guano trade, appropriating much of the profit for itself; Argentina, unlike Peru, did not have a large indigenous population and was therefore much more dependent on labor immigration; Argentina's immigrants came mostly from Europe, while Peru's came from China and Japan. (anthology, textbook, study guide)

30. The "disappeared" refers to people who were abducted and subsequently disappeared under repressive military governments. In Argentina, at least 10,000 persons disappeared under military rule between 1976 and 1983, leaving a bitter legacy for the subsequent civilian governments. (program, textbook, study guide)

Essay Questions

1. Students should demonstrate familiarity with the major similarities and differences between Argentina and other Latin American countries. Argentina lacks a peasantry, a history of conquest, a struggle over land; it is a highly "European" nation due to the volume of immigration from Europe. Nevertheless, it faced problems similar to those of other Latin American countries in attempting to pursue economic development: dependency, economic vulnerability, inability to develop strong domestic industries, debt, and inflation. Nationalism has been an important unifying theme for Argentina throughout the twentieth century, as was demonstrated by the strength of Peronism and the popularity of the Malvinas War. It continues to be critical for building a strong, stable nation in the postmilitary period.

2. The shift to a more industrialized society helped develop new economic groups. A burgeoning working class spread across several industries, and was not just concentrated in transportation; the middle sectors grew and diversified to include professionals, small business owners, shopkeepers, and others; and a new class of entrepreneurs and industrialists developed. These groups resented the monopolization of power by the "old" elites, especially the landowners, and pressured to gain their share of social, economic, and political power. Populism emerged as the most effective political movement to give voice to these new actors and their concerns, basing its appeal on multiclass coalitions, nationalism, and a combination of proindustrial and prolabor policies.

3. Perón was at least partly responsible for the escalation in violence, due to his pitting the working class against the military, the Church, and the aristocracy. The militancy of Peronism and the strident demands of organized labor remained undercurrents in Argentine politics even when Peronism itself was outlawed. The military intervened with increasing frequency after 1955, and each time had to take a harder line to repress labor, impose economic austerity, and re-establish order. The country also saw the development of a revolutionary left that was not interested in compromise or political participation, only in conducting its own terror campaign against military and government targets within the major cities. The Cold War and the success of the Cuban Revolution strengthened the military's conviction that Argentine society and politics were rotten from within, and national security doctrine gave the armed forces the moral responsibility to ferret out the subversives, leading to the excesses of the "dirty war."

Unit 4

Capital Sins: Authoritarianism and Democratization

UNIT SUMMARY

Unit 4 examines key economic and political experiences shared by several major Latin American countries over the last 30 years: the rise of military regimes, the push for rapid economic development, the crippling debt crisis, and the eventual return to democratic government. The television program and text focus exclusively on Brazil, while the anthology also includes some information on two other bureaucratic-authoritarian regimes, Chile and Argentina, as well as on the Alliance for Progress, the basis for U.S. policy toward the region during the early 1960s.

LEARNING OBJECTIVES

After completing this unit, students should be able to:

- Understand the inherent problems with import-substituting industrialization policies, and the various measures Brazil's leaders used to respond to those problems.

- Recognize the links between economic and social issues and the rise of military governments in Brazil and other Latin American countries during the midtwentieth century.

- Identify the central characteristics of bureaucratic-authoritarian regimes and understand how these governments in Brazil and elsewhere in Latin America differed from early military dictatorships.

- Identify the benefits and costs of Brazil's "economic miracle."

- Understand the process by which Brazil's military government left power.

- Explain some of the lingering problems that confront elected governments in Brazil and other former military dictatorships.

OVERVIEW

This unit focuses on the various strategies that Brazil's leaders have employed in order to bring about economic growth. It discusses the failures of the import-substituting industrialization phase and the decision to push for rapid growth via export diversification and an influx of foreign capital. The program and anthology give various perspectives on the bureaucratic-authoritarian period as experienced by military leaders, Brazilian industrialists, workers, consumers, and peasants. Some of the human rights abuses under the military are described in the program and anthology readings, as are continuing environmental issues in the Brazilian Amazon.

The program also looks at the transition to civilian government, and outlines some of the challenges confronting Brazil's civilian leaders. Some of the questions posed include how to restore economic growth and handle a huge debt burden, while also seeking to address the country's enormous poverty.

The text provides a historical overview of economic, social, and political developments in Brazil since independence. Students should use this information to place the experiences of the most recent decades in context. They should focus on the pressures on the Brazilian economy, the deep-rooted desire for growth and development, the military's role in politics, and the public's increasing demands for greater social justice and democracy.

Since this unit covers some difficult economic concepts, you may want to cover briefly the history of the International Monetary Fund and the World Bank and introduce students to such concepts as debt forgiveness and debt-for-nature swaps (see Activity 3, below).

STUDENT READING ASSIGNMENT

Modern Latin America, 3d ed.
In chapter 2: *Phase 4: Stagnation in Import-Substituting Growth, 1960s–1980s*, pp. 56–59, *Phase 5: Crisis, Debt, and Democracy*, pp. 59–62, and *A Framework for Comparison*, pp. 66–67.

Chapter 5, "Brazil: Development for Whom?" pp. 144–84.

Americas: An Anthology, chapter 4, pp. 72–103.

Writing Assignments/ Discussion Questions

1. The introduction to the anthology article "When Executives Turned Revolutionaries" states that some members of the Brazilian elite were willing to sacrifice democracy to restore social order and economic and political stability. If the society in which you lived became chaotic and politically unstable, which of your civil rights would you be willing to give up for order and stability?

2. Recent awareness of the earth's degraded natural environment has focused attention on the Amazon basin, which for centuries has been the home of many indigenous peoples as well as millions of species of plants, insects, and animals. The Brazilian Amazon has been a rich source of revenue for domestic companies and multinational corporations, especially logging and ranching interests. Huge tracts of land in the Amazon have also drawn migrant farmers from the impoverished and arid northeast, whose slash-and-burn techniques have caused widespread international concern. In addition, gold miners in search of wealth have contaminated rivers and fish with mercury. Which interests do you think can be accommodated and still preserve the rain forest resources? Which cannot? Are certain claims on natural resources more valid or moral than others? Why or why not?

3. How might each of the following people view the foreign debt crisis: a peasant in northeastern Brazil; a Brazilian government official; an industrialist in São Paulo; a North American banker. How do the origins and costs of the debt differ according to each person's vantage point? Should Brazil continue making payments, accept even more years without growth, or announce another debt moratorium? What other strategies might work, and why?

SUGGESTED ACTIVITIES

1. Have students imagine that the U. S. economy is in serious decline, inflation rates are up to 100 percent, and they and their families and friends are in danger of being homeless, without enough money for food or basic necessities. Have them imagine that public protests against food shortages and for higher pay are being held daily, causing mass confusion on the streets and rioting. Then present students with a chance to vote for a new government, one promising stability and help for the economy, but one that would be run with the help of the military and would be in power for ten years. Have students vote either for or against the new government and justify their choice.

2. After reading the excerpt from *Child of the Dark*, by Carolina Maria de Jesus, in the anthology chapter for this unit, have students write their own diary entries about life in a *favela* from the point of view of a resident from an affluent part of Rio de Janiero.

3. Tell students that they are residents of a large nation on the equator with great poverty, a vast tract of rain forest, and an enormous national debt. Divide students into groups and assign each group one the following roles: migrant farmers, environmentalists, loggers, ranchers, IMF loan officers, rubber tappers, and economic advisors. Have groups research the economic role they play in the destruction or preservation of the Brazilian rain forest. Then have students regroup so there is one representative of each role in each new group. In their new groups, have students negotiate a sustainable solution to Brazil's foreign debt that meets the needs of the greatest number of people while preserving the rain forest.

RESOURCES

Nonfiction

Canak, William, ed. *Lost Promises: Debt, Austerity and Development in Latin America.* Boulder, Colo.: Westview Press, 1989. This collection of essays focuses on the impact of the debt crisis on different aspects of Latin American societies such as organized labor, urban growth rates, and other factors.

Collier, David, ed. *The New Authoritarianism in Latin America.* Princeton: Princeton University Press, 1979. A collection of essays by leading scholars which looks at the causes and nature of bureaucratic-authoritarian regimes, and the relationship between socioeconomic issues and the rise of authoritarian rule.

da Costa Viotti, Emilia. *The Brazilian Empire.* Chicago: University of Chicago Press, 1985. History of the society of Brazilian elites in the nineteenth century, covering economic relations, regional conflicts, race relations, land policies, and ideology.

Dassin, Joan, trans. *Torture in Brazil: A Report.* New York: Vintage Books, 1986. This report, prepared by the Archdiocese of São Paulo, details human rights abuses and torture during the Brazilian military governments from 1964 to 1979. It is based on *Brasil: Nunca Mais* ("Brazil: Never Again"), the findings of a five-year research project documenting human rights abuses.

Davis, Shelton. *Victims of the Miracle: Development and the Indians in Brazil.* New York: Cambridge University Press, 1977. In this highly critical view of Brazil's "economic miracle," the author claims that the suffering of the indigenous Brazilian peoples and the devastation of the rain forest resulted directly from the economic development policies of the military government.

de Jesus, Carolina Maria. *Child of the Dark.* New York: Mentor Books, 1964. True story of daily life in a *favela* written by a poor Brazilian woman. Excerpted in the anthology.

Diamond, Larry, Juan Linz, and Seymour Martin Lipse, eds. *Democracy in Developing Countries: Latin*

America. Vol. 4. Boulder, Colo.: Lynne Rienner, 1989. Compares the perspectives of leading scholars on the issue of democracy in Latin America.

Evans, P. E. Liedke, and E. Liedke Filho. *Political Economy of Contemporary Brazil: A Study Guide.* Albuquerque: Latin American Institute, University of New Mexico, 1985. Includes a brief background on the political economy of contemporary Brazil and an annotated bibliography.

Fishlow, Albert. "The State of Economics in Brazil and Latin America: Is the Past Prologue to the Future?" In *Americas: New Interpretive Essays,* edited by Alfred Stepan. New York: Oxford University Press, 1992. An examination of how Latin American states need to restructure their economies in the face of a changing world market, written by a member of the *Americas* academic advisory board as an optional addition to this unit.

Golden, Tim. "Brazil's Gold Rush Brings a Brutal Clash of Cultures," *Miami Herald,* July 25, 1989. Describes how many of the indigenous groups in the Amazon are threatened by mining.

Linz, Juan, and Alfred Stepan, eds. *The Breakdown of Democratic Regimes: Latin America.* Baltimore: Johns Hopkins University Press, 1978. This collection of essays explains how and why democratic regimes failed and authoritarian rule emerged in various countries in Latin America.

Malloy, James M., ed. *Authoritarianism and Corporatism in Latin America.* Pittsburgh: University of Pittsburgh Press, 1977. This collection of essays by leading scholars analyzes the organization of different political regimes, such as populist and bureaucratic-authoritarian governments in Latin America.

Mendes, Chico. *Fight for the Forest.* London: Latin American Bureau, 1989. In this extended interview conducted weeks before his murder in 1988, Mendes talks about the rubber tappers' lives, their political struggle and alliances with local indigenous groups and the environmental lobby, and their campaign to save the rain forest. (Available from Monthly Review Press, 122 West 27th St., New York, NY 10001.)

O'Donnell, Guillermo. *Modernization and Bureaucratic-Authoritarianism: Studies in South American Politics.* Berkeley: University of California Press, 1979. This seminal work on bureaucratic-authoritarianism and import-substituting industrialization (ISI) examines the relationship between socioeconomic crisis and the rise of authoritarian rule.

Skidmore, Thomas, *Politics in Brazil, 1930–1964.* New York: Oxford University Press, 1967. This book examines the political, economic, and social forces at work in Brazil since the 1930s which led to the breakdown of democracy and the overthrow of Brazilian president João Goulart in 1964.

Skidmore, Thomas. *The Politics of Military Rule in Brazil, 1964–1985.* Princeton: Princeton University Press, 1988. This comprehensive study of different military governments since 1964 highlights the role of internal divisions of the military in the movement toward a return to democratic rule.

Stallings, Barbara, and Robert Kaufman, eds. *Debt and Democracy in Latin America.* Boulder, Colo.: Westview Press, 1989. A collection of general articles and case studies that focus on how various types of regimes have dealt with foreign debt.

Stepan, Alfred. *Rethinking Military Politics: Brazil and the Southern Cone.* Princeton: Princeton University Press, 1988. A study of the military's role in the transition from authoritarian rule in the Southern Cone and the continued presence and role of the military in the new democracies.

Stepan, Alfred, ed. *Authoritarian Brazil.* New Haven: Yale University Press, 1973. Book of essays by leading scholars examining the origins of military rule in Brazil from a historical and comparative perspective, highlighting the role of economic-structural factors, political factors, and shifts in military control.

Stepan, Alfred, ed. *Democratizing Brazil: Problems of Transition and Consolidation.* New York: Oxford University Press, 1989. These essays focus on Brazil's transition to a democratic government and chronicle the first years of the new democracy. Articles discuss such topics as trade unionism, women in politics, the role of the Brazilian church, the economics of *abertura,* the debt crisis, and grass-roots popular movements in the *favelas.*

Vesilind, Priit. "Brazil: Moment of Promise and Pain." *National Geographic* 171:3 (March 1987). An overall view of Brazilian people and culture, and of the impact of economic development on the poor.

Wirth, John L. *The Politics of Brazilian Development, 1930–1954.* Stanford, Calif.: Stanford University Press, 1970. Three case studies—foreign trade, the steel industry, and the oil industry—are used to analyze the way policy decisions were made in the Vargas era.

Fiction

Amado, Jorge. *Gabriela, Clove and Cinnamon.* New York: Avon Books, 1968. The story of Gabriela, who comes from the backlands of Brazil and is hired by the owner of the town's most popular café to replace his cook. The café owner soon finds himself with the most prosperous business—and the most sought-after woman—in town.

Machado de Assis, Joaquim M. *The Devil's Church and Other Stories.* Translated by Jack Schmit and Lorie Ishimatsu. Austin: University of Texas Press, 1977. Brazilian writer Machado de Assis (1839–1908) is considered to be an early modernist and the father of modern Brazilian fiction. This collection of 19 stories is set in Brazil in the second half of the nineteenth century.

Films

Unless otherwise indicated, all films listed are available in VHS video format.

Bye Bye Brazil. 105 minutes, 1980 (Portuguese, with English subtitles). In the words of director Carlos Diegues, this film, set in northeast Brazil, is "about a country which is about to come to an end in order to make way for another which is about to begin." Released on Warner Home Video and available in most video-rental outlets.

How Nice to See You Alive. 100 minutes, 1989. Film by Lucia Murat about the suspension of civil rights in Brazil after the 1964 military coup. Using a mix of fiction and documentary, the film interviews eight women who were political prisoners. Available from Women Make Movies, 225 Lafayette Street, New York, NY 10012; (212) 925-0606.

In the Name of Progress. 60 minutes, 1991. This fourth episode of the 10-part environmental television course *Race to Save the Planet* investigates the consequences of Western-style industrial development in India and Brazil, and profiles slain activist Chico Mendes and his work to help preserve Brazil's rain forest and ensure a sustainable living for the rubber tappers who live in it. Available for purchase ($29.95) from The Annenberg/CPB Project, P.O. Box 2345, S. Burlington, VT 05407-2345; (800) LEARNER.

Pixote. 127 minutes, 1981. (Portuguese, with English subtitles.) This film is a poignant, blunt portrait of the lives of a group of street children in Brazil. Director Hector Babenco based the script on life stories, and cast real street children as the film's the main characters. Educational institutions may purchase the film on VHS video for $250 through New Yorker Films, 16 W. 61st Street, New York, NY 10023; (212) 247-6110. Available in some video-rental outlets.

They Don't Wear Black Ties. 120 minutes, 1981 (Portuguese, with English subtitles). Set during a period of military dictatorship in Brazil, this film chronicles a union strike at a factory and the conflict it causes within one working-class family. Available for purchase (video, $250) through New Yorker Films, 16 W. 61st Street, New York, NY 10023; (212) 247-6110.

Other Resources

Favelas of Rio de Janeiro. This 28-slide media packet depicts the *favelas* as a housing alternative for the poor of Brazil, and attempts to dispel many of the misconceptions concerning the *favelas'* residents, their jobs, and social support networks. Contains a teacher's guide, suggested readings, and classroom activities. The cost is $10. Available from: Latin American Curriculum Resource Center, Tulane University, New Orleans, LA 70118; (504) 865-5164.

TEST BANK

Questions reflect content from the programs, textbook, study guide, and anthology.

Multiple Choice

*Mark the letter of the response that **best** answers the question or completes the statement.*

_____ 1. Brazil's economy during the colonial period emphasized the export of which commodity?

    a. Silver
    b. Sugar
    c. Tin
    d. Rice

_____ 2. Although there was an abundance of labor that could have been mobilized from within the country to handle Brazil's large increases in agricultural production at the turn of the century, the Brazilian government instead chose to encourage immigration from:

    a. Europe.
    b. Africa.
    c. North America.
    d. the Caribbean.

_____ 3. Reliance on coffee in the years 1890–1945 posed which of the following problems for Brazil?

    a. Supplies could not keep up with rising world demand.
    b. Brazil didn't have enough land for the large coffee plantations.
    c. Brazil didn't have enough labor to sustain a large volume of coffee production.
    d. The world market price fluctuated dramatically, affecting Brazil's earnings.

_____ 4. Which of the following events in the late 1970s and early 1980s contributed to the weakening of public support for military government in Brazil? (*Mark all that apply.*)

    a. continued rapid economic growth that increased hopes for democracy.
    b. public realization of the high costs of Brazil's foreign debt.
    c. a slow-down in economic growth and a wave of industrial strikes.
    d. The military government's refusal to even discuss the possibility of *abertura*.

_____ 5. Which of the following statements are true of the Brazilian "economic miracle" of 1968–1974? (*Mark all that apply.*)

    a. The benefits of growth were shared equally throughout society.
    b. Economic growth averaged 10 percent or better over the "miracle" years.
    c. The miracle relied largely on the growth of import industries such as automobile production.
    d. Income equality increased significantly during the years of the miracle.

_____ 6. One of the major difficulties of import-substituting industrialization policies was that:

    a. they were not capital-intensive.
    b. Latin American governments did not adequately protect the fledgling industries.
    c. imports remained high while export competitiveness decreased, leading to a foreign exchange crisis.
    d. the new industries were very labor intensive and couldn't find enough skilled workers to do the necessary jobs.

_____ 7. In 1960, many heads of state attended the inauguration of the new capital of Brazil, which was called:

    a. São Paulo.
    b. Brasília.

c. Rio de Janeiro.

d. Rio Grande do Sol.

_____ 8. Most of the Brazilian military opposed the succession of João Goulart to power in 1961 because:

a. they did not believe he had a constitutional right to power.

b. they thought he was too conservative.

c. they feared his populist and leftist orientation.

d. they wanted to keep Vargas in power.

_____ 9. The Alliance for Progress was instituted because the United States:

a. wanted to forestall any new revolutionary takeovers in Latin America.

b. wanted to assist Brazil in repaying its huge foreign debt.

c. wanted to avoid the establishment of any other bureaucratic-authoritarian regimes in Latin America.

d. wanted to respond to Latin American countries' desire for a military alliance with the United States.

_____ 10. Bureaucratic-authoritarianism refers to regimes that often:

a. promote human rights and social organizations.

b. have large social service bureaucracies.

c. came to power only in Brazil and Chile.

d. are directly operated by the military, which represses most political activity.

_____ 11. Which of the following statements describe Brazil's economic miracle of 1968–74? *(Mark all that apply.)*

a. Economic growth averaged 10 percent or better.

b. Income inequality increased as the gap widened between the poor and the rich.

c. The benefits of growth were distributed equitably throughout society.

d. It was achieved by focusing on production of industrial goods for domestic consumption and export.

_____ 12. The two oil shocks of the 1970s, which aggravated trade and budget deficits, forced most Latin American governments to:

a. free political prisoners.

b. adopt devaluation policies.

c. borrow heavily from abroad.

d. stop importing oil.

_____ 13. The "debt crisis" was the result of a chain of events triggered by the worldwide recession of 1980–82, including the rise of interest rates on Latin American loans, the decline in Latin American export earnings, and the suspension of new lending by creditors. Which country was the first to announce its inability to continue debt payments?

a. Brazil

b. Argentina

c. Mexico

d. Chile

_____ 14. Some of the "social costs" of military rule in Brazil were: *(Mark all that apply.)*

a. the repression of labor movements.

b. persistent unemployment.

c. an influx of migrants to the northeast.

d. a more unequal distribution of wealth and income.

_____ 15. In a 1978 interview excerpted in the anthology, Luis Ignacio da Silva ("Lula") said the union movement he led differed from previous union movements because:

a. it received financial and technical assistance from the state.

b. it was met with less repression from the military government.

c. union workers no longer had to strike for higher wages.

d. workers had developed a greater sense of class consciousness.

_____ 16. According to the anthology article "Deforestation and the Rights of Indigenous Peoples," lumbering on indigenous lands:

a. poses a minimal threat because it is confined to a small area in just one state.

b. is essential for Brazil's economic development.

c. decreases self-sufficiency in indigenous communities.

d. is opposed by the indigenous leaders because profits are too small.

Identification/Short Answer

Define or describe the following terms, concepts, or persons, or answer the following questions. Answers should be no longer than a few sentences.

17. Getúlio Vargas:

18. After the transition from authoritarian rule, what are some of the social and economic problems facing new civilian governments?

19. Briefly describe what the bureaucratic-authoritarian regimes that came to power in several Latin American countries in the 1960s and 1970s viewed as their "mission."

20. Why was General Ernesto Geisel an important figure in Brazil's eventual return to democratic rule?

21. Which three countries had the largest external debt in Latin America in the 1980s?

22. Petrodollars:

23. Pharaonic projects:

24. Export diversification:

25. List some problems with import-substituting industrialization policies which became apparent in the 1960s.

ESSAY QUESTIONS

1. During the years of the economic miracle, Brazil's finance minister, Delfim Neto, said, "A cake has to rise before it can be sliced and served up." What were some of the long-term problems that resulted from this policy of grow now, distribute later?

2. Describe the characteristics of Brazil's bureaucratic-authoritarian regime. Why did it come to power, and why were so many Brazilians content to live with such restrictions of their civil and political rights?

3. In his interview on the program, Lula says, "There's a contradiction between economic development and political underdevelopment." Does the experience of Brazil prove that political repression is necessary for economic growth? Draw upon recent events in China, Eastern Europe, and the former Soviet Union to illustrate other aspects of the relationship between democratic government and economic progress.

ANSWER KEY

Test Bank

Answers indicate sources.

1. b (textbook)
2. a (textbook)
3. d (textbook)
4. b, c (program, anthology, textbook, study guide)
5. b, c (program, anthology, textbook, study guide)
6. c (anthology, textbook, study guide)
7. b (textbook)
8. c (anthology, textbook, study guide)
9. a (anthology)
10. d (anthology, textbook, study guide)
11. a, b, d (program, textbook, study guide)
12. c (anthology, textbook, study guide)
13. c (textbook)
14. a, b, d (program, anthology, textbook, study guide)
15. d (anthology)
16. c (anthology)
17. Prominent Brazilian populist leader and president during the 1930s–50s. Founder of the *Estado Nôvo*. (program, anthology, textbook, study guide)
18. Students should generally mention debt, socioeconomic inequalities, unemployment, urban poverty, and the need to restore economic growth, among other issues. (program, anthology, textbook, study guide)
19. The military governments' doctrine of national security justified their taking and holding state power in order to prevent Communist takeovers, promote economic growth, fight corruption, and protect democracy. (program, anthology, textbook, study guide)
20. He launched the political opening known as *abertura*, and committed Brazil to the return of democratic rule; he was a member of the legalist, reformist faction of the military. (textbook, study guide)
21. Argentina, Brazil, Mexico. (textbook)
22. Term used to describe the abundance of bank deposits from oil-exporting countries which were used to finance loans to Latin American countries. (program, study guide)

23. Huge development schemes launched by Brazil's military government in the 1970s, financed primarily by foreign loans, and generally viewed as symbols of waste and corruption. (program, study guide)
24. Export diversification is the effort made by many Latin American countries to expand the range of exported goods, moving in particular away from primary goods toward manufactures. (textbook, study guide)
25. Students should list and describe the four main problems cited in the text:
    a. Latin America remained dependent on other countries for imported capital goods in order to produce manufactured goods.
    b. There was an imbalance of trade—that is, Latin America's main products underwent a steady decline, so that over time the countries could only purchase smaller and smaller quantities of capital goods.
    c. The demand for Latin American manufactured goods was limited.
    d. There was only a limited number of jobs created because of the relatively high degree of technology involved in Latin American industry. (textbook)

Essay Questions

1. Students should mention the inequalities that resulted as benefits were restricted to a small elite; the widened gap between the rich and the poor; the chronic social problems in the areas of health care, education, housing, and employment; and the resentment among those who were left out of the "miracle."
2. Brazil's bureaucratic-authoritarian regime emerged after 1964, when the military toppled the Goulart government to prevent what it perceived as a dangerous drift toward socialism. As it had not done in earlier coups, the military after 1964 remained in power in the belief that it was the most appropriate institution to manage Brazil's modernization and growth. All popular sectors were excluded from power—at least until the military began the gradual transition back to electoral politics in 1970—and labor activity was tightly controlled. Never-

theless, many Brazilians accepted the loss of democratic, participatory government as a necessary cost of achieving social and economic stability. Probably the most important reason for the military government's popularity was the sustained growth of the Brazilian economy, especially during the period from 1968 to 1974, known as the "Brazilian miracle."

3. Students should recognize that although economic growth occurred during the bureaucratic-authoritarian period, it had occurred earlier under democratically-elected president Juscelino Kubitschek, and reoccurred later under José Sarney. Also, Brazil was not the most repressive of the bureaucratic-authoritarian regimes in Latin America, although it did try to control labor. Therefore, there is not a causal link between political repression and economic growth. Other examples students may cite to show that links between economic growth and political democracy are complex include China, where economic reforms led to broad demands for democracy that were violently crushed, and the former Soviet Union, where the change to political democracy was initially accompanied by economic chaos and public dissatisfaction.

Unit 5

Continent on the Move: Migration and Urbanization

UNIT SUMMARY

Unit 5 explores the causes and effects of migration, one of the most important forces transforming Latin America and the Caribbean in the twentieth century. The unit considers in particular migration in Mexico, where domestic and international forces have caused millions of people to move out of rural villages in search of jobs, whether in Mexico City, the world's largest urban area, in new industrial cities along the United States–Mexico border, or across the border in the United States.

LEARNING OBJECTIVES

After completing this unit, students should be able to:

- Recognize that migration is caused by a variety of political, economic, and social factors, and is affected by both domestic and international policies.

- Describe the impact of Mexico's political and economic development on domestic and international migration patterns.

- Understand that lack of access to land and the inability to make a living by farming are important underlying reasons for much of the rural-to-urban migration in Mexico and elsewhere in the Americas.

- Identify some of the benefits and costs of rural-to-urban migration for migrants.

- Discuss the impact of migration on Mexico's largest cities.

- Draw connections between migration in Latin America and the Caribbean and the larger processes of economic and social change in the hemisphere.

OVERVIEW

After centuries of absorbing numerous waves of migrants, particularly from Europe and Africa, Latin America and the Caribbean have been transformed during the twentieth century by new migratory patterns moving people both internally and internationally, within and outside of the region. Unit 5, "Continent on the Move: Migration and

Urbanization," analyzes the forces underlying this massive internal migration and ties them to the impact that modernization and development have had on the region.

Students should understand that migration is not caused only by internal, domestic conditions, although such issues as access to land, housing policies, and industrial growth are very important. The experience of Latin American and the Caribbean countries shows that migratory patterns are also affected by the movement of international capital within the region, international economic forces that emphasize or undermine production of certain goods, and international agreements such as those that created the *braceros* program or the *maquiladora* industries.

Two other central themes in this unit are the importance of land, especially land ownership—which was a key factor in both the Mexican Revolution and to the subsequent rural-to-urban migration within Mexico—and the effect of explosive urban growth on Mexico City and other major Latin American cities. The anthology readings complement the television program by providing a vivid glimpse of modern Mexico City, depicting the enormous contrasts between the wealthy and the poor, and describing the squalid and unhealthy living conditions of millions of the city's poorest residents.

The chapter assigned in the textbook is a political and economic history of Mexico since independence, with particular emphasis on the Mexican Revolution and the postrevolutionary period. The textbook creates the context for the program and the anthology readings, and gives students an understanding of how Mexico's complex political, social, and economic history is connected to migration. The subject of the Mexican Revolution is not covered in the study guide or in the test bank of this unit, since it will be discussed in Unit 11, "Fire in the Mind: Revolutions and Revolutionaries."

The anthology readings and program concentrate on the perspectives of those who migrate, their motivations, and their experiences while the textbook provides important historical information on social, political, and economic change in twentieth century Mexico. Readings in the anthology also illustrate the widespread nature of the migration phenomenon and its effect throughout Latin America and the Caribbean.

STUDENT READING ASSIGNMENT

Modern Latin America, 3d ed.
Chapter 7, "Mexico: The Taming of a Revolution," pp. 221–53.

Americas: An Anthology, chapter 5, pp. 104–36.

WRITING ASSIGNMENTS/ DISCUSSION QUESTIONS

1. Internal migration has contributed to increasing urbanization in Mexico and throughout Latin America and the Caribbean. By the end of this century, Latin America will be predominantly urban, and will contain two of the world's largest cities, Mexico City and São Paulo. What kind of changes has this massive movement of people from rural to urban areas had on Latin American societies, and what further changes are likely to result? Should the governments of the region encourage people to stay in the countryside? What kinds of measures could make rural villages, such as Zacatecas, more attractive places for young people to remain?

2. Reading 5.5 in the anthology, "The Perilous Journey of Nicaraguan Migrants," illustrates some of the many risks and physical and psychological dangers confronting would-be migrants to the United States. How does this reading, along with films such as *El Norte* (listed in the Resources section), affect students' perceptions of those who migrate illegally to the United States? Does it reinforce or alter their views? Have students discuss the conditions that might push migrants to take such risks in order to seek a better life. Could students see themselves undertaking similar journeys? Why or why not?

3. The program "Continent on the Move" includes a scene of peasants marching together with poor urban residents to protest the agrarian policies of Mexican president Salinas de Gortari. Given the poor conditions in the Mex-

ican countryside, are you surprised by the peasants' strong negative reaction to Salinas's plans? The PRI has always attempted to keep peasants and working-class citizens separate in order to prevent alliances. Do you think the coalition between *campesinos* and residents of poor *barrios* could pose a significant threat to the Mexican political system?

SUGGESTED ACTIVITIES

1. Have students write up a comprehensive plan of measures to address the major urban problems of Mexico City from the perspective of a minister of urban planning or a member of the Asamblea de Barrios, the organization of Mexico City's poor residents. The plans should include an analysis of the economic and political obstacles to their plans.

2. The anthology contains a selection about the movement of Guatemalan refugees into Mexico to escape brutal repression in their communities. Have students research the dilemmas faced by Mexico in coping with the refugees and their needs. Some possible research questions:

- How should a poor country like Mexico balance the needs of refugees with those of its own citizens who might lose land, jobs, or other resources to the large numbers of refugees?

- What was the international community's response?

- What was Mexico's initial reaction to the refugees? Did the policy change over time? Why or why not?

- Did Mexico request or receive international aid to cope with the refugees? Was the aid sufficient?

- Does Mexico have different policies on migration for economic reasons as opposed to migration due to political persecution? How were its policies affected by the flow of refugees and consequent economic, social, political, and environmental conflicts?

RESOURCES

Nonfiction

Calderon de la Barca, Fanny. *Life in Mexico: The Letters of Fanny Calderon de la Barca*. Edited by Howard T. Fisher and Marion Hall Fisher. Garden City, N.Y.: Doubleday, 1966. Originally published in 1843, the letters and journal entries of Fanny Calderon de la Barca provide a detailed and descriptive account of life in nineteenth-century Mexico. The author, a Scot, was married to a Spanish diplomat who served as Spain's first minister to Mexico.

Fernández-Kelly, M. Patricia and Alejandro Portes. "Continent on the Move: Immigrants and Refugees in the Americas." In *Americas: New Interpretive Essays*, edited by Alfred Stepan. New York: Oxford University Press, 1992. An examination of the causes and consequences of the migration of more than 5 million people per year across national borders within the Americas, written by two members of the *Americas* academic advisory board as an optional addition to this unit.

Fernández-Kelly, María Patricia. *For We Are Sold, I and My People: Women and Industry in Mexico's Frontier*. Albany: State University of New York Press, 1983. The hidden human dimensions of present-day multinational manufacturing procedures are revealed in this examination of *maquiladoras*, the hundreds of assembly plants that since the 1960s have been part of the Mexican government's development strategy.

Fried, Jonathan L., Marvin E. Gettleman, Deborah T. Levenson, and Nancy Peckenham, eds. *Guatemala in Rebellion: Unfinished History*. New York: Grove Press, 1983. An anthology covering contemporary Guatemalan history from varying viewpoints, including primary sources.

Friedrich, Otto. "A Proud Capital's Distress." *Time*, August 6, 1984, 26–30, 33–35. This article provides a description of Mexico City's plight—overcrowding, poverty, pollution, and corruption—and discusses the Mexican and U.S. governments' attempts at political reform and economic development.

Helper, Susan, and Philip Mirowski. "Mexico's Desperate Experiment," *Dollars and Sense* (September 1989). Critically asks the question, will *maquiladoras* save the Mexican economy? Examines the role of multinational corporations, the benefits for employees, and political linkages.

Mangin, William. "Young Towns of Lima." *The World and I* (June 1989). Examines the hundreds of permanent squatter settlements in the environs of Lima, Peru, and dispels many myths about these "young towns."

Merrick, Thomas W., with PRB (Population Reference Bureau Incorporated) staff. "Population Pressures in Latin America." *Population Bulletin* 41:3 (July 1986). Analysis of population data in Latin America; examines growth rate in both urban and rural areas, and includes statistics on life expectancy, infant mortality, contraceptive use, and national population policies for each country.

Oster, Patrick. *The Mexicans*. New York: Morrow, 1989. Brief descriptions of the different Mexican social classes by a journalist.

Reavis, Dick J. *Conversations with Moctezuma*. New York: Morrow, 1990. After immersing himself in Mexico for a year, the author provides a vivid description of Mexico's past and a glimpse of its troubled future.

Richardson, Bonham C. "Caribbean Migrations, 1838–1985." In *The Modern Caribbean*, edited by Franklin W. Knight and Colin A. Palmer. Chapel Hill: University of North Carolina Press, 1989. From the colonial period to the present, Richardson discusses the variety of people, destinations, and reasons for migrating, and the results in the Caribbean and new communites where Carribean emigrants settle.

"The World's Urban Explosion."*Unesco Courier* (March 1985) 24–29. General survey of the four themes addressed at the international symposium

"Metropolis 84": demography and town planning; economic and technological change; transport; and culture and the environment.

Fiction

Castellanos, Rosario. *Another Way To Be: Selected Works of Rosario Castellanos*. Athens: University of Georgia Press, 1990. Poetry and fiction that examine the role of women in modern Mexico.

Cisneros, Sandra. *Woman Hollering Creek*. New York: Random House, 1990.
Collection of 20 short stories, including "Eyes of Zapata," the tale of the Mexican Revolution as told by the mistress of General Zapata.

Fuentes, Carlos. *A Change of Skin*. Translated by Sam Hileman. New York: Farrar Straus Giroux, 1968. As four people drive from Mexico City to Veracruz, the narrator exposes the object of each one's search: redemption for ex-Nazi Franz; experience for his Mexican lover, Isabel; success for the poet Javier; and love for Javier's wife, Elizabeth.

Fuentes, Carlos. *The Death of Artemio Cruz*. Translated by Sam Hileman. New York: Farrar Straus Giroux, 1988. This novel conveys the sweep of modern Mexican history through the eyes of one man.

Rulfo, Juan. *Pedro Paramo*. New York: Grove/Weidenfeld, 1990. A young man searches for his father, who he discovers is the corrupt political boss of an impoverished town in southern Mexico.

Sainz, Gustavo. *The Princess of the Iron Palace*. New York: Grove Press, 1985. Gustavo Sainz is a leader of a group of Mexican writers known as "The Wave" who gained notice in the 1960s. The teenage protagonist of this novel is exuberant, cynical, and ambitious.

Yáñez, Agustin. *The Edge of the Storm*. Arlington: University of Texas Press, 1963. The saga of an isolated village in Mexico in 1909 and 1910, just before the revolution.

Films

Unless otherwise indicated, all films listed are available in VHS video format.

El Norte. 139 minutes, 1984. (Spanish, with English subtitles) This movie chronicles the illegal immigration of a Guatemalan brother and sister through Mexico into the United States. Available in most video-rental outlets.

Guatemala: Roads of Silence. 59 minutes, 1988. (Spanish, with English subtitles.) Examines the plight of Guatemalan indigenous peoples caught in the crossfire of the government's counterinsurgency campaign. Guatemalans have fled by the thousands into neighboring countries to escape the violence. Winner of the Silver Caravel at the Bilbao Film Festival. Available on videocassette for rental ($90) or purchase ($395) from: The Cinema Guild, 1697 Broadway, New York, NY 10019; (212) 246-5522.

Hour of the Star. 96 minutes, 1986. This film tells the story of a young woman who migrates from the countryside of northeast Brazil to São Paulo. Multi-award winner at the Brazilian Film Festival. Available for rental ($20) from: Facets, 1517 West Fullerton, Chicago, IL 60614; (800) 331-6197.

Mexico and the U.S.: Ambivalent Allies. 30 minutes, 1988. Part of the World Beat series. An examination of the U.S. relationship with Mexico, including economic ties and common problems such as immigration, drugs, debt, and trade. Available for purchase ($39.95) through May 1995 from PBS Video; phone: (800) 424-7963; fax: (703) 739-5269.

Time of Women. 20 minutes, 1988. (Spanish, with English subtitles.) Filmed in Santa Rosa, Ecuador, this film tells the story of a village from which thousands of people have emigrated to the United States in search of better lives. It explores the "push factors" involved in migration and the strength of the rural women who stay behind. Available from: Women Make Movies, 225 Lafayette Street, New York, NY, 10012; (212) 925-0606.

Three short films on population issues in Latin America are available from the Population Reference Bureau for a $10 rental fee. They may be ordered by writing: Film Librarian, Population Reference Bureau, 777 14th Street N.W., Suite 800, Washington, DC 20005.

> *Immigration: What We Promised, Where to Draw the Line.* 15 minutes, 1986. (3/4″ or 1/2″ videocassette.) Addresses the United States' attraction for immigrants and the effects of immigration on U.S. society.

> *Lessons for the Future.* 17 minutes, 1980. This 16-mm film presents the case studies of three teachers as they discuss family planning with their students.

> *Mexico in the Year 2000.* 12 minutes, 1979. (16 mm.) This film, produced in cooperation with the Mexican government, describes the rapid increase in Mexico's population and the difficulties Mexico will face in providing social and economic services to its people.

Other Resources

Guatemala, I Carry Your Name. This 25-minute slide/tape presentation chronicles the plight of the displaced as a result of the Guatemalan government's "counterinsurgency" drive. Available from: Oxfam America, 115 Broadway, Boston, MA 02115; (617) 482-1211.

TEST BANK

Questions reflect content from the programs, textbook, and anthology.

Multiple Choice

*Mark the letter of the response that **best** answers the question or completes the statement.*

_____ 1. Social and kinship networks are especially important to migrants because they: *(Mark all that apply.)*

    a. help ease the transition from rural villages to new urban environments.

    b. are responsible for the growing numbers of young people who are choosing to remain in the rural villages of their birth.

    c. attract new migrants to follow in the footsteps of relatives and friends who have gone ahead to new locations.

    d. are a source of jobs, housing, and other assistance for new migrants.

_____ 2. The single largest type of migration that occurs in the Americas as a whole is:

    a. urban to rural.

    b. rural to urban.

    c. among various Latin American and Caribbean countries.

    d. from Latin America and the Caribbean to the United States.

_____ 3. Mexico's agrarian reform program during the 1930s:

    a. was emulated elsewhere in Latin America because of its economic success.

    b. emphasized the establishment of large estates for ranching and agro-export industries.

    c. broke up the *latifundios* and distributed the land to groups of peasant families under the *ejido* system.

    d. was a political failure that ultimately led to President Lázaro Cárdenas's resignation.

_____ 4. Which of the following criticisms have been made about the *maquiladora* industries? *(Mark all that apply.)*

    a. They maintain inadequate health and safety standards for workers.

    b. They split up families by requiring their female employees to live in company-sponsored, dormitory-style housing.

    c. They have a top-heavy management structure that keeps the number of jobs created unnecessarily low.

    d. They are responsible for several serious cases of environmental pollution, such as dumping of toxic wastes.

_____ 5. Why did Mexico and the United States go to war in 1845?

    a. The United States objected to Mexico's invasion of California and sought to restore its sovereignty over the territory.

    b. Mexico attacked Texas in the famous battle at the Alamo.

    c. Mexicans considered the annexation of Texas an invasion of Mexican territory and attacked U.S. troops along the border.

    d. The United States refused to pay Mexico the agreed-upon purchase price for the territories of Texas, California, and the Colorado River Valley.

_____ 6. Migration from Mexico to the United States: *(Mark all that apply.)*

    a. has long been considered by many Mexicans to be an essential safety valve for absorbing unemployed laborers.

b. was formalized by means of the *braceros* program.

c. ended abruptly when Congress passed the Simpson-Rodino Act in 1986.

d. is expected to cease entirely once Mexico signs the North American Free Trade Agreement.

_____ 7. The Mexican Miracle:

a. resulted from the discovery of oil reserves in the late 1970s.

b. resulted in a greater economic growth rate in the capital than in other cities.

c. prompted a massive movement of single women to the border to look for *maquiladora* jobs.

d. emphasized the need to provide parcels of land for all who qualified in order to reduce rural-to-urban migration.

_____ 8. Which of the following is true of the Mexican economy in the 1950s and 1960s?

a. Tijuana, Ciudad Juárez, and other border cities grew faster than Mexico City.

b. Severe austerity measures led to a deep recession and a drop in per capita income.

c. The Mexican peso had to be devalued several times as a result of rapid inflation.

d. Inequalities of income grew as the wealthy profited from rapid economic growth.

_____ 9. The discovery of vast deposits of oil in the late 1970s in Mexico had which of the following effects? (*Mark all that apply.*)

a. Mexicans believed they would have new economic power in the world market.

b. The increasing price of oil throughout the early 1980s surpassed all expectations for potential oil revenues.

c. The Mexican government became increasingly reliant on oil revenues to finance its spending programs.

d. International lenders remained skeptical of Mexico's economic stability and refused to provide substantial amounts of loans.

_____ 10. According to the program and the anthology, which of the following is true of the impact of migration on Mexico City? (*Mark all that apply.*)

a. Mexico City grew rapidly, but is still able to provide adequate jobs and housing for the migrants.

b. Mexico City's economy was able to keep growing even during the depression of the 1980s.

c. Mexico City now has a huge percentage of its population living in extreme poverty in slums and squatter communities.

d. Migration intensified the rate of urban growth in Mexico City, which will have more than 20 million residents by the year 2000.

_____ 11. Mexico's 1982 announcement that it was unable to continue payment on its debt:

a. led to a cutoff of credit from the world's largest financial institutions, such as the International Monetary Fund.

b. brought about a significant economic recovery with the investment of funds formerly sent out of the country to service the debt.

c. brought about a major "rescue package" of new loans conditional upon Mexico's acceptance of a severe austerity program.

d. resulted in a steady increase in per capita income over the course of the 1980s.

_____ 12. *Maquiladoras*:

a. made their largest contribution to the Mexican economy in the 1960s.

b. had a major impact on occupational structure and migration patterns in Mexico.
c. resulted from the Mexican government's import-substituting industrialization policies.
d. are in the process of being phased out due to pressure from U.S. labor groups.

_____ 13. Mexican proponents of the North American Free Trade Agreement: (*Mark all that apply.*)

a. argue that it will create new jobs in a wide range of industries.
b. believe it will decrease Mexico's historic economic dependence on the U.S. market.
c. hope that the pact will encourage U.S. professionals, such as doctors and engineers, to migrate to Mexico.
d. expect it to lead to diversification of the Mexican economy.

_____ 14. Which of the following is true of Mexican president Salinas's radical proposals for agrarian reform?

a. He promised to increase dramatically the pace of land distribution.
b. His decision to abolish the system of communal land ownership had great appeal for the *ejidatarios*.
c. He announced there would be no further distribution of land to the *ejidos*.
d. His plans were criticized by the agro-export industries, which would lose an important source of labor.

_____ 15. Most migration in Latin America consists of:

a. the movement of those seeking greater political freedom.
b. the movement of refugees escaping civil war and revolution.

c. the movement of unemployed professionals in an international "brain drain."
d. the movement of labor in search of jobs.

_____ 16. Poor residents of Mexico City complain that the government:

a. is unresponsive to their needs for improved housing and other services.
b. has cracked down too hard on the informal economy, eliminating important sources of income.
c. has tried to force them to leave their homes and return to the countryside.
d. refuses to allow them to form self-help organizations such as the Asamblea de Barrios.

_____ 17. Since the revolution, Mexico's political system has been characterized by:

a. a bureaucratic-authoritarian government in which the military dominates and political activity is severely circumscribed.
b. a weak central authority elected nationally which is counterbalanced by strong local and regional bosses, or *caudillos*.
c. a multiparty democratic system that has exchanged power regularly among the top three parties.
d. an official party that has swung back and forth between liberal and conservative policies but retained dominance.

_____ 18. Migration in the Caribbean in the twentieth century: (*Mark all that apply.*)

a. dates back to the construction of the Panama Canal and has only increased over the course of the century.
b. is characterized by the push-and-pull effect of U.S. capital on labor.

c. is disrupting traditional ways of life, which until recently kept families in the same place for generations.

d. usually involves the transfer of families from one island to another.

_____ 19. Which of the following is considered a "pull" factor?

a. Government policies that make it difficult for people to earn a living by farming.

b. The availability of housing, education, and entertainment in major urban areas.

c. The fact that most migrants have to earn a living in the informal economy.

d. The inability of political dissidents to state their views publicly.

_____ 20. Since the revolution, Mexico's rural economy has been characterized by:

a. rising production of basic foods, enabling the country to have a thriving industry exporting corn and beans.

b. a decline in investment in agro-export industries and ranching.

c. a split between the peasant economy, with poor land and low investments, and the wealthy agro-export industries.

d. the virtual elimination of the *campesinos* due to official encouragement of rural-to-urban migration.

21. Treaty of Guadalupe Hidalgo:

22. Why does the program narrator say that "Mexico City became a showcase of the worst of underdevelopment and the worst of overdevelopment"?

23. List two important benefits of the growth of *maquiladoras* in Mexico.

24. *Coyote*:

25. Kinship networks:

26. What are remittances and why are they an important aspect of migration?

27. Name two other types of migration besides rural-to-urban which are common in contemporary Latin America, and give an example of each type.

Identification/Short Answer

Define or describe the following terms, concepts, or persons, or answer the following questions. Answers should be no longer than a few sentences.

28. Lázaro Cárdenas:

29. Define and give two examples (one from the program and one from the anthology) of the informal economy.

30. Superbarrio Gómez:

ESSAY QUESTIONS

1. How does the story of Marcela and Atanacio related in the program "Continent on the Move" illustrate the history of internal migration in Mexico? Why did they leave their homes in Zacatecas? How did their lives change in the city? What are their prospects for the future?

2. Mexico's view of the United States has historically been a blend of suspicion and admiration; independence and dependence; caution and embrace. Trace the major historical events that occurred between the United States and Mexico since Mexico's independence from Spain which may have contributed to this sensitivity.

3. How are government policies and international economic trends linked to migration in Latin America and the Caribbean?

ANSWER KEY

Test Bank

Answers indicate sources.

1. a, c, d (program, anthology, study guide)
2. b (program, anthology, study guide)
3. c (program, textbook, study guide)
4. a, d (program, anthology)
5. c (textbook)
6. a, b (textbook, study guide)
7. b (program, textbook, study guide)
8. d (program, textbook, study guide)
9. a, c (program, textbook, study guide)
10. c, d (program, anthology)
11. c (textbook, study guide)
12. b (program, anthology, textbook, study guide)
13. a, d (program, study guide)
14. c (program)
15. d (anthology, study guide)
16. a (program)
17. d (program, textbook)
18. a, b (anthology)
19. b (anthology, study guide)
20. c (program, textbook, study guide)
21. The 1848 Treaty of Guadalupe Hidalgo brought a formal end to the war between Mexico and the United States. According to its terms, the United States agreed to pay Mexico $15 million and took about half of Mexico's territory, including the states of Texas and California and the Colorado River valley. (textbook)
22. Mexico grew so rapidly that it was not able to meet the basic needs of many of its residents; one result is that millions live without potable water, sewers, or adequate housing. At the same time, the wealthy saw a huge jump in their incomes. Mexico City now has beggars coexisting with chic designer shops, horrible pollution problems, and other consequences of having grown too much, too fast. (program)
23. Although the *maquiladoras* have been much criticized, they have created thousands of jobs in an economy that desperately needs employment for its population. The location of the assembly plants has also helped redirect the flow of migrants into Mexico City and has drawn a new wave of migration from the center and south of Mexico to the border area. (program, anthology, textbook, study guide)
24. Slang term for someone who engages in the profitable and dangerous business of guiding illegal immigrants across the border into the United States. Some *coyotes* bring families the entire length of Central America, while others work exclusively along the United States-Mexico border areas. (anthology, study guide)
25. A system of close friendships and relationships that facilitates relocation and employment for migrants. By providing food and shelter and finding employment for their friends and relatives, those who are already in the cities can encourage migration to the urban centers. Often, those who live in border towns provide a "stepping stone" into the United States. (program, anthology, study guide)
26. Remittances are sums of money sent home by migrants. They represent an important source of income for the families, as well as a major source of foreign exchange for the country. In some countries, the value of remittances is greater than any single foreign aid package, making it very difficult for governments actively to discourage international migration. (program, anthology, study guide)
27. Types of migration include: refugees from civil wars and other violence (for example, Guatemalans fleeing across the border to Mexico); political dissidents seeking civil freedoms (such as Cuban exiles in the United States or exiles from the Southern Cone living in Mexico); temporary migrants who do not move their homes and families but may leave for months at a time in search of temporary jobs (such as sugar cane harvesters in the Caribbean or construction workers in Mexico); and middle- and upper-class professionals who leave their countries because of the lack of opportunities (such as Mexican executives who live in the United States but operate *maquiladora* plants in Mexico). (anthology, study guide)
28. Mexican president from 1934 to 1940 who distributed about 50 million acres of land to landless Mexicans in the country's most famous phase of agrarian reform. The land

came from large estates, or *latifundios*, and was distributed as communal property to *ejidos*, groups of peasant families. (program, textbook, study guide)

29. The informal economy refers to economic activities that are not regulated. It is a critical source of employment and services for many of those who migrate to Mexico City and are unable to find factory work. Examples given in the program include shoemakers, printers, and minivan drivers, among others. Examples in the anthology include women who take in laundry or prepare food for sale on the street, coyotes, and garbage pickers. (program, anthology)

30. A man costumed like the comic book hero Superman who has taken it upon himself to meet with poor residents and to attempt to intercede for them with government authorities. He is a symbol of the abandonment of the poor by the city and of the desperation of poor residents. (program)

Essay Questions

1. In their answers, students should integrate the story told in the program with information on migration gathered from the textbook, anthology, and study guide. Both push and pull factors were involved in Marcela and Atanacio's decision to leave Zacatecas for Mexico City. The land was poor, and it was hard to make a living. At the same time, when they moved in the 1970s, industrial growth made Mexico City's economy very dynamic, and they looked forward to a better life. In the city, their lives did improve: Atanacio had no trouble finding a job; they were able to build a new home, get municipal services, and send their children to schools. However, they were hurt along with millions of other Mexicans by the economic shock of the 1980s, and Atanacio was murdered, evidence of rising urban violence. As a result, the family looked back to the countryside for the possibility of improving their lives.

2. Students' answers should draw from the textbook, program, and study guide. There is much to draw on for this answer, depending on the students' level of familiarity and comprehension of the material. At a minimum, students should cite the Mexican-American War as an underlying historical event that has encouraged Mexican suspicion and lack of trust in the United States. Students should also discuss economic factors such as Mexican dependence on the United States as a major trading partner and source of foreign investment, while seeking to "play the oil card" to achieve greater independence; and the U.S.-engineered "rescue" of the Mexican economy after the debt crisis in a manner that both helped and hurt ordinary Mexicans. Other issues that could be used as illustrations are the conflicting signals in international migration (the *braceros* versus the Simpson-Rodino Act), the mixed blessing of the *maquiladoras*, and the fears and hopes raised by the North American Free Trade Agreement.

3. Domestically, government policies can sometimes produce the effect of attracting more migrants to the urban centers by holding out the prospect of social services, employment opportunities, education, low-cost housing, and industrialization. Government economic choices of where to invest (or what to neglect) also set up situations that may push or pull migrants. Internationally, government policies of permitting migration under certain prescribed conditions also affect migratory patterns. Finally, the movement of international capital among industries and countries tends to pull an internationalized migrant labor force along with it.

Unit 6

Mirrors of the Heart: Color, Class, and Identity

UNIT SUMMARY

"Mirrors of the Heart" examines the complex issue of racial and ethnic identity in Latin America. The television program, set in Bolivia, the Dominican Republic, and Haiti, explores how race and ethnicity interact with gender, class, occupation, and generational factors. It also considers the impact on identity of urbanization, industrialization, the international media, and modern consumer culture in contemporary Latin America. The text and anthology readings complement the program by establishing the historical context and by extending the examination of race, class, and ethnicity to other countries in the region: Peru, Guatemala, and the English-speaking Caribbean.

LEARNING OBJECTIVES

After completing this unit, students should be able to:

- Explain the historical and contemporary role of racial and ethnic factors in defining the identities of various peoples in Latin America.

- Recognize that identity is not static and is never defined by just one factor but instead by a combination that includes, but is not limited to, race, ethnicity, and class.

- Understand that racial and ethnic identities are continually in flux, adapting to new social realities and interacting with other factors such as class, gender, age, religion, occupation, and political affiliation.

- Describe how race and ethnicity in Latin America and the Caribbean have been used to define particular groups as a means of consolidating power and exerting control, as well as to defend against conquest, exploitation, and marginalization.

- Recognize that processes of social change have had an ongoing impact on racial and ethnic identities in contemporary Latin America and the Caribbean.

- Understand how concerns for self-determination by ethnic and race-based cultural movements continue to shape complex definitions of identity for peoples throughout the region.

OVERVIEW

"Mirrors of the Heart" looks at identity in three very different countries: Bolivia, Haiti, and the Dominican Republic. In Bolivia, the emphasis is on the indigenous people, whose original cultures predate the European conquest and who today continue to make up approximately three-quarters of the country's population. In Haiti and the Dominican Republic, as in much of Caribbean, the key influence has been African, since both countries experienced massive importation of enslaved Africans after the virtual elimination of their original indigenous populations.

Perhaps the most important point for students to understand is the fact that for peoples of all colors, races, and ethnic backgrounds, identity is not fixed. Race and ethnicity are not timeless, physical attributes but rather changing gauges of social differences and cultural diversity. Race and ethnic background are important contributors to individual identity, along with such factors as age, sex, occupation, and class, or whether a person lives in a rural village or major industrial city. The program and anthology highlight the many different interpretations of what it means to call oneself Aymara, black, mulatto, Hispanic, or any other group in modern Latin America. These labels have been used to discriminate in work, housing, and education, but also to create group cohesion and pride and to struggle for equity and political goals. A key factor shaping changes in identity has been rural to urban migration. In the highly urban, industrial, and rapidly changing societies of contemporary Latin America, identity is continually being redefined.

The textbook readings on Haiti and the Dominican Republic briefly recount the two countries' histories and help give students an understanding of the roots of tension between the two countries today. There is no textbook reading on Bolivia, but the introduction to chapter 6 on Peru contains a general discussion of the indigenous peoples of the Andes. A similar introduction is assigned in chapter 10 in order to highlight the similarities and differences between indigenous peoples' experience of colonialism in the two regions.

An important concept introduced in the anthology is that of negritude, the French Caribbean literary and cultural movement that began in the 1930s and continues to be influential today. The anthology also broadens the discussion of ethnic and racial identity to: Guatemala, Peru, and the English-speaking Caribbean.

STUDENT READING ASSIGNMENT

Modern Latin America, 3d ed.
In chapter 6, "Peru: Soldiers, Oligarchs, and Indians," pp. 185–87.

In chapter 9, *Haiti: Slave Republic, Voodoo Dictatorship*, pp. 290–94, and *The Dominican Republic: Unfinished Experiment*, pp. 295–97.

In chapter 10, "Central America: Colonialism, Dictatorship, and Revolution," pp. 308–11.

In the epilogue, *What Will Happen to the Non-European Cultures in Latin America?* pp. 403–4.

Americas: An Anthology, chapter 6, pp. 137–172.

WRITING ASSIGNMENTS/ DISCUSSION QUESTIONS

1. Contrast the perceptions of Blas Jiménez, Carlos Pérez, and Altagracia Sánchez as examined in the program on the issues of black identity in the Dominican Republic. How do their comments help to illustrate the points made by Eric Williams in his essay on racism in the Caribbean?

2. There are many possible interpretations of the scenes in the program of hair being straightened in the Dominican Republic and permed in Bolivia. One view might be that in both cases people are trying to change or escape their identities by adopting a physical characteristic of the more privileged ethnic/racial group. Another might be that in both cases people are attempting to be modern and Western, participating in a consumer culture that transcends national boundaries, imitating cultural images imported through the media from Europe or

the United States. Still a third view might emphasize the ways young people experiment with different looks to have fun, share the latest look with their peers, appear economically successful, or resist parental authority. Which explanations would you support? Can people have a variety of reasons for their choices? How would you explain these scenes?

3. As members of the Mamani family sit down to lunch in the program, a debate develops over the quincentenary of Columbus's arrival in the Americas. Ramiro feels, "We shouldn't celebrate; it's ridiculous to celebrate the conquest. It ruined our lives." Johnny asserts, "We should throw out this idea of colonialism...We should recognize the importance of Spanish culture." Which viewpoint do you support? Why?

4. Compare and contrast the situation of the Aymara in Bolivia with that of Dominican blacks. In what ways are their experiences comparable? In what ways different? Which group faces greater obstacles to mobility and social acceptance today? How important does race and ethnicity seem to be in determining each group's identity?

SUGGESTED ACTIVITIES

1. Have students brainstorm together or individually what factors they consider to determine race and ethnicity. What makes someone a different race? Then have students write a short paragraph that describes themselves according to the factors they have listed. Have students discuss or write about what elements of their personality are not included in their paragraphs. What are the weaknesses of using race as an important factor in defining populations? Is classifying people according to race a valid system? For distant learners, instructors could compile and distribute copies of the descriptions.

2. Have students research the Civil Rights Act of 1964, and write brief summaries of the political arguments both for and against the legislation,

and their impressions of the legislation and how it has affected U.S. society since it became law.

3. Have students select an event that involved racial conflict and research newspaper articles to determine how the conflict evolved and how elements of race entered into it. Possible topics include the U.S. government reaction to the tens of thousands of Haitian refugees that fled the country in the wake of the September 1991 coup that forced President Jean-Bertrand Aristide from office, the Los Angeles riots of May 1992, conflicts in the Southwest involving Mexican-American migrant labor, Native American conflicts in the Northwest, or any local event that has received newspaper coverage.

4. Have students research how Native Americans have been portrayed in the United States, in history books and in popular media. If possible, have students interview members of Native American organizations, to get their perspectives, and contrast it with what is commonly believed.

RESOURCES

Nonfiction

Allen, Catherine J. *The Hold Life Has: Coca and Cultural Identity in an Andean Community*. Washington, D.C.: Smithsonian Institution Press, 1988. Ethnographic study of the social, ceremonial, and spiritual uses of coca leaves in a Quechua community in Peru. Contrasts the white elite's perception of coca leaves with that of the indigenous peoples.

Bourque, Susan C., and Kay Barbara Warren. *Women of the Andes: Patriarchy and Social Change in Two Peruvian Towns*. Ann Arbor: University of Michigan Press, 1981. Shows the interplay of gender, class, and ethnic identity in agrarian and conventional settlements, with a focus on community political debates, and economic and family dynamics.

Barrios de Chungara, Domitila with Moema Viezzer. *Let Me Speak! Testimony of Domitila, a Woman of the Bolivian Mines.* New York: Monthly Review Press, 1978. A very readable autobiographical account of the family life and political struggles of today's miners.

Bastien, Joseph W. *Healers of the Andes: Kallawaya Herbalists and Their Medicinal Plants.* Salt Lake City: University of Utah Press, 1987. Survey of the ancient medical tradition *Kallawaya*, which still survives in the Andes; explores the social and cultural contexts of this medical tradition as well as the efficacy of some of the cures.

Coulthard, Gabriel. *Race and Colour in Caribbean Literature.* London: Oxford University Press, 1962. An appreciation of Caribbean society as analyzed through its novels, short stories, and poetry.

Crandon-Malamud, Libbet. *From the Fat of Our Souls: Social Change, Political Process, and Medical Pluralism in Bolivia.* Berkeley: University of California Press, 1991. Examines the medical care options in a village in highland Bolivia. The choices people make are influenced by their social and political significance, in addition to health considerations. Social status and ethnic identity can be negotiated or reinforced by choosing one practitioner over another.

Harrison, Regina. *Signs, Songs, and Memory in the Andes: Translating Quechua Language and Culture.* Austin: University of Texas Press, 1989. An important study of the linguistic and cultural richness of the indigenous culture and world view in the Andes.

Hill, Jonathan D., ed. *Rethinking History and Myth: Indigenous South American Perspectives on the Past.* Urbana: University of Illinois Press, 1988. A collection of essays on indigenous constructions of culture and history.

Isbell, Billie Jean. *To Defend Ourselves: Ecology and Ritual in an Andean Village.* Prospect Heights, Ill.: Waveland Press, 1978. A classic view of Andean religion in everyday life that considers how Andean people transform their understandings of the world as they migrate to urban culture.

Leyburn, James. *The Haitian People.* New Haven: Yale University Press. 1941. The classic book on Haiti; a starting point for research into the country's history.

Maingot, Anthony P. "Haiti and Aristide: The Legacy of History." In *Current History* (Feb. 1992), pp. 65–69. Places contemporary Haitian politics within a historical context.

Maingot, Anthony P., "Race, Color, and Class in the Caribbean." In *Americas: New Interpretive Essays,* edited by Alfred Stepan. New York: Oxford University Press, 1992. An exploration of the numerous permutations of race, color, and class in the Caribbean, written by a member of the *Americas* academic advisory board as an optional addition to this unit.

Mamami Condori, Carlos. "History and Pre-history in Bolivia: What About the Indians?" In *Conflict in the Archaeology of Living Tradition,* edited by Robert Layton, pp. 46–59. Boston: Unwin Hyman, 1989. An important analysis of indigenous identity by an Aymara anthropologist that considers the indigenous view of Bolivian history, archaeology, and the struggle for indigenous rights in the face of Bolivian nationalism.

Meyerson, Julia. *Tambo: Life in an Andean Village.* Austin: University of Texas Press, 1990. An accessible source on community culture and social life in an Andean community that describes rural life.

Moody, Roger, ed. *The Indigenous Voice: Visions and Realities,* vols 1 and 2. London: Zed, 1988. Short statements from a variety of sources that reflect indigenous politics and critique social change.

Rappaport, Joanne. *The Politics of Memory: Native Historical Interpretations in the Colombian Andes.* Cambridge: Cambridge University Press, 1990. How Andean individuals and culture have shaped local history, identity, and social change. This book looks at how the concerns of the present shape understandings of the past and create history.

Smith, M.G. *The Plural Society in the British West Indies.* Los Angeles: University of California Press, 1965. These essays initiated the debate over the nature of Caribbean social stratification.

Spalding, Karen. *Huarochirt: An Andean Society Under Inca and Spanish Rule*. Stanford: Stanford University Press, 1984. An excellent study of Andean politics before and after the Spanish conquest, which shows Andean adaptation, resistance, and transformation.

Stein, William W., ed. *Peruvian Contexts of Change*. New Brunswick, N.J.: Transaction Books, 1985. Essays by North American and Peruvian authors on social conditions in modern Peru. Includes studies of slum living in Lima, class stratification in peasant communities, and the social standing of men and women.

Stern, Steve J., ed. *Resistence, Rebellion, and Consciousness in the Andean Peasant World, Eighteenth to Twentieth Centuries*. Madison: University of Wisconsin Press, 1987. A well-known collection of articles on the responses of Andean peoples to the economic and political transformation of their lives that occurred with the Spanish conquest, colonization, and the formation of New World Latin American national culture.

Tannenbaum, Frank. *Slave and Citizen: The Negro in the Americas*. New York: Knopf, 1946. Tannenbaum opened up a new debate on the nature of race relations by distinguishing between the Protestant legal interpretation of slaves as chattel and the Catholic interpretation of slaves as human beings.

Warren, Kay Barbara. "Transforming Memories and Histories: The Resurgence of Indian Identity." In *Americas: New Interpretive Essays*, edited by Alfred Stepan. New York: Oxford University Press, 1992. An analysis of how contemporary Mayan communities are exploring, redefining, and reasserting their identities, written by a member of the *Americas* academic advisory board as an optional addition to this unit.

Weiner, Annette B. and Jean Schneider, eds. *Cloth and Human Experience*. Washington, DC: Smithsonian Institution Press, 1989. A classic analysis of the cultural importance of cloth in Incan rule, expansion, and control over indigenous populations long before the conquest.

Williams, Eric. *Capitalism and Slavery*. Chapel Hill: University of North Carolina Press, 1944. Williams'

thesis that the abolition of slavery in Brittain was due to changed economic relations rather than humanitarian sentiment was very influential on Latin American and Caribbean society.

Fiction

Alegría, Ciro. *Broad and Alien is the World*. Chester Springs: Dufour, 1987. A deeply sympathetic portrayal of Peru's highland Indians and their struggles against exploitation.

Astorias, Miguel Angel. *Men of Maize*. New York: Delacorte Press, 1975. Mythic, magical novel of an indigenous rebellion in Guatemala. Much of this book is a reworking of Mayan legends. Astorias won the Novel Prize for literature in 1967.

Astorias, Miguel Angel. *Mulata*. New York: Delacorte Press, 1967. Mythic treatment of the conflicts between ancient communal life and the demands of the modern world faced by Guatemala's indigenous population.

Depestre, René. *A Rainbow for the Christian West*. Amherst: University of Massachusetts Press, 1977. The poetry of a black Haitian political activist who wrote mainly from exile after 1952.

Vargas Llosa, Mario. *Aunt Julia and the Scriptwriter*. New York: Avon, 1985. Semiautobiographical novel from Peru's most famous author.

Films

Unless otherwise indicated, all films listed are available in VHS video format.

Bitter Cane. 75 minutes, 1983. Produced by Haiti Films. Covers the history of Haiti from its successful revolution in 1804 through the Duvalier dictatorships. Includes interviews with ordinary Haitian citizens who describe their lives. Available for rental ($95) from The Cinema Guild; (212) 246-5522.

Blood of the Condor. Directed by Jorge Sanjines. 1969. 74 minutes. 16-mm. A Quechua chief in Bolivia discovers that American medical workers are sterilizing native women to keep the indigenous population down. Available for rental ($250 plus $20 shipping/handling) from New Yorker Video, 16 West 61st Street, New York, N.Y. 10023; (212) 247-6110.

Burn. 1969. 112 minutes, 1969. Political drama about Sir William Walker who is sent by the British to instigate a slave revolt on a Portuguese-controlled, sugar-producing Carribbean island, based in part on Haiti. Available in most video-rental outlets.

Bye Bye Brazil. Directed by Carlos Diegues. 1980. 110 minutes. This comedy drama about traveling entertainers functions as a travelogue of Brazil, exploring jungles and port towns. Available in most video-rental outlets.

Los Olivados. Directed by Luis Bunuel. 1950. 88 minutes. Story of juvenile delinquency among the slums of Mexico, enforced with surreal dream sequences. Available in most video-rental outlets.

Mountain Music of Peru. 60 minutes, 1984. Directed by John Cohen. Documentary on the musical traditions in Peru dating back to the Inca Empire and the role music plays in preserving indigenous culture. Available for rental ($95) from The Cinema Guild: (212) 246-5522.

Xica da Silva. Directed by Carlos Diegues. 1978. 107 minutes. The story of the strong-willed black slave Motta who seduces the new Royal Diamond Contractor in corrupt, repressive, colonial Brazil. Available in most video-rental outlets.

TEST BANK

Questions reflect content from the programs, textbook, and anthology.

Multiple Choice

*Mark the letter of the response that **best** answers the question or completes the statement.*

_____ 1. People of African descent make up the majority of the population in: (*Mark all that apply.*)

a. Haiti.
b. the Dominican Republic.
c. Argentina.
d. Bolivia.

_____ 2. Which of the following is an example of resistance measures by indigenous and/or enslaved peoples in Latin America and the Caribbean during the colonial period? (*Mark all that apply.*)

a. Occasional revolts and armed rebellion
b. Flight to remote areas
c. Work slowdowns and legal challenges
d. Widespread refusal to allow the *derecho de pernada*

_____ 3. For most island nations in the Caribbean, economic development has been characterized by: (*Mark all that apply.*)

a. a reliance on manufacturing and import-substituting industrialization.
b. a reliance on agricultural production for export, especially sugar.
c. increasing reliance on tourism as a means of earning foreign exchange.
d. a rise in self-sufficiency and a decline in the influence of foreign countries.

_____ 4. *Noirisme*, or negritude, refers to:

a. the negative characteristics of Haitians, according to mulattos in the Dominican Republic.
b. a political ideology restricting civil rights to those with African ancestry.
c. a literary and cultural movement emphasizing African influence in the Caribbean.
d. a musical tradition that was the basis for the development of reggae music in Jamaica.

_____ 5. According to Aimé Césaire, the goal of negritude was: (*Mark all that apply.*)

a. to force the last European colonists out of the Caribbean islands.
b. to emphasize the contributions of blacks to Caribbean cultures.
c. to gain political power for blacks in Caribbean states.
d. to struggle against the alienation and inferiority felt by most blacks.

_____ 6. François ("Papa Doc") Duvalier: (*Mark all that apply.*)

a. created a special paramilitary force known as the Tontons Macoutes.
b. used and manipulated racial issues as part of his formula for political power.
c. attempted to enhance Haiti's independence from the United States by casting UN votes with the nonaligned movement.
d. identified strongly with Haiti's French heritage and pushed most blacks out of public office.

_____ 7. Haiti and the Dominican Republic share which of the following?

a. A colonial history of Spanish domination
b. A significant African cultural influence

c. The continuing existence of indigenous groups

d. A primarily French colonial heritage

_____ 8. Dominican Republic dictator Rafael Leonidas Trujillo: (*Mark all that apply.*)

a. used his political position to gain personal wealth.

b. used *Hispanidad* to connect himself with Europe, modernity, and progress.

c. sought a rapprochement with Haiti in order to increase his political appeal among the Dominican Republic's blacks.

d. attempted to increase Dominican pride in the nation's African heritage by fostering negritude.

_____ 9. According to the program, temporary labor migrants from Haiti living in the Dominican Republic show which of the following characteristics?

a. They have been thoroughly incorporated into society at large.

b. They have been unable to practice their own cultural traditions due to widespread prejudice and racism.

c. They have been forcibly prevented from returning to Haiti since their labor is essential to the sugarcane industry.

d. They have been restricted in large part to miserable living conditions in sugar plantation *bateys*.

_____ 10. According to Eric Williams, race relations in the Caribbean:

a. are very similar to those in the United States.

b. are characterized by an apartheid-like system of racial separation in public facilities.

c. have a legacy of laws similar to the "Jim Crow" laws in the United States, but lack the U.S. experience of the civil rights movement.

d. are not burdened with any overt legal discrimination.

_____ 11. Merengue is significant in the Dominican Republic because it: (*Mark all that apply.*)

a. is viewed by nearly all Dominicans as an example of their shared cultural legacy with Haiti.

b. has recently been used as a symbol of African heritage by the Dominican proponents of negritude.

c. has frequently been a vehicle for social and political commentary.

d. dates back to the colonial period and is an important symbol of the Dominican Republic's European roots.

_____ 12. According to the text, cultural heterogeneity in Latin America: (*Mark all that apply.*)

a. is likely to be eliminated in the Andean region.

b. will survive because of an increasing emphasis on individual rights by the World Bank and the IMF.

c. may be an impediment to improving literacy rates and other social indicators.

d. is threatened by the impact of modern communications.

_____ 13. According to Mario Vargas Llosa, the indigenous peoples of Peru: (*Mark all that apply.*)

a. cannot obtain the benefits of modern, Western society without also losing their Indian identities.

b. are holding the nation back by their slowness in adopting more urban, industrial ways.

c. represent a valued part of Andean national identity and must be protected and preserved at all costs.

d. should be restricted to their traditional homelands and prevented from mixing with modern Peruvian society.

_____ 14. Until the midtwentieth century, indigenous peoples in Bolivia:

   a. had no voting rights as citizens of the country.
   b. obtained limited rights to land ownership from reformist political leaders.
   c. tended to vote according to landowners' wishes, perpetuating the elite monopoly on power.
   d. were invited into the national government only as a means of co-optation.

_____ 15. Which of the following statements is/are true of the 1952 revolution in Bolivia? (*Mark all that apply.*)

   a. It legalized the debt peonage system, which had been practiced for years on the country's haciendas.
   b. It resulted in significant land reform.
   c. It removed the right to vote from the country's indigenous peoples.
   d. It resulted in the nationalization of Bolivia's largest mines.

_____ 16. An important change in the lives of Bolivia's Calcha people today is that: (*Mark all that apply.*)

   a. Calcha men now work the land.
   b. women no longer weave all their family's clothing.
   c. men and women now are migrating in search of jobs.
   d. women are less likely to be the heads of households.

_____ 17. The bowler hat worn by Aymara women developed out of:

   a. the Spanish imposition of a dress code to identify indigenous people.
   b. the required uniform for indigenous workers on the Bolivian railroad.

   c. Aymara admiration of the dress of Englishmen working in Bolivia.
   d. the desire of Aymara women to imitate the fashions of Bolivia's upper classes.

_____ 18. As depicted in the program, most Aymara in La Paz and other Bolivian cities:

   a. have been fully integrated into the larger society.
   b. have recreated their own indigenous society within the urban setting.
   c. have almost no access to modern means of communication.
   d. are known as *K'aras* for their attempts to become Westernized.

_____ 19. Women from Aymara communities: (*Mark all that apply.*)

   a. are often the financial heads of their families.
   b. are not permitted to farm traditional lands in the *altiplano*.
   c. are generally not involved in managing family finances.
   d. never wear traditional dress anymore, especially in the cities.

_____ 20. Indigenous peoples of the Andes: (*Mark all that apply.*)

   a. were ingenious in their use of a variety of measures to resist European domination.
   b. found that the Spanish ignored the important differences among them and considered them all to be "Indians."
   c. can no longer speak their native languages.
   d. are in imminent danger of extinction as urbanization continues.

Identification/Short Answer

Define or describe the following terms, concepts, or persons, or answer the following questions. Answers should be no longer than a few sentences.

21. Eric Williams:

22. Aimé Césaire:

23. Hispaniola:

24. *Pollera*:

25. Why did Trujillo choose to emphasize *Hispanidad*, and how did it enhance his position of power?

26. What does Mario Vargas Llosa mean when he says "we are all the conquistadors"?

27. What was Dominican bandleader Luis Senior protesting when he declared, "This outlandish statement is unpatriotic!"?

28. What is the significance of the Mamani family's making *chuño*?

29. Name four Caribbean islands that belonged to four different European colonial powers:

30. *Derecho de pernada*:

ESSAY QUESTIONS

1. Using the examples of Señora Mamani and Doña Sara, discuss the sources of change in their lives. Are they themselves sources of change as well?

2. How have the different colonial experiences of the Caribbean nations contributed to divisions among them? What similarities in history and culture do they share?

3. Discuss the pros and cons of Vargas Llosa's argument that the indigenous groups of Peru need to be completely assimilated into the larger society. Why does he believe this to be essential? How do you think the Mamani family would react to his argument?

ANSWER KEY

Test Bank

Answers indicate sources.

1. a, b, c (program, anthology, textbook)
2. a, b, c (program, anthology, textbook, study guide)
3. b, c (textbook)
4. c (anthology, textbook)
5. b, d (anthology)
6. a, b (textbook, study guide)
7. b (program, anthology, textbook, study guide)
8. a, b (program, anthology, textbook, study guide)
9. d (program)
10. d (anthology)
11. b, c (anthology)
12. c, d (textbook)
13. a, b (anthology)
14. a (program, study guide)
15. b, d (program)
16. b, c (anthology)
17. c (program)
18. b (program)
19. a (program)
20. a, b (program, anthology, textbook, study guide)
21. Historian, founder of the People's National Movement in the 1950s in Trinidad. Became chief minister in 1956, prime minister of Trinidad and Tobago upon its independence from Britain in 1962 until 1981, heading his government for 25 years. (anthology)
22. Poet, native of Martinique, considered one of the founders and foremost exponents of negritude. He served as mayor of Fort-de-France, President of the Provincial Council, and delegate to the National Assembly in Paris. (anthology)
23. Island in the Caribbean that is divided between Haiti and the Dominican Republic. (program, textbook, study guide)
24. Type of full skirt traditionally worn by Bolivian indigenous women; originally a style of clothing imposed by the Spanish to differentiate the peasant population, but it has become distinctively indigenous and today is a source of pride to many Aymara and Quechua women. Also marks differences in family economic status. (program, study guide)
25. He wanted to associate himself with the cultural ideal of modern, Western, white society. He also wanted Dominicans to feel superior to the rest of the Caribbean because of their Spanish heritage, and to look to him to protect and preserve that heritage. (program, textbook)
26. He disagrees with the reluctance of national elites to accept any responsibility for the terrible conditions of poverty and underdevelopment of the indigenous people in the Americas. (anthology)
27. He was protesting the assertion that the merengue had African roots and was an example of the African cultural heritage of the Dominican Republic. (anthology)
28. Making *chuño* has symbolic importance as an example of the family's continued links to the land, indigenous religion, and ancient Aymara practices. The return of the Mamani family to make *chuño* shows how they draw on their family history and reweave it into their urban contemporary Aymara ethnicity as members of middle-class Bolivian society. (program)
29. Any four of the following: Jamaica, Barbados, Trinidad and Tobago (Britain); Haiti, Guadeloupe, Martinique (France); Aruba, Curaçao (Holland); the Dominican Republic, Puerto Rico, Cuba (Spain); Virgin Islands (Denmark). (textbook)
30. Term for the hacienda owner's sexual rights to the women on his estate. The landowners' rape of indigenous women, which they justified by the *derecho de pernada*, was partly responsible for the growth of the mestizo population in countries with large indigenous populations. Carried out against the wishes of local populations, the *derecho de pernada* epitomizes the brutal nature of colonial domination of indigenous groups by elites of European descent. (program)

Essay Questions

1. Students should use the program and anthology to discuss some or all of the following: Doña Sara and Señora Mamai are examples of how gender and family roles have changed, along with other aspects of culture, although women sometimes do not appear to be considered the equals or partners of men; men now frequently migrate to look for jobs, leaving women as the heads of household; Calcha women now are working the land and have given up their labor-intensive work in weaving; Aymara women are still responsible for earning the family's income, but their means have changed (Señora Mamani now drives a truck, whereas she used to farm).

2. Students should draw on the text, program, and anthology. Similarities are that the island nations are small and vulnerable to foreign pressures, have dependent economies, and they face similar challenges in asserting their independence and nationhood; most only recently became independent, and some are still tied to the former colonial power. The shared African heritage due to the importance of slavery throughout the region has given Afro-Caribbean movements, such as negritude or *noirisme*, widespread appeal. There are also many important differences. Many of the countries speak different languages, have different religions, and have different political systems depending on whether they were colonized by Spain, France, Britain, or Holland. Relations between Haiti and the Dominican Republic are complicated by the fact that Haiti was established in 1697 when Spain granted one half of the island of Hispaniola to France, and the ceding of Santo Domingo in 1797, followed in 1822 by Haiti's postrevolutionary invasion and occupation of the Dominican Republic. Some nations are more "black" than others, although all have significant African antecedents. Most do not have a large or powerful military, although this is not true for the Dominican Republic or Cuba.

3. Vargas Llosa believes that the multicultural nature of modern Peruvian society may be quaint and picturesque, but it is also part of the reason for the country's continued underdevelopment. Indigenous peoples need to obtain the benefits of modernization, he argues, and this can only occur if they become fully integrated into society; integration while maintaining separate identities is impossible. One can only speculate about the Mamani family's views on the subject, but based on their success in La Paz and their obvious pride in Aymara culture and identity, it seems unlikely that most of the family would completely agree with Vargas Llosa's claim that there is no place for indigenous culture in the modern world. For example, in their discussion of the quincentenary, one son argues that modern society has brought some good things, but another son and the father stress that their own culture has an older history and is very important. They seem to have been able to strike an acceptable balance between retaining their identity as Aymara and adopting many aspects of modern, urban life.

Unit 7

In Women's Hands:
The Changing Roles of Women

===

UNIT SUMMARY

Unit 7 focuses on major changes in the roles of women in the Americas during the past 40 years. Using the example of Chile, it explores the phenomenon of increased political activism by women of all social classes and backgrounds, as well as the increased participation of women in the labor market due to economic crises.

The text and program trace the political, social, and economic history of Chile, concentrating especially on the years since 1970: the Allende government, the Pinochet regime, and the subsequent return to democracy. In interviews with several Chilean women, students are exposed to women who actively supported Allende and were later tortured under the military government; women who opposed Allende and supported the military regime; and women who were drawn into politics because of their direct experience of economic and personal loss. The unit's anthology readings broaden the focus to include a wide variety of experiences of women from different ethnic and class backgrounds in Argentina, Bolivia, Brazil, El Salvador, Guatemala, Honduras, and Mexico, along with Chile.

LEARNING OBJECTIVES

After completing this unit, students should be able to:

- Analyze how class and race influence what women do both inside the household and in the labor market in Latin America and the Caribbean.

- Understand the effects of economic, political, and social changes on different types of families, especially on what women must do to contribute to family survival.

- Describe various ways in which women in the Americas are involved in the political process.

- Understand the ways in which women's traditional roles have both helped and constricted their efforts to respond to economic and political situations in their countries.

- List some of the factors that brought about the coup against Salvador Allende, and the political and economic changes that military rule brought to Chilean society.

- Describe some of the issues that prompted Chilean women on both ends of the ideological spectrum to become politically active during the Allende and Pinochet years.

OVERVIEW

The program in this unit has the dual purpose of exploring changes in women's roles, especially increased political consciousness and activism, and discussing the dramatic experience of the past 20 years in Chile, where a long tradition of democratic government was supplanted by one of Latin America's most brutal military dictatorships.

Women profiled in the program come from different classes and articulate the variety of positions women took during the Allende and Pinochet periods. The effectiveness of women in opposing the military government is especially noted, although women who supported and worked for Pinochet are also represented.

The program briefly describes economic changes that have encouraged more women to enter the formal and informal labor markets. The anthology readings expand upon this theme, providing several case histories of women who work as wage laborers, domestics, and other occupations in order to feed their families. The differences in women's experiences based on their class and ethnic origins are made very clear, as is the effect that organizations of poor women (peasants, rural laborers, and poor urban housewives) have had on the consciousness of Latin American feminism.

The text traces the history of Chile since independence. Students should be especially aware of the reasons for Chile's long-standing tradition of civilian government. They should also consider how the inherent strains and polarization built up over the years, culminating in the traumatic experience of the Popular Unity government and the coup led by General Pinochet.

STUDENT READING ASSIGNMENT

Modern Latin America, 3rd ed.
In chapter 2: *Women and Society*, pp. 62–66.

Chapter 4, "Chile: Socialism, Repression, and Democracy," pp. 112–43.

Americas: An Anthology, chapter 7, pp. 173–207.

WRITING ASSIGNMENTS/ DISCUSSION QUESTIONS

1. To what degree has the increased involvement of Latin American women in economic and political activities led to changes within the traditional family structure? What are some of the factors that indicate how, if at all, women's position within the home has changed?

2. In your view, are Latin American women more or less politically active than their counterparts in North America? What lessons might North American women draw from the experiences of women in Latin America and the Caribbean?

3. Many women's advocates argue that the *maquiladoras*, international packaging and assembling plants in Latin America that primarily employ women, are a modern technological version of *machismo*. Others say these industries are important and beneficial to women. Review the information on the *maquiladora* industry provided in Unit 5, and explain the factors that proponents of each view cite in support of their arguments. What do you think, and why?

SUGGESTED ACTIVITIES

1. Drawing on examples from the anthology and program, discuss how the cultural norms of *machismo* and *marianismo* affect Latin American women in both the home and the labor market. Then have students compare these traditional roles with the roles of men and women in the United States. Have students research the numbers of men and women, and their average salaries, in different professions, such as doctors, lawyers, journalists, construction workers, factory workers, agricultural workers, teachers, social workers, and artists. Then have students draft short descriptions of the masculine and feminine cultural ideals in the United States, based on their data.

2. Have students identify a community advocacy group in their area that is composed largely of

women. Consider health groups concerned with such social issues as housing, health care, literacy, and community improvement. Interview women involved in the organization and find out why they became involved, what their organization is working to accomplish, and whether they have been able to extend their impact beyond their immediate community. Have students compare the organizations and women they studied with women's organizations and women activists in Chile, using information from the readings and the program.

RESOURCES

Nonfiction

Abreu, Luz María. "The Experience of MUDE Dominicana in Operating a Women-Specific Credit Program." In *Women's Ventures: Assistance to the Informal Sector in Latin America,* edited by Marguerite Berger and Mayra Buvinic, 161–73. West Hartford, Conn.: Kumarian Press, 1989. This essay explains how poor urban women formed an organization to generate income and direct resources to women to develop microenterprises.

Agosin, Marjorie. *Scraps of Life.* Trenton, N.J.: Red Sea Press, 1987. Moving account of the *arpillera* movement in Pinochet's Chile.

Alvarado, Elvia. *Don't Be Afraid, Gringo.* Translated by Medea Benjamin. New York: Harper and Row, 1987. This autobiography of a Honduran *campesina* outlines the dual pressures placed on women by rural poverty and *machismo.* It also illustrates ways rural women are organizing themselves to enact social change on the local level.

Alvarez, Sonia E. "Contradictions of a 'Woman's Space' in a Male Dominated State: The Political Role of the Commission on the Status of Women in Postauthoritarian Brazil." In *Women, International Development, and Politics: The Bureaucratic Mire,* edited by Kathleen Staudt, 37–78. Philadelphia: Temple University Press, 1990. This essay describes and analyzes the problems of keeping women's agendas in the public eye after democratization.

Bernaria, Lourdes, and Martha Roldan. *The Crossroads of Class and Gender: Industrial Homework, Subcontracting, and Household Dynamics in Mexico City.* Chicago: University of Chicago Press, 1987. This book explores the interaction between economics and social relations by looking at the effect of working at home on gender and family dynamics.

Bourque, Susan C., and Kay Barbara Warren. *Women of the Andes: Patriarchy and Social Change in Two Peruvian Towns.* Ann Arbor: University of Michigan Press, 1981. This book links women's structural subordination in the Peruvian Andes with the social, economic, and political realities of Peruvian life. It shows the importance of women in maintaining the kinship and friendship networks crucial for survival in both rural and urban areas.

Bunster, Ximena, and Elsa M. Chaney. *Sellers and Servants: Working Women in Lima, Peru.* New York: Praeger, 1985. This book illustrates the development and interaction of the two main sources of employment for poor women in Lima, Peru: street selling and domestic service. In intensive interviews, working mothers describe their experiences in their own words.

Burkett, Elinor C. "In Dubious Sisterhood: Class and Sex in Spanish Colonial South America." In *Women in Latin America: An Anthology from Latin American Perspectives.* Riverside, Calif.: Latin American Perspectives, 1979. This essay illustrates how women from all classes shared ideas of what was expected of them by the male-imposed social standards. However, the women's social status determined what they were able to do.

Chaney, Elsa M. *Muchachas No More: Household Workers in Latin America and the Caribbean.* Philadelphia: Temple University Press, 1989. Presents the history of domestic service in Latin America and the Caribbean, the ideology and reality of domestic service today, the organization of women who work in domestic service, and their relation to the state. Includes testimonies of domestic workers from Brazil, Colombia, Peru, and Venezuela.

Chuchryk, Patricia M. "Subversive Mothers: The Women's Opposition to the Military Regime in

Chile." In *Women, the State, and Development,* edited by Sue Ellen M. Charlton, Jana Everett, and Kathleen Staudt, 130–51. Albany: State University of New York Press, 1989. By tracing the growth of various mothers' organizations in Chile during the Pinochet military regime, this essay shows how women used their traditional roles to resist and subvert the political system.

Ehlers, Tracy Bachrach. *Silent Looms: Women and Production in a Guatemalan Town.* Boulder, Colo.: Westview Press, 1990. This intimate portrait of women in an entrepreneurial indigenous town in highland Guatemala addresses issues of female subordination and power as the economy changes.

Ellis, Pat, ed. *Women of the Caribbean.* London: Zed Books, 1986. All of the essays included in this collection are written by Caribbean women. The introduction provides an overview of women's experiences in Caribbean society within the context of race, ethnicity, and class. Women's changing roles within the formal and informal sectors are described and explored.

Flora, Cornelia Butler. "Women in Latin American Fotonovelas: From Cinderella to Mata Hari." *Women's Studies: An International Quarterly* 3:1 (1980): 95–104. This article traces the shifting image of women in one of the most common forms of popular culture in Latin America.

Gross, Susan Hill, and Marjorie Wall Bingham. *Women in Latin America,* 2 vols. St. Louis Park, Minn.: Glenhurst Publications. 1985. This double-volume text describes the role and status of women in Latin America and the Caribbean from pre-Columbian times to the twentieth century. Offering a unique perspective, its premise is that "women have led very different lives, depending on factors such as time, place, class, life stage, and individual talents." A teacher's guide with discussion questions, suggested activities, and unit tests is provided along with the two textbooks.

Jaquette, Jane S., ed. *The Women's Movement in Latin America: Feminism and the Transition to Democracy.* Boston: Unwin Hyman, 1990. These essays illuminatingly describe the political roles and organizations of women in South America.

Levy, Marion Fennelly. "Reyna de Miralda: Organizing Peasant Women in Honduras." In *Each in Her Own Way: Five Women Leaders of the Developing World.* Boulder, Colo.: Lynne Rienner, 1988. A peasant woman leader tells how she used grassroots political organizing techniques to empower women first in her community, then in her region, to address their common needs.

Mcleod, Ruth. "The Kingston Women's Construction Collective: Building for the Future in Jamaica." In *Seeds: Supporting Women's Work in the Third World,* edited by Ann Leonard, 163–194. New York: Feminist Press, 1989. This essay describes a project to integrate low-income women into Jamaica's construction industry.

Miller, Beth, ed. *Women in Hispanic Literature: Icons and Fallen Idols.* Berkeley: University of California Press, 1983. A historic overview of the wide variety of portrayals of women in Hispanic fiction from the eleventh century to the 1970s.

Miller, Francesca. *Latin American Women and the Search for Social Justice.* Hanover, N.H.: University Press of New England, 1991. A pioneering synthesis of the experience of Latin American women and social and political change.

Nash, June, and Helen I. Safa. *Women and Change in Latin America.* South Hadley, Mass: Bergin and Garvey, 1986. A collection of essays dealing with theoretical and practical issues surrounding women in Latin America: production for the market, social reproduction and biological reproduction, production in industrial and agricultural change, migration, and political action and the state.

Navarro-Aranguren, Marysa. "The Construction of a Latin American Feminist Identity." In *Americas: New Interpretive Essays,* edited by Alfred Stepan. New York: Oxford University Press, 1992. An analysis of the new feminist voice in Latin America, and its potential affect on the world feminist movement, written by a member of the *Americas* academic advisory board as an optional addition to this unit.

Navarro-Aranguren, Marysa. "Latin American Feminism." In *Americas: New Interpretive Essays,* edited by Alfred Stepan. New York: Oxford University Press, 1992. An analysis of the new feminist voice in Latin America, and its potential effect on the world feminist movement, written by a member of the *Americas* academic advisory board as an optional addition to this unit.

New American Press, ed. *A Dream Compels Us: Voices of Salvadoran Women.* Boston: South End Press, 1989. Salvadoran women speak of their experiences working for change in popular organizations, in women's organizations, with guerrilla groups, in liberated zones, and in exile. This collection of relatively short readings includes some very radical analysis of women's condition in El Salvador.

Partnoy, Alicia, ed. *You Can't Drown the Fire: Latin American Women Writing in Exile.* Pittsburgh: Cleis Press, 1988. Latin American women in exile write of their painful experience of exile, torture, and death through personal testimonies, letters, poems, and stories.

Patai, Daphne. *Brazilian Women Speak.* New Brunswick, N.J.: Rutgers University Press, 1988. Contemporary and historical views of women from various locales and classes.

Safa, Helen I. and Cornelia Butler Flora. "Production, Reproduction, and the Polity: Women's Strategic and Practical Interests." In *Americas: New Interpretive Essays*, edited by Alfred Stepan. New York: Oxford University Press, 1992. An exploration of the role of women in organizing the community to fulfill family survival needs, written by two members of the *Americas* academic advisory board as an optional addition to this unit.

Fiction

Allende, Isabel. *The House of the Spirits.* Translated by Magda Bogin. New York: Knopf, 1988. In her first novel, Allende traces the lives of three generations of Chilean women from the early to the late twentieth century. Written in the magic realism style, the novel skillfully weaves the family intrigues and the romantic relationships of these women with the general sociopolitical changes that the country experienced during those decades.

Cruz, Sor Juana Inés de la. *Dreams.* Mexico: Imprenta Universitaria, 1951. The author, one of the most important literary figures of colonial Latin America, epitomized the women who entered the convent in order to pursue intellectual and literary growth.

Cruz, Sor Juana Inés de la. *A Sor Juana Anthology.* Translated by Alan Trueblood. Cambridge: Harvard University Press, 1988. This anthology of the major poems and treatises of the Mexican nun includes a foreword by Octavio Paz and a complete translation of Sor Juana's famous poem, "First Dream."

Ferré, Rosario. "When Women Love Men." In *Contemporary Women Authors of Latin America*, edited by Doris Meyer and Margarite Fernández Olmos. Brooklyn, N.Y.: Brooklyn College Press, 1983. This story by a Puerto Rican author explores the issues of women's traditional roles as wives and mothers.

Kincaid, Jamaica. *Lucy.* New York: Farrar Straus Giroux, 1990. This novel is a series of stories about a Caribbean woman's adaptation to her new home in the United States. She settles in a large metropolitan city as the governess for a wealthy family with four children. Through Lucy's unique perspective, the reader learns about her life in the islands as well as her impressions of North American society.

Swartz-Bart, Simone. *The Bridge of Beyond.* Translated by Barbara Bray. London: Heinemann, 1982. This historical novel, recounted in the first person, examines women's strength and empowerment through the matrilineage of one black family in Guadaloupe.

Vigil, Evangelina, ed. *Woman of Her Word: Hispanic Women Write.* Houston, Tex.: Arte Publico Press, 1983. Anthology of short stories that reflect a diverse selection of Latin American women writers—Mexican, Puerto Rican, Cuban, Costa Rican, Chilean, and others.

Films

Unless otherwise indicated, all films listed are available in VHS video format.

Carmen Carrascal. 30 minutes, 1982. This movie follows the daily life of an artisan woman in Colombia. The viewer has an opportunity to see firsthand the creative and ingenious fashion in which Third World women survive and provide for their families. The film richly illustrates the weavings, baskets, wall hangings, and crafts that are made by women in Third World countries and exported for First World consumption. Available for rental ($75) from Women Make Movies, 225 Lafayette Street, New York, NY 10012; (212) 925-0606.

Hell to Pay. 52 minutes. 1988. This Bolivian film explores the issue of international debt. Of central concern is Decree 21060, issued by the Bolivian government, and the effects it has had on peasant women. Available for rental ($90) from Women Make Movies, 225 Lafayette Street, New York, NY 10012; (212) 925-0606.

Lucía. 160 minutes, 1969. (Spanish, with English subtitles.) Tells the story of three generations of Cuban women. All three are named Lucía, but they live under very different social circumstances during very different eras in Cuba's history: an 1895 peasant uprising, the 1932 revolt against the dictator Gerardo Machado, and the Castro years. Available for rental (16 mm, $175) or purchase (video, $125) from New Yorker Films, 16 W. 61st Street, New York, NY 10023; (212) 247-6110.

A Man When He Is a Man. 66 minutes, 1982 (Spanish, with English subtitles). Through interviews with Latin American men of various ages, this documentary explores the cultural ideal of *machismo*. Available for rental (16mm, $130; video $90) or purchase (video, $350) from Women Make Movies, 225 Lafayette Street, New York, NY 10012; (212) 925-0606.

Miss Universe in Peru. 32 minutes, 1986. Director Grupo Chaski filmed the 1982 Miss Universe pageant hosted by Peru. This documentary juxtaposes the glamour of the beauty contest with the realities of Peruvian women's lives, while providing a critique of multinational corporate interests. Available for rental ($90) from Women Make Movies,

225 Lafayette Street, New York, NY 10012; (212) 925-0606.

The Official Story. 112 minutes, 1985. Chronicles a woman's political awakening and the legacy of the *desaparecidos* in Argentina. Winner of the Academy Award for best foreign film. Available in most video-rental outlets.

Other Resources

Meeting the Third World Through Women's Perspectives. This global education unit is intended for use in high schools, but the fine slides, activities, and handouts are effective and useful supplemental teaching resources. Available in filmstrip ($45) or video format ($50), with an accompanying teacher's guide, from Social Studies School Service, 10200 Jefferson Blvd., Rm. Y71, P.O. Box 802, Culver City, CA 90232-0802; (800) 421-4246.

Nazzari, Muriel. "Women in Latin America." In *The Cross-Cultural Study of Women*, edited by Margot J. Duley and Mary I. Edwards, 376–405. New York: Feminist Press, 1986. An annotated bibliography of the condition of Latin American women from colonial times to the twentieth century. The topics covered include images and status of Latin American women, their role in politics, feminism in Latin America, family patterns in contemporary Latin America, fertility and population control, women in the labor force, the impact of modernization on the condition of women, and Latin American women under socialism.

Pérez Duarte, Alicia. "Reproductive Rights in Mexico." In *The Future for Women in Development: Voices from the South*, edited by Nancy O'Rourke. Proceedings of the Association of Women in Development Colloquium, Ottawa, Canada: The North-South Institute, 1991. This essay discusses the current struggle of women in Mexico to gain access to family planning resources and to influence the legal structure to achieve that access. Available from the North-South Institute, 55 Murrary St., Suite 200, Ottawa, Canada K1N 5M3; (613) 237-7435 (fax).

TEST BANK

Questions reflect content from the programs, textbook, study guide, and anthology.

Multiple Choice

*Mark the letter of the response that **best** answers the question or completes the statement.*

_____ 1. During the period of European conquest, indigenous women:

    a. tried to keep their communities together and resisted domination by the European invaders.

    b. had children with European men in order to create a racially and ethnically mixed society, a goal of colonial administrations.

    c. were no longer economically unproductive because they had an opportunity to work for Europeans.

    d. fostered an appreciation of indigenous customs among the European invaders.

_____ 2. In colonial Latin America, Hispanic women's behavior was carefully controlled: (*Mark all that apply.*)

    a. in order to protect the purity of European bloodlines.

    b. because they needed to be taught aristocratic ways in order to become the social equals of the European men.

    c. to maintain the hierarchical structure of the colonial empire.

    d. because the colonial societies placed a very high value on women and wanted to protect them from violence.

_____ 3. After 1920, Chile's copper industry: (*Mark all that apply.*)

    a. had an ownership that was concentrated in foreign hands.

    b. was controlled by only three companies, each of which was a subsidiary of a U.S. corporation.

    c. created large profits that were invested domestically and helped Chile's industrial development.

    d. was capital- and technology-intensive, and did not create high numbers of jobs for Chilean workers.

_____ 4. Like other elected governments before it, the 1970–73 Popular Unity government:

    a. was a fragile coalition of many parties.

    b. was strong because it had won with such a large majority of the vote.

    c. remained immensely popular due to its economic policies.

    d. was replaced by another elected government in a constitutional transition.

_____ 5. Under Salvador Allende's Popular Unity government of 1970–73, women: (*Mark all that apply.*)

    a. responded to the government's call to work in the poor urban squatter settlements (*poblaciones*).

    b. were prevented from expanding their activities beyond the spheres of family and home.

    c. of the upper and middle classes took to the streets to protest the shortage of consumer goods.

    d. and their families suffered because of shortages and inflation, despite the Allende government's attempted economic reforms.

_____ 6. Women's groups in Chile opposed the government of:

    a. socialist Salvador Allende.

    b. military dictator Augusto Pinochet.

c. both Allende and Pinochet, although each was favored by some sectors.

d. neither Allende nor Pinochet; women's groups did not involve themselves in politics.

_____ 7. Chilean women:

a. still can't vote in national elections.

b. won the right to vote in national elections in 1949.

c. won the right to vote in national elections in 1903.

d. won the right to vote in national elections in 1878.

_____ 8. The 1973 military coup was welcomed by many Chileans because: (*Mark all that apply.*)

a. they feared a military intervention by the United States if Allende were not deposed.

b. they were frightened by the economic upheaval and the social conflict.

c. they were willing to give up democracy temporarily for the sake of order.

d. Chile had a long history of military rule and most of the population was comforted by the move away from democracy.

_____ 9. General Augusto Pinochet's regime: (*Mark all that apply.*)

a. was one of Latin America's most repressive military governments, with many thousands arrested, subjected to torture, killed, or disappeared.

b. presided after 1983 over a period of economic stabilization and growth.

c. maintained social control by providing many social services to keep urban and rural workers satisfied.

d. provoked many women, even those who had never before been politically active, to organize and demonstrate against the government.

_____ 10. Latin American and Caribbean women: (*Mark all that apply.*)

a. have been pushed into grassroots political movements by economic crises and political repression over the past twenty years.

b. have until quite recently been divided by vast differences based on class and ethnicity.

c. usually initially become politically active over such issues as violence against women, divorce laws, and reproductive rights.

d. have a strong political presence and hold a significant number of important political positions.

_____ 11. As a result of the economic and political turmoil of recent years: (*Mark all that apply.*)

a. poor women have developed informal networks of mutual aid.

b. traditional ties of kinship and godparenthood (*compadrazgo*) were weakened as women searched for new ways to meet their economic needs.

c. women staged protests against governments to find out about their "disappeared" relatives and to end the repression.

d. women formed alliances with political parties and have influenced electoral politics.

_____ 12. Women in Latin America generally meet for intellectual and political discussion:

a. with other women in informal groups.

b. with men in political parties.

c. with men in unions.

d. in formal, feminist political parties and advocacy groups similar to women's organizations in North America and Europe.

_____ 13. Women who work for large agricultural businesses in El Salvador and elsewhere in the region: (*Mark all that apply.*)

    a. earn high wages and have access to benefits because of the financial stability of their employers.

    b. sometimes must leave their homes and family members to follow the harvest of many crops.

    c. work under harsh and unhealthy conditions.

    d. are often sexually harassed by management.

_____ 14. Which of the following statements about women in the Bolivian highlands are true? (*Mark all that apply.*)

    a. They are largely illiterate.

    b. They are often unable to speak Spanish or relate to a Westernized urban culture.

    c. They are stigmatized by urban and upper classes for their ethnicity and for their poverty.

    d. They have never become politically organized.

_____ 15. The communal kitchens (*ollas comunes*) in poor neighborhoods in Chile:

    a. were developed with foreign aid.

    b. were created as a way for the Pinochet government to give away surplus agricultural products.

    c. built solidarity among women who saved their families from starvation despite having few resources.

    d. were created by political opposition parties.

_____ 16. Feminism in Latin America: (*Mark all that apply.*)

    a. is restricted to upper-class women who have contact with feminist groups in the United States and Europe.

    b. has tried to protect women's right to stay in the home and care for the family.

    c. is notable for the multiclass solidarity it has built among women from many different backgrounds.

    d. has awakened many poor and uneducated women to the harmful effects of *machismo.*

_____ 17. According to Rigoberta Menchú, domestic servants in Guatemala City: (*Mark all that apply.*)

    a. can be pressured to submit to the sexual demands of their employers as a condition of employment.

    b. are treated well by the mistress of the house because they share a common bond of *marianismo.*

    c. are sent out of the house overnight on Saturdays, forcing many girls into prostitution.

    d. are educated and dressed well, so that they make a good impression on visitors.

_____ 18. Carolina María de Jesus, who lived in a Brazilian *favela* :

    a. was a social worker who later became a member of Congress.

    b. worked constantly for enough money to get food for her family.

    c. didn't have to work because she got enough social welfare benefits to feed and clothe her family.

    d. had relatively easy life and was able to devote her time to writing about the *favela.*

Identification/Short Answer

Define or describe the following terms, concepts, or persons, or answer the following questions. Answers should be no longer than a few sentences.

19. March of the Empty Pots:

20. *Machismo*:

21. Sor Juana Inés de la Cruz:

22. *Madres de la Plaza de Mayo*:

23. How have women's traditional roles been a problem for them in the midst of economic and political change in their societies?

24. Who are "the disappeared" (*desaparecidos*) and what do they have to do with the activism of Latin American women?

25. What group of women workers in Latin America best reveals how middle- and upper-class women must face the issues of class in feminist struggle?

26. What Latin American country has a feminist movement similar to that in the United States? What issues are important in this movement?

27. How have poor women's organizations such as the peasant women's federations in Honduras and Bolivia helped to increase feminist consciousness?

28. General Augusto Pinochet:

29. *Arpilleras*:

30. *"Somos más"*:

ESSAY QUESTIONS

1. Describe the historical process that led Chile to turn its back on its democratic past for nearly 30 years. What were some of the tensions that Allende's election illustrated, and why did so many Chileans accept and support the Pinochet government?

2. Using any three women portrayed in the program as examples, illustrate different ways in which Chilean women were affected by the Allende and Pinochet periods. For example, did women become active in politics? Did they experience a change in traditional roles?

3. Describe the impact of *machismo* in Latin America. What are the most visible signs of its continued impact on women? What are the signs of its being challenged?

4. Why is it that feminist movements in Latin America have generally been able to unite women across boundaries of race, ethnic group, and class?

ANSWER KEY

Test Bank

Answers indicate sources.
1. a (anthology)
2. a, c (anthology, study guide)
3. a, b, d (program, textbook)
4. a (program, textbook, study guide)
5. a, c, d (program)
6. c (program, study guide)
7. b (textbook)
8. b, c (program, textbook, study guide)
9. a, b, d (program, textbook, study guide)
10. a, b (anthology, study guide)
11. a, c, d (program, anthology, study guide)
12. a (anthology)
13. b, c, d (program, anthology)
14. a, b, c (anthology)
15. c (program, anthology)
16. c, d (program, anthology, study guide)
17. a, c (anthology)
18. b (anthology)
19. Protest against the Allende government in which middle-class and well-to-do women took to the streets, banging on empty pots, to protest the beginnings of consumer shortages. (program)
20. A cultural norm that exalts male virility, superiority, and control, especially over women. Traditionally linked with *marianismo*, which idealizes women as the custodians of virtue, piety, and spirituality. It has been the ideological basis of male-female relations in Latin America for centuries but is now widely questioned. (anthology, study guide)
21. A seventeenth-century Mexican nun, considered to be one of the most gifted poets of Latin America. She also wrote impassioned letters to elders in the Church hierarchy, arguing for better treatment of women. (anthology)
22. Literally, mothers of May Square in Buenos Aires, where the presidential palace is located. Women gathered weekly in the Plaza de Mayo to protest the arrest, disappearance, and execution of their loved ones under military rule. (program, anthology, study guide)

23. They are obliged to work but still have tremendous duties in the home. Their income must go to the family, not to enhance their own independence. They have been reluctant to become involved in politics, especially formal political parties, and few women are in official positions of power. (program, anthology, textbook)
24. The *desaparecidos* are the people who were arrested and subsequently disappeared under repressive military governments. Most of the thousands who disappeared in Brazil, Argentina, Guatemala, and Chile are now presumed to have been killed by the military or police. Women protested these disappearances with marches and vigils. In Chile, women also commemorated the missing with appliquéd, embroidered wall hangings known as *arpilleras*. The trauma of the *desaparecidos* also provoked many women to protest actively against military rule. (program, anthology, study guide)
25. The exploitation of domestic workers, which includes long hours, low pay, no benefits, exposure to discrimination, and sexual harassment or abuse, has become important in Latin America. Middle- and upper-class women who are feminists must also recognize the oppression of women by women within their societies. (anthology)
26. Argentina's feminist movement is like that of the United States because it is more restricted to intellectual, educated women and does not have a broad popular base. Equal pay for equal work and the liberalization of divorce laws are two important feminist demands in Argentina. (anthology)
27. The anthology readings show how once women come together in their own groups to talk and share experiences, they begin to see the problems they have in common with other women, such as domestic violence and all of the harmful effects of *machismo*. They also become more assertive of their rights, gain more confidence, and begin to question and confront men, whether their husbands or their employers. (anthology)
28. General who led the coup against Chilean president Salvador Allende in 1973 and remained dictator until 1990. Even though he was replaced with a civilian government, Pinochet retained control over the armed forces

and remained very powerful. His government was marked by high levels of repression and human rights abuses but also by economic growth in its final years. (program, textbook, study guide)

29. Appliquéd tapestries sewn by Chilean women illustrating their personal experiences of torture, hunger, unemployment, and the arrest and disappearance of their loved ones. This work, supported by the Chilean Catholic Church, not only created solidarity and relieved loneliness among the women, but also served as a source of income and a means of bringing international attention to human rights violations in Chile. (program, anthology, study guide)

30. Literally, "We are more," or "There are more of us." Chant used by women's groups in angry street demonstrations against the unelected Pinochet government in the mid-1980s. (program, study guide)

Essay Questions

1. In responding to this question, students should demonstrate an understanding of the Chilean political system, which by the time of Allende's election was increasingly polarized. Although he came to power with only 36 percent of the vote, as a long-time standard-bearer for the Left, Allende had a radical agenda of reforms that he was determined to set in place. His policies raised high expectations among Chile's working class and poor citizens, but many of the elite were frightened at the prospect of socialism. Chileans across the board were hurt by the inflation and scarcity of goods that resulted from Allende's economic policies. As opposition to his presidency mounted from the conservative sectors and from the middle and upper classes, many supporters also took to the streets in pro-Allende demonstrations. Chileans felt the country was being torn apart, and many welcomed the restoration of order promised by the 1973 coup. Although they may not have expected the military dictatorship to last

17 years, the fact that economic growth was steady during most of the period led many Chileans to accept and support the Pinochet government.

2. Students should draw upon cases of women in the program to show how women did not have one single political view: some supported Allende while others, mostly those in privileged positions, feared and opposed him. Some women were inspired by Allende to leave their homes and work actively for social change. Some of them were later arrested and tortured as "subversives" under Pinochet. Women who had been very traditional wives and mothers were drawn into politics almost against their will by the Pinochet government's policy of "disappearing" its opponents. Overall, women have emerged from the dictatorship much more organized and politically aware.

3. *Machismo* is a cultural norm that came to Latin America with the Spanish and has governed male-female relationships for centuries. *Machismo* elevates the ideal of man as superior to and dominant over woman; the corresponding ideal for women is to be passive, submissive, obedient, and chaste. Fortified by *machismo*, Latin American men have crafted a society that tolerates, even encourages, alcoholism, domestic violence, male promiscuity, and adultery. The anthology readings and conversation with agricultural workers in the program show how women are becoming more aware of *machismo* and its impact, but still must cope with husbands, fathers, and lovers who are abusive, make unreasonable demands, and take no responsibility for their children or households.

4. Although class- and race-based divisions among the region's women are very great, women in Latin America also share many experiences that transcend these differences. All are subject to the code of *machismo*; all have a strong desire to protect their families; all have been pushed into new roles by economic and political pressures. As their former isolation in the household ends, women are forging common bonds in the workplace and in unions, protest movements, soup kitchens, and other formal and informal organizations.

Unit 8

Miracles Are Not Enough: Continuity and Change in Religion

UNIT SUMMARY

Unit 8 offers historical and contemporary perspectives on the role of religion in Latin America and the Caribbean. It explores the varied nature of religious practices and the dynamism and diversity that characterize religion in the Americas. Ideas of continuity and change are considered particularly in the case of the Catholic Church, which has remained strong despite, or perhaps because of, the many transformations it has undergone during five centuries in the Americas. The program, set in Brazil and Nicaragua, illustrates the range of religious alternatives available, the ease with which Latin Americans move from one religious belief system to another, and the important relationship between religion and major social questions of the day. The textbook assignments on El Salvador and Nicaragua focus especially on churches' response to revolutionary upheaval; these readings will be considered in greater detail in Unit 11, "Fire in the Mind: Revolutions and Revolutionaries."

LEARNING OBJECTIVES

After completing this unit, students should be able to:

- Understand that the diversity of religions and religious beliefs in Latin America and the Caribbean is a reflection of the region's cultural complexity.

- Recognize that adaptation to local conditions and beliefs has allowed religion to play an evolving and dynamic role in Latin American and Caribbean society.

- Explain the historical and institutional basis for the decision by the Latin American Catholic Church in the late 1960s to take a more prominent role in support of profound political, economic, and social change in the region.

- Be familiar with the role of the Catholic Church in the Americas today and recognize some of the tensions that the Church's activism has produced.

- List some of the reasons for the growth of Pentecostalism and spiritism over the last 50 years, and explain the principal ways in which these religions differ from Catholicism and mainline Protestantism.

OVERVIEW

Religion has always played a vital role within Latin American and Caribbean societies, and it continues to have great importance for millions of people in the region today. The multicultural complexity of the Americas is clearly reflected in the diversity of religious beliefs in the region. While Catholicism is predominant, there are many other religions practiced today by people of all classes and races.

The anthology readings examine the roots of various religious traditions in the Americas, the evolving role of the Catholic Church, and the active commitment to social and economic justice that churches have promoted in the second half of the twentieth century. Among the important concepts and events described in this unit are liberation theology, *comunidades eclesiales de base*, or base Christian Communities (CEBs), Vatican II, the Latin American Bishops Conference (CELAM), spiritism, and Pentecostalism.

The anthology also explores the complex religious landscape that characterizes the region today, focusing especially on the example of Brazil, the world's largest Catholic country. Brazilians also practice numerous religious alternatives, including many with African and indigenous roots. The textbook assignments consider the response of the churches to revolutionary situations in El Salvador and Nicaragua, including the repression of church activists.

Along with the program, the readings help students understand that although approximately 90 percent of Latin Americans continue to identify themselves as Catholics, many engage in non-Catholic religious practices. Among the other religious alternatives presented are those based on African beliefs, such as *Candomblé*, spiritist religions with European and African roots, such as *Umbanda*, and a variety of Pentecostal movements.

The program considers the role of religion in two very different societies: Brazil and Nicaragua. Interviews with Catholics who supported the Sandinista revolution in Nicaragua and with Brazilian Catholics provide insight into some of the tensions that have resulted from the mainline denominations' efforts to become more relevant to their members' daily lives and struggles.

STUDENT READING ASSIGNMENT

Modern Latin America, 3d ed.
In chapter 10: "Nicaragua: From Dynasty to Revolution," pp. 326–30, and "El Salvador: From Stability to Insurgence," pp. 332–37.

Students should also review pp. 179–84, assigned in Unit 4.

Americas: An Anthology, chapter 8, pp. 208–40.

Writing Assignments/ Discussion Questions

1. Do religious organizations have a moral obligation to take strong and vocal positions on important social issues such as human rights, poverty, and oppression? Or should religious organizations stay out of politics and instead focus on the spiritual needs of individuals?

2. Compare and contrast the roles of religion in the United States and in Americas. Do you think institutional churches in the United States have more or less influence on important political, social, and economic issues than their counterparts in Latin America and the Caribbean? Why?

3. How are some Latin Americans able to participate in more than one religious tradition whose beliefs and practices may conflict with one another? What might this indicate about the role of religion in their lives?

SUGGESTED ACTIVITIES

1. Have students recreate the Valladolid debate, with one student playing Bartolomé de las Casas, another playing Juan Ginés de Sepúlveda, and the rest taking the part of the board of theologians, asking questions. After both sides have been presented, have students vote

in favor or against the conquest and subsequent treatment of the Indians, justifying their answers according to the mores of the time.

2. Students may not be aware that various types of spiritist religions, such as *Vodún* and *Santería*, are practiced within the United States, especially among communities of immigrants from Latin America and the Caribbean. Have students research the presence and extent of such religious alternatives in this country and present their findings to the group. If your class is located in a major urban area, students may be able to visit stores specializing in religious artifacts to learn more about the beliefs and practices of spiritists.

RESOURCES

Nonfiction

Brown, Diana DeGroat. *Umbanda: Religion and Politics in Urban Brazil.* Ann Arbor, Mich.: University Microfilms International Research Press, 1986. A basic textbook on contemporary *Umbanda.*

Bruneau, Thomas C., Chester E. Gabriel, and Mary Mooney, eds. *The Catholic Church and Religions in Latin America.* Montreal: McGill University Center for Developing-Area Studies, 1984. Examines the influence of Catholicism on non-Catholic religious practices and vice versa.

Carrasco, David. *Religions of Mesoamerica: Cosmovision and Ceremonial Centers.* New York: Harper & Row, 1990. An analytical description of indigenous religions in the area that is today Mexico and Central America.

Cole, Jeffrey A. *The Church and Society in Latin America.* New Orleans: Tulane University Press, 1984. A collection of essays covering Protestantism and Catholicism in both the colonial and national periods.

Crahan, Margaret E. "Church and State in Latin America: Assassinating Some Old and New Stereotypes." *Daedalus* 120:3 (Summer 1991): 131–58. An overview of church-state relations in Latin America with an emphasis on contemporary ecclesial views of what constitutes moral political and economic systems.

Crahan, Margaret E. "Cuba and Nicaragua: Religion and Revolution." In *World Catholicism in Transition,* edited by Thomas M. Gannon, S.J., 265–82. New York: Macmillan, 1988. A comparative analysis of the involvement of churches in the Cuban and Nicaraguan revolutions including changing positions over time. Suggests the general issues that arise when churches confront revolution.

Crahan, Margaret E. "Religion : Reconstituting Church and Pursuing Change." In *Americas: New Interpretive Essays,* edited by Alfred Stepan. New York: Oxford University Press, 1992. An evaluation of the prospects for the Latin American Church as it confronts new external and internal pressures, written by a member of the *Americas* academic advisory board as an optional addition to this unit.

Crahan, Margaret E. "Religion, Revolution and Counterrevolution: The Role of the Religious Right in Central America." In *Democracy and the Right in Latin America,* edited by Douglas Chalmers, Maria do Carmo Campello de Souza, and Atilio Borón. Westport, Conn.: Praeger, 1992. An analysis of the role of the religious right in the United States and Central America during the crises in the latter region in the 1980s.

Dorr, Donal. *Option for the Poor: A Hundred Years of Vatican Social Teaching.* Maryknoll, N.Y.: Orbis Books, 1983. A survey of Catholic positions on social issues since the late nineteenth century, including an analysis of Vatican II and Medellín.

Eagleson, John, and Philip Scharper, eds. *Puebla and Beyond.* Maryknoll, N.Y.: Orbis Books, 1980. A description and analysis of the 1979 Latin American Catholic bishops' conference at Puebla, Mexico, together with some of the basic documents.

Farriss, Nancy. *Maya Society Under Colonial Rule: The Collective Enterprise of Survival.* Princeton: Princeton University Press, 1984. A landmark study of how indigenous peoples used the structures imposed on them as well as traditional beliefs and practices to survive, beginning in the sixteenth century.

Gannon, Thomas M., S.J., ed. *World Catholicism in Transition*. New York: Macmillan, 1988. A collection of essays analyzing the role of the Catholic Church in the modern world with special attention to Asia, Africa, and Latin America.

Gutierrez, Gustavo. *The Truth Shall Make You Free: Confrontations*. Maryknoll, N.Y.: Orbis Books, 1990. The most current of the leading liberation theologian's works available in English. Reflects some modifications of Gutierrez's earlier positions.

Hennelly, Alfred T., S.J., ed. *Liberation Theology: A Documentary History*. Maryknoll, N.Y.: Orbis Books, 1990. Contains selections from the most influential liberation theologians, as well as responses to their work.

Levine, Daniel H. "Is Religion Being Politicized? And Other Pressing Questions Latin America Poses." *Political Sociology* (Fall 1986): 825–31. Tackles the issues involved in the charges that religion in Latin America, and particularly the Catholic Church, is becoming too political.

Levine, Daniel H. *Religion and Political Conflict in Latin America*. Chapel Hill: University of North Carolina Press, 1986. Focuses on grassroots Catholicism and popular religiosity.

Mainwaring, Scott. *The Catholic Church and Politics in Brazil, 1916–1985*. Stanford, Calif.: Stanford University Press, 1986. First-rate analysis of Catholicism in twentieth-century Brazil.

Mainwaring, Scott, and Alexander Wilde, eds. *Progressive Church in Latin America*. Notre Dame, Ind.: University of Notre Dame Press, 1988. Examines progressive church movements in Central America, Brazil, and Peru and their evolution over time.

McGovern, Arthur F. *Liberation Theology and Its Critics*. Maryknoll, N.Y.: Orbis Books, 1989. Contains a brief history and analysis of liberation theology and then examines the principal controversial issues it generated.

Murphy, Joseph M. *Santería: An African Religion in America*. Boston: Beacon Press, 1988. Describes the

spiritist religion of *Santería* and its influence in the Cuban-American communities in Miami and New York.

Sigmund, Paul E. *Liberation Theology at the Crossroads: Democracy or Revolution?* New York: Oxford University Press, 1990. An analysis of the origins and evolution of liberation theology in Latin America and some of the controversies generated by it.

Stoll, David. *Is Latin America Turning Protestant? The Politics of Evangelical Growth*. Berkeley: University of California Press, 1990. Argues that Protestantism, especially Pentecostalism, is spreading rapidly in Latin America. Stoll's statistics have been challenged by a good number of scholars as being overstated.

Tamez, Elsa, ed. *Through Her Eyes: Women's Theology from Latin America*. Maryknoll, N.Y.: Orbis Press, 1989. Collection of essays on women's views of liberation theology, particularly its relevance to the problems of women in Latin America.

van Duk, Frank Jan. "The Twelve Tribes of Israel: Rasta and the Middle Class," *New West Indian Guide* 62: 1, 2 (1988). This article describes the rise and growth of the Kingston-based Twelve Tribes of Israel—the largest, best-organized, and best-disciplined group within Rastafarianism.

Wafer, Jim. *The Taste of Blood: Spirit Possession in Brazilian Candomblé*. Philadelphia: University of Pennsylvania Press, 1991. An analysis of African-Brazilian spiritism and who is attracted to it.

Williams, Philip J. *The Catholic Church and Politics in Nicaragua and Costa Rica*. Pittsburgh: University of Pittsburgh Press, 1989. Examines contemporary trends within the Nicaraguan Catholic Church and compares them with those in the Church in Costa Rica.

Fiction

Carpentier, Alejo. *Explosion in a Cathedral*. Translated by John Shirrock. Boston: Little, Brown, 1963. This international best-seller by a Cuban author recounts the origins of the Haitian revolution and the interplay of various motivations, including the challenge of freemasonry to the Catholic Church and to traditional society.

Esquivel, Julia. "They Have Threatened Us with Resurrection: Parable." In *You Can't Drown the Fire: Latin American Women Writing in Exile*, edited by Alicia Partnoy, pp. 190–97. Pittsburgh: Cleis Press, 1988. A poem by a Guatemalan Protestant political activist about repression in her country.

Greene, Graham. *The Power and the Glory*. New York: Penguin Books, 1962. Graham Greene's classic novel set in Mexico after the 1910–17 revolution recounts the story of a priest caught up in the anti-clericalism of the period.

Mistral, Gabriela. *Selected Poems of Gabriela Mistral*. Translated and edited by Foris Dana. Baltimore: Johns Hopkins University Press, 1971. Poems by the first Latin American writer to receive the Nobel Prize for literature. This Chilean poet's work is suffused with religious imagery and references as she discusses death, grief, children, and nature.

Partnoy, Alicia. *The Little School: Tales of Disappearance and Survival in Argentina*. Pittsburgh: Cleis Press, 1986. The chapter entitled "Religion" is a meditation on religion and political activism, and on the interplay of religions, as well as belief and nonbelief.

Films

Unless otherwise indicated, all films listed are available in VHS video format.

Bahia: Africa in the Americas. 58 minutes, 1988. This documentary explores the impact of African culture on Brazil, with emphasis on the *Candomblé* religion. Available for rental ($40, plus $6 shipping and handling) from: The University of California Extension Media Center, 2176 Shattuck Avenue, Berkeley, CA 94704; (510) 642-0460.

Christmas Customs in Latin America. 15 minutes, 1986. Educational Filmstrips. This short video is a mixture of live action and still pictures which explores

the Christmas season in Latin America as a time for music, ritual, and rejoicing. Available in VHS format for purchase only ($49.95 plus $3 shipping) from: Educational Video Network, 1401 19th Street, Huntsville, TX 77340; (409) 295-5767.

Divine Horsemen: The Living Gods of Haiti. 52 minutes, 1985. Originally filmed from 1947 to 1951 by Maya Deren, this video describes the *Vodún* religion of Haiti. The viewer attends the rituals of the Rada, Petro, and Congo cults, and observes ritual offerings, songs, and dances. Available for purchase only ($29.95 plus $4 shipping) from: Mystic Fire Video, Box 1092 Cooper Station, New York, NY 10276; (212) 941-0999 or (800) 292-9001. Available in most video-rental outlets.

Highland Maya: A Case in Economic Anthropology. 29 minutes, 1983. Part of the *Faces of Culture* series, this film explores the syncretic blend of Maya religious beliefs and Catholicism, as well as the complex interrelationship between economics and religion known as the "cargo" system found among the highland Maya of Mexico and Guatemala. Available for rental ($35 for five business days, plus $3 shipping) from: Coast Telecourses, 11460 Warner Avenue, Fountain Valley, CA 92708-2597; (714) 241-6109.

Hotel Cuba. 27 minutes, 1984. Uses recollections of immigrants and archival photographs to describe the experiences of Old World Jews who came to Cuba following World War I. Available for rental ($5) from: Florida Endowment for the Humanities, 1718 East Seventh Avenue, Suite 301, Tampa, FL 33605; (813) 272-3473.

The Mission. 128 minutes, 1986. Robert De Niro and Jeremy Irons star in this epic tale of eighteenth-century Jesuit missionaries in Brazil and the disaster that results when they try to convert the indigenous tribes living in Brazil's interior. Available in most video-rental outlets.

Popol Vuh: The Creation Myth of the Maya. 29 minutes, 1989. VHS video. This animated film recounts the creation myth of the Maya in ancient Guatemala. Available for rental ($60 plus $7 shipping) from: University of California Extension Media Center, 2176 Shattuck Avenue, Berkeley, CA 94704; (510) 642-0460.

TEST BANK

Questions reflect content from the programs, textbook, and anthology.

Multiple Choice

*Mark the letter of the response that **best** answers the question or completes the statement.*

_____ 1. The Popol Vuh is an example of:

    a. the Catholic Church's efforts to convert indigenous peoples.

    b. religious beliefs of indigenous peoples in Central America which predate the conquest.

    c. the impact of African religious belief systems in the Americas.

    d. religious justification for Aztec human sacrifice.

_____ 2. The debate between Bartolomé de las Casas and Juan Ginés de Sepúlveda at Valladolid:

    a. was resolved by the establishment of the *patronato real* system for managing Church/state relations.

    b. was an indication of the moral obligation some church people felt to defend the rights of indigenous populations.

    c. revealed the general indifference of Church and royal authorities to the moral issues raised by the conquest.

    d. revolved around the question of whether it was proper for the Church to amass significant wealth in the Americas.

_____ 3. The wealth of the Catholic Church in Latin America: *(Mark all that apply.)*

    a. is considered one of the most important issues facing believers in the region today.

    b. was of great concern to many newly independent governments in Latin America during the nineteenth century.

    c. was used in part to help the less fortunate, since churches in the colonial and early independence periods tended to be the primary providers of social services.

    d. was one of the most important issues discussed at CELAM II, when the Latin American bishops decided the Church should divest itself of its large landholdings, monasteries, and other wealth.

_____ 4. Which of the following statements is true of the Church's position during the colonial period and through the nineteenth century on the issue of slavery? *(Mark all that apply.)*

    a. The Church forbade slavery and threatened to excommunicate any who continued to hold slaves after about 1700.

    b. The Church as an institution owned slaves, although many clergy and church people questioned the morality of slavery.

    c. The Church was a stalwart defender of slavery and tended to side with the Portuguese and Spanish monarchs against those who wanted slaves to be able to purchase their freedom.

    d. Slavery, like other social issues, prompted diverse views within the Church which tended to evolve over time.

_____ 5. The proportion of Latin Americans who identify themselves as Catholic is approximately:

    a. 30 percent.
    b. 50 percent.
    c. 75 percent.
    d. 90 percent.

_____ 6. Which of the following is an example of the adaptation of Catholicism to local beliefs? (*Mark all that apply.*)

a. The identification of Roman Catholic saints with deities of indigenous and/or African religions.

b. The use of mediums to speak directly with the Holy Spirit at Catholic masses.

c. The practice of *Umbanda* among a wide variety of classes and races in Brazil.

d. The fact that popular feast days frequently coincide with saints' days and are celebrated together.

_____ 7. Pentecostalism in Latin America:

a. became very popular in the wake of World War II but is now on the decline.

b. emphasizes the action of mediums to communicate directly with the spirit world.

c. has drawn most of its followers from spiritist religions such as *Umbanda*.

d. is growing in popularity as an alternative to standard institutional religions.

_____ 8. Many Brazilians in urban areas:

a. have rejected newer Pentecostal and spiritist churches in favor of involvement in traditional Catholic parishes.

b. no longer attend Catholic and Protestant churches because they have joined *Candomblé* and *Umbanda* centers.

c. are likely to practice more than one religion depending on their needs at any one time.

d. are uninterested in the spiritist religions, which they identify with poor blacks from the northeast.

_____ 9. Which of the following is true of *comunidades eclesiales de base*? (*Mark all that apply.*)

a. They represent an effort to connect religious beliefs and practices to the concerns of daily life.

b. Their popularity results in part from believers' desire to experience church community in a smaller, more personal setting.

c. They illustrate the growing popularity of spiritist religions among the lower classes.

d. They are an example of the adaptation of Catholicism to indigenous beliefs.

_____ 10. For the Latin American Catholic Church, concern with social justice for the poor:

a. only became important after the pope used Vatican II to pressure the Latin American bishops to become active on social issues.

b. was increasingly emphasized by church people at the grassroots level after Vatican II but was never shared by the Church hierarchy.

c. was a trend associated with liberation theology but can no longer be said to characterize Church activities in the region.

d. has historical roots dating from the conquest but became more of an institutional concern since the early 1960s.

_____ 11. An important theologian considered one of the originators of liberation theology was:

a. Pope John XXIII.

b. Paulo Freire.

c. Gustavo Gutierrez.

d. Bartolomé de las Casas.

_____ 12. Which of the following statements is true of liberation theology? (*Mark all that apply.*)

    a. It was criticized for advocating revolution to overthrow the established order.
    b. It was based on a new interpretation of the social meaning of Christ's teachings.
    c. It had a relatively short life and has in general been repudiated by most Latin American intellectuals, who reject its sanctioning of violence.
    d. It has continued to be a subject of scholarship and has been the focus of extensive debate outside as well as within Latin America.

_____ 13. The CELAM meeting in 1968 was significant because:

    a. it marked the first time that Latin America's bishops had gathered to discuss policy matters.
    b. it brought bishops from the United States, Europe, and Latin America together to discuss how to implement the changes of Vatican II.
    c. it led to the public association of the Latin American Catholic Church with the struggles of the poor and advocacy of social change.
    d. it resulted in the formal acceptance by the bishops of Latin Americans' desire to have more than one religious affiliation.

_____ 14. Iemanjá, the goddess of water in some African religions, is connected in popular Brazilian culture to:

    a. the Virgin Mary.
    b. Saint Theresa.
    c. the Aztec goddess Tonantzín.
    d. the Virgin of Guadalupe.

_____ 15. The growth and number of religious alternatives practiced in Latin America are indications of:

    a. the likelihood that Catholicism will be eliminated from the region by the end of the twentieth century.
    b. the fact that religion in general is increasingly seen by poor and middle-class Latin Americans as irrelevant to their daily needs.
    c. the fact that Latin Americans continue to view the institutional churches as the most reliable source of stability and comfort in the midst of rapid social change and economic hardship.
    d. the continuing dynamism and importance of religion in the region, even in an increasingly secular and modern world.

_____ 16. Which of the following is true of institutional churches' positions during revolutionary uprisings in Nicaragua and El Salvador in the late 1970s?

    a. Their traditional alliances with national elites led Nicaraguan and Salvadoran bishops to declare their countries' revolutionary movements illegitimate.
    b. Catholic and Protestant church hierarchies in both countries supported the guerrilla army's Marxist ideology.
    c. Revolutionary uprisings posed a dilemma for the churches, which had to decide how to reconcile support for nonviolence with the need to replace authoritarian governments.
    d. Church hierarchies remained silent on the legitimacy of armed struggle and remained neutral and uninvolved bystanders.

_____ 17. Mainline Catholic and Protestant churches in Latin America today are:

    a. backing away from their commitment to justice, peace, and human rights because of the repression that church people have suffered in many countries.

b. beginning to confront the need for greater justice within their own institutions as well as in society at large.

c. endorsing armed revolts such as Peru's Sendero Luminoso as the only promising means of achieving socioeconomic justice.

d. considered to be largely irrelevant in terms of the major social and political issues in their countries.

_____ 18. One of the most important reasons for the influence of the Catholic Church over the centuries has been that:

a. schools tended to be run by the Church, and Catholic universities trained most of Latin America's intellectuals.

b. most of the clergy came to Latin America from the United States, where they had a superior educational background.

c. the Church's presence and power were concentrated in the rural areas where the majority of Latin Americans lived until very recently.

d. political authorities were mindful of Church authority because of the high attendance of their citizens at church services.

_____ 19. Which of the following statements describe *Umbanda*? (*Mark all that apply.*)

a. The spirits include those of ancient Amazonian Indians and African slaves.

b. It is a uniquely Brazilian combination of indigenous, African, and European religious beliefs.

c. There is no connection between the *orixás* of *Umbanda* and the Christian saints.

d. It is practiced most extensively by Afro-Brazilians in Bahia.

_____ 20. Brazilian Cardinal Paulo Evaristo Arns: (*Mark all that apply.*)

a. was a vocal defender of workers' right to strike during the late 1970s and early 1980s.

b. was originally archbishop of Recife, in the Brazilian northeast, where he became aware of the importance of land reform.

c. publicly criticized the human rights practices and legitimacy of the military government.

d. was forced to back down from his progressive social positions after numerous church workers became the targets of government repression.

Identification/Short Answer

Define or describe the following terms, concepts, or persons, or answer the following questions. Answers should be no longer than a few sentences.

21. Briefly describe the significance of Vatican II.

22. Gustavo Gutierrez:

23. *Umbanda*:

24. *Patronato real*:

25. Why are CEBs considered an important pastoral innovation?

26. What are some of the reasons cited by individual Brazilians for the appeal of Pentecostal churches?

27. Cardinal Miguel Obando y Bravo:

28. Iemanjá:

29. What was the basis for Bartolomé de las Casas's argument in the Valladolid debate?

30. Why did Catholic Church relations with some Latin American states deteriorate after the wars of independence?

ESSAY QUESTIONS

1. Explain the origins of the Latin American Catholic Church's move toward open support for significant transformation of oppressive social, political, and economic structures. Was this more of an evolution or an about-face? How is the "preferential option for the poor" articulated at Medellín connected to the repression and assassinations of church people in El Salvador and elsewhere?

2. Consider the following excerpt from Gustavo Gutierrez's *A Theology of Liberation*:
   What the groups in power call "advocating" class struggle is really an expression of a will to abolish its causes, to abolish them, not cover them over, to eliminate the appropriation by a few of the wealth created by the work of the many. . . . It is a will to build a socialist society, more just, free, and human. . . . To "advocate" class struggle, therefore, is to reject a situation in which there are oppressed and oppressors. . . . Neutrality is impossible. When the Church rejects the class struggle, it is objectively operating as a part of the prevailing system.
   How might these words lend themselves to different interpretations of the intentions of liberation theology?

3. Using your impressions from the program as well as the anthology, describe in your own words the appeal that religious alternatives such as Pentecostalism and spiritism offer to Latin Americans. What do you predict for the future of religion in the region? Is Catholicism likely to lose its dominance?

ANSWER KEY

Test Bank

Answers indicate sources.

1. b (anthology)
2. b (anthology, study guide)
3. b, c (anthology)
4. b, d (anthology)
5. d (anthology, study guide)
6. a, d (program, study guide)
7. d (program, anthology, study guide)
8. c (program, anthology)
9. a, b (program, anthology, study guide)
10. d (anthology, study guide)
11. c (anthology, study guide)
12. a, b, d (anthology, textbook, study guide)
13. c (anthology, study guide)
14. a (study guide)
15. d (program, anthology, study guide)
16. c (program, textbook)
17. b (anthology, study guide)
18. a (anthology, study guide)
19. a, b (program, anthology, study guide)
20. a, c (program, textbook)
21. Vatican II was an important worldwide meeting of Roman Catholic prelates called by Pope John XXIII. The council, which met in Rome from 1962 to 1965, brought major changes to Catholic practices and emphasized Church support for peace, justice, and human rights in an effort to make the Church more relevant to the lives of its members. It was a stimulus for the Church in Latin America to become more outspoken in its defense of the poor. (program, anthology, study guide)
22. One of the earliest and most important liberation theologians, who argued beginning in the 1960s that the Church had a responsibility to participate in class struggle, to take action against the various forms of oppression in society, and to work for the establishment of a more just society. (anthology, study guide)
23. Brazilian religion with roots in European spiritism and African beliefs, adapted and modified by interaction with Catholic, indigenous, and other religious beliefs. *Umbanda* emphasizes the use of mediums (*orixás*), who receive the spirits from the gods and speak to the petitioner in answer to prayers and offerings. The spirits include *petros velhos* (the spirits of Africans enslaved in Brazil during colonial times) and *caboclos* (the spirits of indigenous people from pre-Colombian times). (program, anthology, study guide)
24. System of royal privileges in Catholic Church matters which emerged in Spain and Portugal prior to 1492 and was subsequently brought to the Americas. Under this system, the Spanish and Portuguese monarchs had certain rights in the areas of Church appointments, finances, and discipline in return for assuming some obligations for maintaining and spreading Catholicism. (anthology, study guide)
25. CEBs are an important innovation because they are an example of the churches' ability to adapt and change in response to modern circumstances. CEBs have spread rapidly in certain countries and have in some cases revitalized participation in Catholic and Protestant churches. They represent an attempt to meet people's needs for greater personal involvement in their religion through the establishment of small, more intimate worship communities. (program, anthology, study guide)
26. Students should mention such factors as Pentecostal churches' identification of evil as the work of the Devil (who can be exorcised by the Holy Spirit); the perceived ability of Pentecostal believers to heal certain afflictions and illnesses through prayer; the powers of prophesy, which believers are thought to have, making potential wrongdoers more cautious in their behavior; and the fact that Pentecostal churches offer a means for coping more successfully with domestic difficulties. (program, anthology)
27. Archbishop of Managua who was highly critical of the Sandinistas for their concentration of power and intolerance of domestic opposition. Obando y Bravo was elevated to cardinal in 1985 and later became instrumental in the search for a negotiated settlement to the *contra* war. (program, textbook)
28. African deity, the goddess of water, who is sometimes identified with the Catholic Virgin Mary. Iemanjá's feast day, December 31, is celebrated widely throughout Brazil with rit-

ual processions and ceremonies along beaches. (study guide)

29. He argued that the indigenous peoples of the Americas were humans, like the Europeans, and therefore were rational beings who could be converted to Catholicism. He compared them to uncultivated soil that needed only labor and cultivation to be fruitful. In other words, there was no reason to destroy them or treat them with brutality. (anthology)

30. The Church continued to have social, political, and economic influence in early postcolonial Latin America due to its operation of schools, hospitals, and humanitarian activities and because of its possession of large sums of money, land, and other capital. It subsequently became a focus of efforts to reduce its influence by some governments, such as that in Mexico, which limited the Church's right to own property. (anthology)

Essay Questions

1. The CELAM declaration of support for the poor was viewed by many as an about-face, but in fact it was part of an evolution in the Latin American Catholic Church and in Catholicism around the world. The Church had become increasingly "politicized" in the twentieth century, struggling to enhance its own relevance in the face of new ideologies (liberalism, Marxism, socialism) and changes in society (secularism, urbanization, industrialization, migration, and so forth). Vatican II in the early 1960s was an indication of the Pope's desire to open the Church to change and to make it more relevant to the daily lives of its believers. The Latin American bishops pushed these forces of change further and set them in the context of the region, but their actions were not com-

pletely unprecedented. However, their sanctioning of struggle against oppressive political, economic, and social structures did promote far greater activism by church people, leading some in power to equate these religious activists with subversive revolutionaries. Thus, for the first time, church people became targets of expression and violence.

2. There is no doubt that these words pose a radical critique of the existing political, economic, and social structure. However, the interpretation of Gutierrez's intentions depends on how literal the reader chooses to be. Did Gutierrez actually mean for church people to become armed revolutionaries? Some thought so, but others saw Gutierrez as proposing a more activist role for the Church, siding with the oppressed against the oppressors, but not necessarily calling for armed struggle. Some powerful economic elites, who had tended to view the Catholic Church as their ally in the past, now accused the Church of trying to destroy society, while some revolutionaries used Gutierrez's words to claim that the Church was now on their side.

3. There is no "correct" answer for this essay. Students should draw on the program and the anthology to discuss the appeal of noninstitutional religions. For example, they might cite the connection of spiritism to African religions for those of African descent, or the ability of Pentecostalist and spiritist believers to experience more direct intervention of the spirits in their lives. It is unlikely that religion in general will become irrelevant in Latin America, given the flexibility and adaptation that have characterized religions in the region. However, students may feel that as society becomes more modern and urbanized, it will also become more secular. The future of religion in Latin America is likely to be dynamic, but its character is difficult to predict.

Unit 9

Builders of Images: Writers, Artists, and Popular Culture

UNIT SUMMARY

Unit 9 examines the diversity, vibrancy, and historical role of various forms of cultural expression in the Americas. The unit illustrates the complex roots of Latin American and Caribbean culture in indigenous, European, and African traditions. The television program and anthology profile different types of art and artists from the realms of literature, painting, music, theater, and cinema, and examine the political and social impact of art in the region.

The unit also includes a brief historical overview of the development and role of Latin American literature, and outlines some of the major questions facing artists throughout the continent today? Is there a distinctly American voice? Should art be autonomous or should it reflect social and political realities? How should artists respond to the pervasive influence of North American culture, as well as to the impact of locally produced mass TV and radio programming?

The reading in *Modern Latin America* discusses the unique history of Puerto Rico and provides some insight into how the country's relationship with the United States has affected its culture, politics, and society.

LEARNING OBJECTIVES

After completing this unit, students should be able to:

- Recognize that the many different forms of cultural expression in Latin America and the Caribbean draw upon a complex heritage of indigenous, African, European, national, and international influences.

- Cite ways in which modern authors and artists in the region have attempted to incorporate distinctly Latin American themes into their work.

- Explain the relationship among social questions, political issues, and literary and artistic expression in the Americas.

- Recognize the contributions of some of the region's most prominent authors, artists, and musicians.

- Understand the cultural impact of higher literacy levels, modernization, and the introduction of modern communications technology.

OVERVIEW

The material presented in this unit illustrates the complex heritage and historical role of Latin American and Caribbean artistic expression. It focuses on the impact of indigenous, African, and European influences, traditional and modern elements, the high culture of the intellectuals, and popular cultures. The important social and political voice of Latin American and Caribbean artists throughout history is discussed, and examples are provided from several different eras, including the present.

An important theme in this unit is the ongoing tension that artists face in three areas: the many popular cultures that co-exist in the Americas today; the role and influence of the United States; and the international mass culture promoted by the region's major media conglomerates. The artists profiled in the program are at the forefront of their fields. Each is struggling to define his or her work as distinctively national, yet the definition of what it means to be Mexican, Puerto Rican, Argentine, or Brazilian is subject to argument. These artists share a desire to be unconventional, to challenge prevailing social and cultural norms via their art.

The text provides some historical perspective on Puerto Rico's relationship with the United States. In conjunction with the program's interviews with Puerto Rican author Luis Rafael Sánchez and artist Nick Quijano, the textbook gives additional insight into how that country's historical relationship with the United States has affected virtually all aspects of its culture, politics, and society.

The anthology gives a very brief outline of the history of Latin American literature. Several important movements, such as Latin American modernism and magic realism, are defined, and examples are provided that illustrate the tendency of Latin American and Caribbean authors to be outspoken political and social critics. The anthology contains excerpts from literature of the nineteenth and twentieth centuries, and includes selections of poetry, prose, and fiction. The works by Rubén Darío, José Martí, and Gabriel García Márquez, in particular, focus on Latin America's place within the world and the threats posed by the influence of other countries, such as the United States.

Students should recognize that this material serves as a very brief introduction to the extraordinarily broad field of culture in the Americas. To expand the students' exposure to the diversity of current artistic expression in the region, extensive resource lists covering films, music, and art are provided.

STUDENT READING ASSIGNMENT

Modern Latin America, 3d ed.
In chapter 9: *Puerto Rico: From Settler Colony to Capitalist Showcase*, pp. 301–3.

Americas: An Anthology, chapter 9, pp. 241–71.

WRITING ASSIGNMENTS/ DISCUSSION QUESTIONS

1. Argentine filmmaker Fernando Solanas works under a dictatorship and is faced with the challenge of confronting and exposing injustice without losing his life. How are artists and their art affected by living under restrictive governments?

2. In the program, Luis Rafael Sánchez says that when recognition comes from abroad it is more important. Does this statement refer only to Puerto Rico, or is the attitude shared to some degree by all of the region's artists? What are the forces that affect artists in Latin America and the Caribbean when they try to be true to their own heritage, rather than creating art solely for export?

3. Why is Mexican actress and theater director Jesusa Rodríguez so controversial within her country? Given what you know about the role of women in Latin American culture, how do you think the fact that she is a woman affects the perceptions and popularity of her work?

4. Many Latin American and Caribbean artists strive to integrate many different influences: European, African, and those that are indig-

enous to the Americas. How does Caetano Veloso incorporate all of these elements in his music?

SUGGESTED ACTIVITIES

1. Assign students a Latin American or Caribbean country and have them visit local libraries and museums to look for art works from that country. Have them bring in slides, prints, or books containing examples of art from their assigned country for the class to view. (An opaque projector will allow you to project color plates from books onto a screen.) Can students identify any political themes or messages in the works? Do the works have any themes in common? What similarities and differences are apparent in works from different Latin American and Caribbean countries? Do any of the works remind students of the work of any well-known North American or European artists? If your class does not meet as a group, have students answer the questions in written form, based on what they have seen in local libraries or museums.

2. Have students read selected chapters from the Oscar Hijuelos novel *The Mambo Kings Play Songs of Love*. Afterward, discuss the extent to which Latin American and Caribbean music have penetrated U.S. culture and affected popular music in this country. Assign students one of the decades from 1950 through 1990 and have them research Latin American and Caribbean influences on U.S. popular music during that period, considering the impact of Cuban-African and Brazilian jazz and such dance crazes as the merengue and lambada. Did Latin American and Caribbean music retain their authentic character in the United States or were they changed by contact with U.S. popular culture? If so, how so?

3. Using the recordings list provided in the Resources section, choose some recordings to play for the class. As they listen to the music, ask students to think about what, if any, aspects of the music makes it sound uniquely Latin American. If possible, compare music from different

areas and different time periods. For distant learners, recommend that they use the recordings list to sample Latin American and Caribbean music through a local library or record store.

4. Assign students one of the countries included in the program (Puerto Rico, Brazil, Argentina, Mexico) and ask them to put together an annotated bibliography of literature from one or more prominent authors. The bibliographies could be exchanged with other students to expand upon the Resources lists included in their study guides.

RESOURCES

Nonfiction

Ades, Dawn. *Art in Latin America*. New Haven: Yale University Press, 1989. A historical overview of the art of the region.

Baddeley, Oriana, and Valerie Foster. *Drawing the Line: Art and Cultural Identity in Contemporary Latin America*. New York: Verso, 1989. By examining such diverse art forms as Mexican murals and Chilean *arpilleras*, the authors try to correct recent stereotypical interpretations of Latin American art while placing it in the context of contemporary modernist art movements.

Burton, Julianne. *Cinema and Social Change in Latin America*. Austin: University of Texas Press, 1986. Interviews with several Latin American filmmakers; includes annotated bibliography of Latin American cinema.

Dorfman, Ariel. *Some Write to the Future*. Durham, N.C.: Duke University Press, 1991. Literary criticism of contemporary Latin American fiction.

Foster, David William. *From Mafalda to Los Supermachos: Latin American Graphic Humor as Popular Culture*. Boulder, Colo.: Lynne Rienner, 1989. Exploration of Latin American popular literature as exemplified by comic books and strips.

Franco, Jean. *An Introduction to Spanish American Literature.* New York: Cambridge University Press, 1969. A historical account of the literary trends in Latin America from the conquest to magic realism, focusing on the social and political contexts.

Franco, Jean. "Remapping Culture." In *Americas: New Interpretive Essays*, edited by Alfred Stepan. New York: Oxford University Press, 1992. A description of the changing cultural terrain in Latin America and the Caribbean, written by a member of the *Americas* academic advisory board as an optional addition to this unit.

Franco, Jean. *The Modern Culture of Latin America.* London: Pall Mall Press, 1967. This book examines the relation of art to the sociopolitical context in Latin America since the nineteenth century. It focuses on the attitude of artists toward society, and on the ways in which this attitude is reflected in their artistic expressions.

Gazarian Gautier, Marie-Lise. *Interviews with Latin American Writers.* Naperville, Ill.: Dalkey Archive Press, 1989. Interviews with 15 Latin American writers, including Isabel Allende, Cabrera Infante, José Donoso, Carlos Fuentes, Mario Vargas Llosa, and Luis Rafael Sánchez. Includes selected bibliography.

History Task Force of Centro de Estudios Puertorriqueños. *Labor Migration Under Capitalism: The Puerto Rican Experience.* New York: Monthly Review Press, 1979. Explains the causes of migration from Puerto Rico and how Operation Bootstrap went from a "miracle" to a "nightmare."

King, John. *Magical Reels: A History of Cinema in Latin America.* New York: Verso, 1990. This survey of Latin American film examines the history of cinema in the region country by country, from the silent era to the present, and shows how Latin American filmmakers have had to compete with the North American movie industry and, often, overcome censorship by the state.

"Latino Film and Video Images." *Centro: Journal of the Centro de Estudios Puertorriqueños* 2:8 (Spring 1990). A collection of articles about Latino filmmakers (with one article on Latina filmmakers). Includes interviews and analysis.

"Latinos in the Media." *Centro: Journal of the Centro de Estudios Puertorriqueños* 3:1 (Winter 1990). A collection of articles on the topic of mass media and their influence on Latino culture.

López, Adalberto. *Puerto Rico and Puerto Ricans: Studies in History and Society.* Cambridge, Mass.: Schenkman, 1987. Collection of essays on Puerto Rico since 1493.

Martin, Gerald. *Journey Through the Labyrinth: Latin American Fiction in the Twentieth Century.* New York: Verso, 1990. In recent years, the works of Latin American writers have begun to reach a wider audience in English translations. This critique provides an overview of the works of Borges, García Márquez, Vargas Llosa, and others, and sets them in the context of the region's cultural and political history.

Rowe, William, and Vivian Schelling. *Memory and Modernity: Popular Culture in Latin America.* New York: Verso, 1991. An overview of Latin America's popular culture, including the samba, carnival, soap operas, oral poetry, and folk theater.

Fiction and Poetry

Agosin, Marjorie. *Women of Smoke.* Pittsburgh: Latin American Review Press, 1988. Collection of poems originally published as *Mujeres de Humo.*

Allende, Isabel. *The Stories of Eva Luna.* Translated by Margaret Sayers Peden. New York: Atheneum, 1991. While lying in bed with her lover, Eva Luna, the main character of Allende's third novel, narrates 23 interwoven stories. These stories about a myriad of characters from fortune-tellers to revolutionaries are a good example of the highly imaginative, magical style that characterizes the Chilean author's writing.

Carpentier, Alejo. *The Kingdom of This World (El Reino de este Mundo).* Translated by Harriet de Onís. London: Deutsch, 1990. This Cuban novelist is one of Latin America's literary masters.

Donoso, José. *The Obscene Bird of the Night.* Translated by Hardie San Martin and Leonard Mades.

New York: Knopf, 1973. In this novel, Donoso explores the remnants of traditional culture in contemporary Chilean society through the oppressive master-servant relationships.

Ferré, Rosario. *The Youngest Doll and Other Stories.* Translated by Marie-Lise Gazarian and Diana Vélez. Norman: University of Oklahoma Press, 1990. A collection of stories first published in Spanish in 1976, this book is an example of the new generation of Puerto Rican writers.

Flores, Angel. *Hispanic Feminist Poems from the Middle Ages to the Present: A Bilingual Anthology.* New York: Feminist Press at the City University of New York, 1986. An anthology of poetry by Latin American women.

Fuentes, Carlos. *The Death of Artemio Cruz.* Translated by Sam Hileman. New York: Farrar Straus Giroux, 1988. This novel conveys the sweep of modern Mexican history through the eyes of one man.

García Márquez, Gabriel. *One Hundred Years of Solitude.* Translated by Gregory Rabassa. London: Cape, 1991. Recounts the lives of the Buendía family in the mythical town of Macondo, Colombia, over a period of 100 years.

Manguel, Alberto, ed. *Other Fires: Short Fiction by Latin American Women.* New York: Crown, 1986. Foreword by Isabel Allende. A collection of short stories by 19 contemporary women writers from Argentina, Brazil, Colombia, Cuba, Mexico, and Uruguay. Includes stories by Clarice Lispector, Silvina Ocampo, Elena Poniatowska, Lydia Cabrera, Beatriz Guido, Lygia Fagundes, Armonía Sommers, and Rosario Castellanos, among others.

Ramírez, Sergio. "To Jackie with All Our Heart." In *Stories.* Translated by Nick Caistor. New York: Readers International, 1986. This short story looks at Latin Americans who forsake their own culture in favor of North American culture.

Sábato, Ernesto. *On Heroes and Tombs.* Translated by Helen Lane. Boston: Godine, 1981. Argentine novelist Ernesto Sabato depicts the obsessions of life in contemporary Buenos Aires.

Sánchez, Luis Rafael. *Macho Camacho's Beat.* Translated by Gregory Rabassa. New York: Pantheon, 1980. Novel about the problem of cultural assimilation and its negative impact on Puerto Rican society.

Santos, Rosario, ed. *And We Sold the Rain: Contemporary Fiction from Central America.* New York: Four Walls Eight Windows Press, 1988. Collection includes title story by Costa Rican author Carmen Naranjo and work by writers from Guatamala, Honduras, Mexico, and other Latin American countries.

Vargas Llosa, Mario. *The Greenhouse.* Translated by Gregory Rabassa. New York: Harper and Row, 1975. This novel tells three apparently unrelated stories, set in Peru's desert, the Andes, and the rain forest. By juxtaposing lives as different as that of a prostitute and a member of an indigenous tribe, Vargas Llosa draws a sharp contrast between life in Peru's traditional societies and in its modern cities.

Vargas Llosa, Mario. *The Time of the Hero.* Translated by Lysander Kemp. New York: Grove Press, 1966. This novel tells the story of a group of cadets at the Leoncio Prado Military Academy in Lima. The actions of an "inner circle" of cadets set in motion a series of events that lead to murder and suicide. The novel exposes the rigid military code of honor and brutal mistreatment that govern life for military cadets at the academy.

Walcott, Derek. *Collected Poems, 1948–1984.* New York: Farrar Straus Giroux, 1986. The work of the Caribbean's foremost playwright and poet reflects the ethnic and cultural diversity of the islands.

Films

Unless otherwise indicated, all films listed are available in VHS video format.

Harvesting New Songs: A Four Part Introduction to the Music of Central America. In this set of four short videos, the folkloric group Sotavento demonstrates the instruments, rhythms, and social influences of music from the Andes, Brazil, the Spanish-speaking Caribbean, Colombia, and Venezuela. Tapes may be purchased ($75 each; $250 for the set) from the Center for Latin America, University of Wisconsin–Milwaukee, P.O. Box 413, Milwaukee, WI 53201.

The Hour of the Furnaces. 240 minutes, 1968 (French and Spanish, with English subtitles). This landmark Solanas film, an open call for armed insurrection, was shown clandestinely for many years. It and another Solanas film, *Tangos: The Exile of Gardel* (125 minutes, 1985), are featured in the program. Both 16-mm films are available for rental, for $325 (*Furnaces*) and $200 (*Tangos*) from New Yorker Films, 16 W. 61st Street, New York, NY 10023; (212) 247-6110.

Manos a la Obra: The Story of Operation Bootstrap. 59 minutes, 1983. (bilingual, with subtitles). The film is available for purchase ($595) or rental ($100) from the Cinema Guild, 1697 Broadway, New York, NY 10019; (212) 246-5522. A companion study guide is available for $7 from the Centro de Estudios Puertorriqueños, Hunter College, City University of New York, 695 Park Avenue, New York, NY 10021; (212) 772-5689.

Pablo Neruda, Poet. 30 minutes, 1972. In an interview shortly before his death, Neruda reads from his poems, explains his work methods, and offers his views on love, hate, life, and death. Available for purchase ($295) or rental ($55) through the Cinema Guild, 1697 Broadway, New York, NY 10019; (212) 246-5522.

Routes of Rhythm with Harry Belafonte. 174 minutes, 1990. Belafonte hosts three 58-minute programs that explore the African and Spanish roots of Latin music (program 1), the musical heritage of the Caribbean (program 2), and the influence of Latin music in the United States and around the world (program 3). The three-tape set is available for purchase ($298) or rental ($150) through the Cinema Guild, 1697 Broadway, New York, NY 10019; (212) 246-5522. Also available separately (call for details).

Teatro! 58 minutes, 1991. This multiaward-winning film follows a grassroots theater company led by a Jesuit priest on the backroads of Honduras to many villages where the citizens have never before seen a play. Available for rental ($85) from Film-makers Library, 124 E. 40th Street, New York, NY 10016; (212) 808-4980.

Voices of Latin America. 60 minutes, 1989. Part of the PBS series "Smithsonian World," this program examines the cultural identity of Latin America through its writers and literature. Dramatizations and interviews, filmed on location in Mexico and Peru, profile the lives of such Latin Americans as Sor Juana Inés de la Cruz, José Martí, and Jorge Luis Borges. Available for purchase ($49.95) from PBS Video, (800) 424-7963; fax: (703) 739-5269.

A World of Ideas with Bill Moyers: Carlos Fuentes. 30 minutes, 1988. In this interview, Fuentes offers his perspective on current Latin American economics and the prospects for the political independence of South American countries. Available for purchase ($39.95) from PBS Video; (800) 424-7963; fax: (703) 739-5269.

Recordings

Blades, Rubén. *Buscando América.* Sarava/Elektra, 1984. *Agua de Luna.* Elektra, 1987. New York–based singer and composer Rubén Blades has been a leading figure in "salsa" music since the 1970s.

Buarque, Chico. *Convite para Ouvir.* RGE Records, 1988. *Chico Buarque and Maia Bethania.* Philips, 1975. Chico Buarque and Maia Bethania are leading figures in contemporary Brazilian music.

Byrne, David. *Rei Momo.* Luaka Bop, 1989. This album is influenced by Brazilian rhythms.

Guerra, Juan Luis. *Bachata Rosa.* Karen Publishing, 1990. Dominican composer-singer Guerra and his group 440 are widely known in Latin America and the U.S. Latino community. Guerra, a U.S.-trained musician, combines traditional Dominican rhythms with international pop music.

Inti Illimani. *Fragments of a Dream.* CBS Masterworks, 1990. *Cancion para Matar Una Culebra.* Monitor, 1987. World-reknowned Chilean group Inti Illimani combines folk-Andean music with contemporary music.

Nascimiento, Milton. *Txai*. Columbia, 1991. *Encontros e Despedidas* ("Meetings and Farewells"). Polydor, 1987. *Sentinela* (with Mercedes Sosa, a foremost Argentinean singer). Verve, 1991. Brazilian singer and composer Nascimiento is one of the most recognized contemporary musicians. His album *Txai* was nominated for a Grammy award in 1992.

Olodum. *10 Years: From the Northeast of the Sahara to the Northeast of Brazil*. Sound Wave/Tropical Storm, 1991. This Brazilian *blocos afro* band recorded with Paul Simon on *Rhythm of the Saints*. On this solo album, they play a variety of songs, including the political anthems "Olodum's Revolt" and "ANC's Hymn."

Palmieri, Charlie, prod. *The Cesta All-Star Salsa Festival*. Musical Productions, 1990. A collection of salsa music by musicians based in New York and Puerto Rico, including Palmieri, Cheo Feliciano, and others.

Piazzolla, Astor. *Tango: Zero Hour*. Pangaea, 1988. Piazzolla was the master of innovative tangos influenced by jazz and other international modern music.

Puente, Tito. *The Mambo King*. RMM Records/Sony, 1991. *Dance Mania*. BGM Records, 1991 (reissue from the original RCA, 1958). Percussionist Tito Puente is a leading figure in Latin jazz.

Rodríguez, Silvio. *Canciones Urgentes. Los Grandes Exitos de Silvio Rodríguez*. Cuba Classics 1 (compiled by David Byrne). Luaka Bop/ Warner Bros., 1991. Cuban composer and singer Rodríguez is the leading figure of the Nueva Trova Cubana.

Simon, Paul. *Rhythm of the Saints*. Warner Bros., 1990. Simon is joined on this recording by Olodum and Nana Vasconcelos, among others.

Sosa, Mercedes. *Gracias a la Vida*. Polydor, 1988. Argentinean singer Mercedes Sosa is a leading figure of the Latin American New Song movement.

Veloso, Caetano. *Estrangeiro*. Elektra, 1989. *Cores Nomes* ("Colors/Names"). Verve, 1982. Featured in the program, Brazilian singer-composer Veloso has been a leading figure of the Brazilian song since the 1960s, widely known for his eclectic approach, which assimilates traditional Brazilian music with international popular music.

Villa-Lobos, Heitor. *Bachianas Brasileiras*. EMI, 1987. In these classical compositions, Villa-Lobos blends Brazilian folk rhythms and tunes with his love of the music of Bach. There are many other recordings of his music.

Other Resources

Arbena, Joseph, H. Schmidt, and D. Vassberg. *Regionalism and the Musical Heritage of Latin America*. Austin: Institute of Latin American Studies, University of Texas, 1980. Developed as a curriculum unit for junior and community colleges, this is an introduction to musical traditions in Latin America. Includes teaching suggestions, bibliography, and list of record albums appropriate for the teaching of the subject.

de Sa Rego, S., and M. Itamar Harrison. *Modern Brazilian Painting*. Albuquerque: Latin American Institute, University of New Mexico, 1985. This annotated bibliography on modern Brazilian paintings also includes a brief introduction on the subject.

Horton, Judith Page. *Latin American Art and Music: A Handbook for Teaching*. Austin: Institute of Latin American Studies, University of Texas, 1989. This teachers' handbook provides information on how to use art and music to explore Latin American values, ideas, and ways of life. It includes units on architecture, dance, music, and the visual arts that address historical and sociological themes. Available for $11.45, including shipping, from the Institute for Latin American Studies, University of Texas, Austin, TX 78712; (512) 471-5551.

Levine, R. *Brazilian Reality through the Lens of Popular Culture*. Albuquerque: Latin American Institute, University of New Mexico, 1985. Background information and annotated bibliography on Brazilian popular culture.

Museum of Modern Art of Los Angeles. *General Patterns of Culture of Latin America*. Excellent collection of slides that surveys topics such as regional markets in Guatemala and Peru, Indian life around Cuzco, native dances of Bolivia, and early Peruvian textiles. Available from: Organization of American States, Audio-Visual Program, 1889 F Street, N.W., Washington, DC 20006; (202) 789-6021.

Oliphant, Dave. *Civilization and Barbarism: A Guide to the Teaching of Latin American Literature.* Austin: Institute of Latin American Studies, University of Texas, 1979. This 94-page curriculum unit is intended to provide college instructors with information about Latin American writers as well as a list of representative works. Available for $4.95 from the Institute of Latin American Studies, Uni-

versity of Texas, Austin, TX 78712-1284; (512) 471-5551.

Seeger, Anthony. *Why Suya Sing: A Musical Anthropology of an Amazonian People.* New York: Cambridge University Press, 1989. An audiocassette is available to accompany this anthropological analysis of the music and verbal arts of an indigenous Amazonian community.

West, D. *Contemporary Brazilian Cinema.* Albuquerque: Latin American Institute, University of New Mexico, 1985. This bibliography provides background information and suggested titles on Brazilian cinema.

TEST BANK

Questions reflect content from the programs, textbook, study guide, and anthology.

Multiple Choice

*Mark the letter of the response that **best** answers the question or completes the statement.*

_____ 1. Which of the following poets is associated with Latin American modernism?

   a. Gabriela Mistral
   b. Pablo Neruda
   c. Rubén Darío
   d. Derek Walcott

_____ 2. The emergence of the modernist period in Latin American literature:

   a. coincided with the rise of independence movements throughout the continent.
   b. was a literary response to the horrors of World War II.
   c. focused on reviving interest in art in Latin American history.
   d. was strongly influenced by developments in Europe.

_____ 3. Which of the following statements is true of Colombian-born writer Gabriel García Márquez?

   a. He wrote *One Hundred Years of Solitude*.
   b. He is the author of *Nuestra America*.
   c. He did not begin writing until the 1980s.
   d. His works praise U.S. cultural influence in the region.

_____ 4. Which of the following statements are true of Chilean poet Pablo Neruda? *(Mark all that apply.)*

   a. He spent several years in exile.
   b. He used poetry as a vehicle to communicate with the working class.

   c. He believed literature should not be influenced by social or political issues.
   d. He was stunned by the reaction of ordinary Chileans to his poetry.

_____ 5. The first Latin American to be awarded the Nobel Prize for literature was:

   a. Gabriela Mistral.
   b. Jorge Amado.
   c. Jorge Luis Borges.
   d. Gabriel García Márquez.

_____ 6. Which of the following Latin American artists are from Mexico? *(Mark all that apply.)*

   a. Jesusa Rodríguez
   b. Nick Quijano
   c. Diego Rivera
   d. Caetano Veloso

_____ 7. The introduction of modern communications technology throughout Latin America and the Caribbean:

   a. raised new barriers between high and popular culture.
   b. enhanced the regionalism of culture in the Americas.
   c. was accompanied by the spread of North American mass culture throughout the Americas.
   d. reintroduced traditional literary forms to the countries of the region.

_____ 8. Argentine writer Jorge Luis Borges was criticized for:

   a. his focus on Argentina as subject matter for his novels.
   b. his use of magic realism.
   c. his lack of identification with Argentine themes.
   d. his use of literature as a vehicle for his political ideology.

_____ 9. Which of the following statements is true of Brazil's Rede Globo? It is:

a. a television network owned by British investors.

b. one of Brazil's smallest newspaper publishing companies.

c. one of Latin America's largest media conglomerates.

d. a national organization of artists.

_____ 10. Which of the following statements express the opinions of Puerto Rican author Luis Rafael Sánchez? (*Mark all that apply.*)

a. When recognition comes from outside, it seems more legitimate.

b. As a people, we have tremendous self-confidence and feel very competent.

c. Puerto Rican identity is under constant siege.

d. Poets, painters, and writers confirm who we are.

_____ 11. Mario Vargas Llosa and Gabriel García Márquez differ in many ways, but they both believe that:

a. Latin American writers and intellectuals should also assume the roles of social critics and political activists.

b. Latin Americans should imitate the literary styles of Europeans and North Americans.

c. Writers should praise the social and political arrangements of their respective countries.

d. Art should remain autonomous and not be a source of commentary on social or political issues.

_____ 12. Which of the following has been an important theme in recent Latin American literature and other cultural forms?

a. The threat of United States' cultural and political domination.

b. The benefits of expanding Latin America's cultural ties to Europe and Asia.

c. The homogeneity and egalitarianism of Latin American societies.

d. The need to look to France and the United States as cultural models.

_____ 13. Why does José Martí say, "It is imperative that our neighbor [the United States] know us"?

a. Because people in the United States should be exposed to the superior quality of Latin American literature.

b. Because ignorance would cause the United States to seek to dominate the region and prevent its unity and development.

c. Because then Latin American countries would receive more economic assistance.

d. Because intercultural understanding is crucial to world peace.

Identification/Short Answer

Define or describe the following terms, concepts, or persons, or answer the following questions. Answers should be no longer than a few sentences.

14. Briefly explain why up until the midtwentieth century the impact and influence of Latin American writers remained limited and "elitist."

15. Derek Walcott:

16. What is Latin American modernism?

17. Cultural imperialism:

18. *Telenovelas*:

19. Identify some of the ways in which cultural expressions from Latin America have influenced popular culture in the United States.

20. Diego Rivera:

21. What is the significance of the program scenes which show Brazilian singer Caltano Veloso interacting with people on the Streets?

22. Why is Coatlicue an important symbol for Jesusa Rodríguez?

23. *Blocos afro*:

24. Operation Bootstrap:

25. Explain what Puerto Rican painter Nick Quijano means when he says, "We are 'the other' so let's admit it, let's celebrate it."

ESSAY QUESTIONS

1. Luis Raphael Sánchez says that poets and painters "affirm who we are." Why is it that Latin Americans feel a need to reaffirm their cultural identity? What are some current and historical efforts by Latin American and Caribbean artists and writers to build their own images?

2. Why do Caetano Veloso and *blocos afro* director Vovo criticize Paul Simon and David Byrne for their popularization of Brazilian music? Do you agree with their perspective? Why or why not?

3. What kinds of challenges are being created for today's artists by the globalization of modern mass culture? Consider both the imported North American culture and the new mass culture being produced and sold within Latin America by its own modern media giants.

4. Briefly explain what is meant by the statement that cultural expression in Latin America and the Caribbean has been marked by an ongoing tension between indigenous and colonial roots, between native and European influences, and between traditional and modern forms of expression.

ANSWER KEY

Test Bank

Answers indicate sources.
1. c (anthology, study guide)
2. d (study guide)
3. a (anthology, study guide)
4. a, b, d (anthology)
5. a (anthology)
6. a, c (program, anthology, study guide)
7. c (anthology, study guide)
8. c (anthology)
9. c (study guide)
10. a, c, d (program)
11. a (anthology, study guide)
12. a (program, anthology, study guide, textbook)
13. b (anthology)
14. Until recently, literacy was restricted to a very small group in most Latin American societies. It was only with the development of mass communications and the spread of literacy that the impact and influence of writers and artists could be felt on a broader, popular basis. (anthology, study guide)
15. West Indian poet and playwright, originally from St. Lucia. Walcott is generally regarded as the Caribbean's most notable poet and playwright. His work emphazies the cultural diversity of the region. (anthology)
16. A literary movement that emerged in Latin America in the late nineteenth century which proclaimed the autonomy of art and literature, especially poetry; influenced particularly by cultural developments in France. (anthology, study guide)
17. Cultural penetration and domination by a major power. Many artists in Latin America and the Caribbean have accused the United States of cultural imperialism due to the pervasiveness of its mass culture, especially through radio and television. (program, anthology, study guide)
18. Television soap operas popularized by the major media giants in Latin America, Rede Globo and Televisa. A televised form of the popular print serials or comic books known as *fotonovelas*. (study guide)
19. Answers may vary. It is important that students recognize the appeal and pervasive influence of Latin American culture in the United States. Drawing from their own experience, students should list a variety of forms—music, drama, art, film, literature—in which Latin American culture has been adapted and popularized within this country. Students should cite the influence of music, dance, art, film, etc. (program, anthology, study guide)
20. A Mexican artist active in the muralist movement, Rivera painted murals in the Detroit Institute of Art, as well as the National Palace in Mexico City. The enormous popular appeal of Mexican muralism drew worldwide attention to Latin American art. (study guide)
21. These scenes show Veloso's efforts to remain in touch with everyday life in his country. He says in the program that the success of Brazilian popular music depends on an exchange between the artists and the public. His own music also reflects that interaction and his acknowledgment of the cultural diversity of Brazilians. (program)
22. Because she recalls the splendor of Mexico's Aztec past and, as a mother figure, continues to be connected to her "children," the Aztec descendants, today. Rodríguez uses Coatlicue to draw attention to the condition of Mexico's indigenous people. She also wants to recreate pride in what is authentically Mexican, not imported from North America or Europe. (program)
23. Afro-Brazilian community music groups in the northeastern state of Bahia. (program, study guide)
24. A program during the 1950s and 1960s under which the U.S. government encouraged investment in Puerto Rico. Not enough new jobs were created, so massive unemployment resulted and more Puerto Ricans migrated to the United States. Now 40 percent of all Puerto Ricans reside in the United States. (textbook)
25. Quijano is acknowledging the inherent qualities that make Latin Americans "different" from North Americans, such as race, color, tradition, language, custom, and history. Rather than feel ashamed of such differences, Latin Americans, he says, should be proud of and should celebrate their own culture through their art, music, dance, literature, and other creative expressions. (program)

Essay Questions

1. Many Latin American artists feel that if people are not proud of their unique historical and cultural identity, they are oppressed, dominated by other nations and cultures. In Latin America and the Caribbean this is illustrated by people's tendency to emulate North American culture rather than value that which is unique to their own countries. As current examples, students could cite any of the artists portrayed in the program or modern novelists whose work appears in the anthology.

2. Their criticism is that once again North Americans and Europeans are taking something from Brazil and exporting it for their own benefit, without fully understanding or respecting Brazilian traditions, but rather using something they find attractive as a new form of cultural imperialism. They also accuse them of not taking risks and letting the influence of Brazilian art significantly change their performances.

3. Challenges of modern mass culture include, but are not limited to, the loss of particular regional, ethnic, and cultural traditions; the focus on consumerism; the rejection of literature in favor of television; and the glorification of U.S. and "white" culture. U.S.–produced mass culture may be seen as more of a threat, since it does not include any reinforcement or support for distinctly Latin American cultural values. However, locally produced mass culture contains many of the same drawbacks as U.S.–produced culture, and the local media giants often serve as vehicles for disseminating U.S.–produced materials with an urban, middle-class perspective.

4. Writers and artists in the Americas have had to balance and borrow from the various cultural heritages that characterize their societies, and have had to try to develop a national identity distinct from outside cultural and political influences. Tensions arise as they try to define their own identity out of such a diverse heritage. Today's artists also confront the choice of whether to be true to their roots, emphasizing their differences with one another, or to produce a more acceptable popular art that reflects the homogeneity of modern cultural expression.

Unit 10

Get Up, Stand Up: The Problems of Sovereignty

UNIT SUMMARY

Unit 10 examines the difficult concept of sovereignty. Using the examples of Panama, Jamaica, and Colombia, it asks that students consider various aspects of sovereignty: freedom from foreign military intervention, autonomy in economic development, independent political decision-making, and legitimacy and effectiveness of national political and legal systems. The question of the U.S. role in the region is addressed, including a discussion of the Monroe Doctrine and its subsequent interpretations to justify U.S. involvement in the region in the early part of this century. Recent U.S. involvement in the internal affairs of the countries of the region, especially in response to the production and shipment of narcotics, is considered from a variety of perspectives. Sovereignty is also explored in the context of domestic guerrilla threats, a theme that will be addressed in greater depth in Unit 11.

LEARNING OBJECTIVES

After completing this unit, students should be able to:

- Define sovereignty and understand why it is such a crucial issue in the countries of Latin America and the Caribbean.

- Identify and describe various measures Latin American and Caribbean nations have relied on to assert and defend their sovereignty.

- Understand the threats that Jamaicans have perceived to their sovereignty and the measures they have taken to protect their national autonomy.

- Explain the unique aspects of Panama's struggle for sovereignty and discuss the role of the United States in that country.

- Name three major domestic and international threats to Colombian sovereignty and explain the recent role of U.S. policy in that country.

OVERVIEW

Unit 10 focuses on the concept of sovereignty in all its manifestations—political, economic, and cultural—and in relation to domestic and external threats. The television program and readings aim to give students some perspective on the reasons for the historic struggles in Latin American and Caribbean nations to attain and defend sovereignty. The question of the U.S. role in the region is especially prominent in this unit. Examples are provided from three countries: Panama, Jamaica, and Colombia. Each has a different historical relationship with the United States and faces a unique combination of threats to national sovereignty.

Panama

Panama's small size and limited resources, combined with the massive U.S. presence (especially through its years of control over the Panama Canal Zone), have made it a country with tremendous difficulties in asserting national sovereignty. The textbook and anthology readings amplify the brief scenes in the program of the 1989 U.S. invasion of Panama, describing the international maneuvering by which Panama became independent; the nationalism associated with the signing of the Panama Canal Treaty in 1978; and the mixed reaction throughout the Americas to the U.S. military invasion that removed General Manuel Noriega from power. Although the readings make clear the desire of most Panamanians to be free of external involvement in their internal affairs, it is also evident that Panama continues to face major barriers in asserting its sovereignty, including new charges of complicity in international drug trafficking which undermine government authority.

Jamaica

Like Panama, Jamaica is also a small country struggling with chronic poverty. Unlike Panama, though, Jamaica was a British colony until 1962 and so came more recently to the broader struggle to maintain sovereignty as a free and independent nation. Jamaica has also not been the site of U.S. military action. Instead, the threats to Jamaican sovereignty are described in primarily economic terms. Michael Manley's experiment with "democratic socialism," his imposition of the controversial bauxite levy, and efforts to pursue an independent foreign policy with regard to Cuba are the focus of the program segment and anthology selection on Jamaica.

The program highlights Manley's overtures to Cuba and anti-imperialist rhetoric. The textbook argues that Manley never intended to pursue a path leading to Communism and connects his economic failures to the politically motivated refusal of the international finance organizations to assist him. Both the text and program make clear the inherent difficulties faced by a small country like Jamaica as it tries to assert sovereignty in today's interdependent, global economy. The transformation of Michael Manley from crusader for democratic socialism to proponent of free market capitalism is a powerful image that underscores the point.

Colombia

The example of Colombia shows that sovereignty is defined as much by internal as by external factors. Unlike Jamaica and Panama, both of which struggled against powerful international forces, Colombia has had to face two major domestic threats: armed guerrilla movements that control major parts of the country's territory, and the drug cartels headquartered in Medellín, which have made themselves a virtual state within the state. In both cases, government authority has been weakened by an inability to end the violence perpetrated by its powerful opponents.

The U.S. relationship with Colombia is defined primarily by the drug issue, since much of the demand for Colombia's cocaine comes from within the United States. In 1989, the United States sought the extradition from Colombia of many of the most notorious narcotraffickers. The program and textbook show how this U.S.–crafted solution to Colombia's internal problems backfired, resulting in the deaths of dozens of judges, police officers, and politicians. Both the program and textbook express some hope that the country's return toward a locally generated approach—no extradition for drug dealers who turn themselves in, and amnesty and political inclusion for guerrillas who lay down their arms—will bring about a relegitimized state and an end to the violence.

In addition to readings devoted specifically to the three focus countries, the anthology chapter also provides excerpts from the Monroe Doctrine and the Roosevelt Corollary to explain the U.S. perspective on its role and obligations in the region. Essays by Argentine Roque Saenz Peña in 1898 and by Michael Manley nearly 100 years later illustrate the continued hostility within the region to the U.S. justification for intervention.

STUDENT READING ASSIGNMENT

Modern Latin America, 3d ed.
In chapter 10: *Panama: A Nation and a Zone*, pp. 321–24.

In chapter 9, *Jamaica: Runaways and Revolutionary Socialism*, pp. 298–301.

In chapter 11, pages 374–75 describe illicit narcotics traffic between Latin America and the United States.

Americas: An Anthology, chapter 10, pp. 272–98.

WRITING ASSIGNMENTS/ DISCUSSION QUESTIONS

1. Discuss the issue of U.S. intervention in Latin America and the Caribbean by asking students the following questions. Was the U.S. explanation for the 1989 invasion of Panama the whole truth? Was the invasion justified? Did the Manley government act properly in its unilateral decision to impose a bauxite levy? Should internationally wanted drug traffickers be extradited to the United States for trial? Have students support their opinions with examples from the program and reading assignments.

2. Ask students to consider the following statement made by President John F. Kennedy on U.S. ties to Latin America:

    This world of ours is not merely an accident of geography. Our continents are bound together by a common history—the endless exploration of new frontiers. Our nations are the product of a common struggle—the revolt from colonial rule. And our people share a common heritage—the quest for dignity and the freedom of man.

    How can this sentiment be used to critique or to support the United States' intervention in Latin America and the Caribbean?

3. The United States does not face the same problems in defending its sovereignty as do Latin American and Caribbean nations. Yet debate in recent years over the issues of the increasingly multicultural nature of U.S. society and the role of foreign (especially Japanese) investment within the United States has taken on many overtones of a debate on national sovereignty. Ask students to consider these and other issues that arouse similar emotions; why and how are these issues connected to sovereignty?

SUGGESTED ACTIVITIES

1. Divide students into two groups, representing U.S. and Latin American and Caribbean interests, to examine the role the United States should play with regard to drug trafficking in Latin America and the Caribbean. Have the first group research current stated U.S. policy regarding drug trafficking in the region, and the second group research the policies of the Latin American and Caribbean countries of Panama, Jamaica, and Colombia. Then have each group generate a policy statement that supports its view, but one that group members also think will be acceptable to the other side. Stage a vote for each policy statement, with equal numbers of each group voting on each policy. After determining which policy gains the most approval, appoint two representatives from each group to meet and come up with a policy acceptable to both sides.

2. Divide students into groups and have each group research one of the following examples of direct and indirect U.S. intervention in Latin America and the Caribbean: the 1954 coup against President Jacobo Arbenz in Guatemala; the Bay of Pigs invasion of Cuba in 1961; the 1965 U.S. invasion of the Dominican Republic; the 1973 coup that overthrew Chilean president Salvador Allende; the funding of the *contras* in Nicaragua in the 1980s; the 1983 invasion of Grenada; the 1989 invasion of Panama. Have them research the following questions:

- Was the intervention direct U.S. military action, U.S. support for antigovernment forces, or economic pressure?

- Was military action preceded by economic pressure? Who was in favor of the intervention? Who was against it?

- What was the stated motivation of the United States? Were there other motivations?

- What was the reaction within the affected country? What were the reactions of other countries in the region?

- How did the action affect the country's later history?

Create a chart on the blackboard that lists the questions and has the specific instances of intervention listed across the top. Fill in the chart with answers from students from each group. For distant learners, students could send in their answers and copies of the complete chart could be circulated.

RESOURCES

Nonfiction

Barry, Tom. *Panama: A Country Guide*. Albuquerque, New Mexico: The Resource Center, 1990. This excellent reference work contains valuable information on society, history, economics, politics, religion, and the environment.

Berquist, Charles, Ricardo Peñaranda, and Gonzalo Sánchez. *Violence in Colombia*. Wilmington, Del.: Scholarly Resources, 1992. Collection of essays by experts on *la violencia* and its consequences.

Dinges, John. "The Case Against Noriega." *Washington Post Magazine*. January 28, 1990. Details the indictments against Noriega, the extent of corruption during his reign in Panama, and his alleged involvement in narcotrafficking.

Dinges, John. *Our Man in Panama*. New York: Random House, 1990. This study of Manual Noriega by an experienced journalist follows Noriega's tangled connections to both the U.S. government and the Colombian drug cartels. Dinges concludes that the United States' efforts to unseat Noriega using propaganda and military force reflect basic flaws in the theory and practice of U.S. foreign policy in the region.

Forbes, John D. *Jamaica: Managing Political and Economic Change*. Washington, D.C.: American Enterprise Institute, 1985. Written by a career U.S. foreign service officer, this short review of post–World War II Jamaica focuses on the period between 1972 and 1983, with a strong emphasis on policy.

Gauhar, Altaf. "Manley Rides the New Wave." *South: The Third World Magazine*. July 1989, pp. 10–11. Gauhar, editor-in-chief of the magazine, interviewed Manley as he was installed back in power after nearly a decade.

Gugliotta, Guy, and Jeff Leen. *Kings of Cocaine: Inside the Medellín Cartel—An Astonishing True Story of Murder, Money, and International Corruption*. New York: Simon and Schuster, 1989. A dramatic exposé of the Medellín cartel.

Hart, Richard. *Slaves Who Abolished Slavery: Blacks in Rebellion*. vol 2. University of the West Indies, Jamaica: Institute of Social and Economic Research, 1985. This second volume is an in-depth study of the maroon wars and of the many slave revolts that were a feature of Jamaica's struggle against slavery.

Holzberg, Carol S. *Minorities and Power in a Black Society: The Jewish Community of Jamaica*. Lanham, Md.: North-South Publishing, 1987. In this study, an anthropologist examines issues of race, ethnicity, and power, and the ways in which a small minority group uses economic power to influence political action.

Kaufman, Michael. *Jamaica Under Manley: Dilemmas of Socialism and Democracy.* Westport, Conn.: Lawrence Hill, 1985. No other study does a better job of exposing the obstacles to change faced by small countries with dependent economies and a privileged economic class supported by the United States. Particularly good on the strengths and weaknesses of the People's National Movement in Jamaica.

Kline, Harvey F. *Colombia: Portrait of Unity and Diversity.* Boulder, Colo.: Westview Press, 1983. This book emphasizes the complexity of Colombian society and history, providing a good background for understanding the difficulties encountered by the government in asserting its sovereignty.

Knight, Franklin W. *The Caribbean: The Genesis of a Fragmented Nationalism.* 2d ed. New York: Oxford University Press, 1990. This study is useful for placing the history of Jamaica in a wider regional context. The final chapter reflects on issues of state and nationalism throughout the Caribbean and suggests that without greater regional cooperation the chances of success for those dependent economies and sovereign ministates will remain dim.

Knight, Franklin W. "The State of Sovereignty and the Sovereignty of States." In *Americas: New Interpretive Essays.* New York: Oxford University Press, 1992. An analysis of the ideas of sovereignty, written by a member of the *Americas* academic advisory board as an optional addition to this unit.

LeFeber, Walter. *The Panama Canal: The Crisis in Historical Perspective.* New York: Oxford University Press, 1989. This short, perceptive review of the relations between Panama and the United States by a leading U.S. diplomatic historian sorts through the record of reaction and rising nationalism with the canal as the focus.

Levi, Darrell E. *Michael Manley: The Making of a Leader.* Athens: University of Georgia Press, 1989. This, the first thoroughly researched biography of Michael Manley, is good both on the principal subject and on the fascinating changes in Jamaican politics, culture, and society during the twentieth century.

Lowenthal, Abraham. *Partners in Conflict: The United States and Latin America.* Baltimore: Johns Hopkins University Press, 1987. A revisionist view of U.S.–Latin American relations, with a stress on recent decades.

Manley, Michael. *Jamaica: Struggle in the Periphery.* London: Third World Media, 1982. This sober evaluation of Jamaica's triumphs and failures in the period 1972–80 was produced by the man who was in charge. Essential to Manley's politics is the quest for respect for individual sovereignty.

Manley, Michael. *The Politics of Change,* rev. ed. Washington, D.C.: Howard University Press, 1990. Manley, a prolific writer, first published this idealistic book in 1973. The revised edition reflects the sobering experience of his political fortunes, both his successes and his failures.

Painter, James. "Bolivians Protest U.S. Militarization of Drug War." *Christian Science Monitor*, April 15, 1991, p. 5. Representatives from Bolivia and the Roman Catholic Church protest U.S. Army instructors' being sent in to train Bolivian infantry battalions to enter the drug war. In the same issue, see Sally Bowen's article, "Leading Peruvians Spurn Antidrug Pact with United States."

Parenti, Michael. "What Will It Really Take To Win The Drug War?" *Political Affairs*, November 1989. (An excerpted version appeared in the May–June 1991 issue of the *Utne Reader*.) This essay takes a critical view of U.S. policy in international narcotrafficking.

Stephens, Evelyne Huber, and John D. Stephens. *Democratic Socialism in Jamaica: The Political Movement and Social Transformation in Dependent Capitalism.* Princeton: Princeton University Press, 1986. The best study of Jamaican politics under Michael Manley. The authors marshal an impressive array of evidence to support their claim that, despite their high overall economic price, Manley's successful policies profoundly affected Jamaica's society and its relations with other countries.

Ugarte, Manuel. *The Destiny of a Continent*. New York: AMS Press, 1970. In this book, originally published in 1925, the Argentine author sets forth his observations and concerns after visiting the United States and Mexico. He was convinced that Latin America was "in danger of being absorbed and dominated" by the United States. His perspective offers an alternative Latin American viewpoint on North American intervention.

Yarbro, Stan. "Colombian Justice System Falters." *Christian Science Monitor*. January 24, 1991, p. 3. This article claims that although drug traffickers turn themselves in as part of a new program encouraging suspects to surrender, judges still face intimidation and the country's judicial system is strained to its limits.

Fiction

Adisa, Opal Palmer. *Bake-Face and Other Guava Stories*. Berkeley, Calif.: Kelsey Street Press, 1986. Collection of short stories set in Jamaica.

Kincaid, Jamaica. *At the Bottom of the River*. New York: Aventura/Vintage Books, 1985. This collection of short stories includes selections that recount the history of the maroons.

Mordecai, Pam, and Mervyn Morris. *Jamaica Woman: An Anthology of Poems*. Portsmouth, N.H.: Heinemann Educational Books, 1980. Poems by 15 contemporary Jamaican women, both well- and lesser-known.

Films

Unless otherwise indicated, all films listed are available in VHS video format.

Giving Up the Canal. 60 minutes, 1990. This film explores Operation Just Cause as the latest chapter in a saga that represents the glory of the United States' technological achievement and the dark vestiges of U.S. colonialism in Central America. Available for purchase only ($59.95) from PBS Video, (800) 424-7963; fax: (703) 739-5269.

Latin America: Intervention in Our Own Back Yard. 30 minutes. This film describes how the United States has used the Monroe Doctrine and Roosevelt's Good Neighbor Policy as a means to control Nicaragua, Haiti, the Dominican Republic, and Panama. Available from Outreach Lending Library, Center for Latin American Studies, University of Florida, 319 Grinter Hall, Gainesville, FL 32611; (904) 392-0375.

The Noriega Connection. 60 minutes, 1991. Originally aired as part of the "FRONTLINE" series, this film examines Manuel Noriega's involvement with the United States. Available for rental ($95) from PBS Video, (800) 424-7963; fax: (703) 739-5269.

Recordings

Marley, Bob, and the Wailers. *Legend: The Best of Bob Marley and the Wailers*.
Island Records, 1984. Includes renditions of "One Love" and "Get Up, Stand Up," both of which are featured in the program.

Marley, Rita. *We Must Carry On*. Shanachie, 1991. After Bob Marley's death, his widow, Rita, emerged as an artist in her own right. On this album, she performs songs written by her late husband.

Mowatt, Judy. *Black Woman*. Shanachie, 1988. This is a classic recording by the woman who is widely recognized as reggae's greatest female artist. A longtime backup vocalist with Bob Marley and the Wailers, Mowatt sings inspirational songs about Black Liberation, women's rights, and Rastafarianism.

Mutabaruka. *Outcry*. Shanachie, 1987. One of Jamaica's most outspoken "dub poets"—artists who recite political poetry over reggae music—Mutabaruka sings about racism, political oppression, war, and hunger.

TEST BANK

Questions reflect content from the programs, textbook, study guide, and anthology.

Multiple Choice

*Select the response that **best** answers the question or completes the statement.*

_____ 1. Prior to the twentieth century, which of the following was the strongest challenge to sovereignty in the Americas?

a. East-West rivalry.
b. International drug cartels.
c. The Monroe Doctrine.
d. Economic and political imperialism.

_____ 2. The Monroe Doctrine: *(Mark all that apply.)*

a. became a justification for U.S. intervention in Latin American domestic affairs.
b. was issued as a warning to Latin American countries not to trade with European countries.
c. argued that the United States had a right to expect other major powers to stay out of the hemisphere.
d. was immediately backed by a strong U.S. military with the ability to enforce its will.

_____ 3. The Roosevelt Corollary:

a. was issued by Franklin D. Roosevelt as an emergency decree during World War II.
b. amended the Hay-Bunau-Varilla Treaty and acknowledged Panama's rights to the canal.
c. was the U.S. response to Latin America's desire for a pledge of nonintervention.
d. was an extension of the Monroe Doctrine by Theodore Roosevelt.

_____ 4. Which of the following statements are true of the Roosevelt Corollary? *(Mark all that apply.)*

a. It gave the United States a role in policing the Western Hemisphere.
b. It gave the United States a role as a debt-collecting agency in the Western Hemisphere.
c. It provided a policy mandate for U.S. intervention in the Caribbean and Central America.
d. It was ratified and issued by the U.S. Congress.

_____ 5. The U.S. relationship with Panama:

a. has always been very friendly due to Panamanians' appreciation of U.S. assistance in their struggle for independence.
b. has been marked by frequent military actions justified by the need to protect the Panama Canal.
c. has been a model for other nations in the region that would like to obtain higher levels of U.S. economic assistance.
d. has helped Panama to eradicate the widespread poverty that is typical of other nations in the region.

_____ 6. Panamanian independence occurred as a result of: *(Mark all that apply.)*

a. a local rebellion, encouraged by the United States.
b. encouragement and support from the Colombian government.
c. the Central American "soccer war."
d. international maneuvering to secure rights to an interoceanic canal.

_____ 7. Which of the following is true of the Panama Canal?

a. Panamanians have been consistently supportive of the U.S. right to administer the canal.

b. Panamanians had proposed an interoceanic canal in their country as far back as the seventeenth century.

c. Panama negotiated the treaty creating the Canal Zone in order to obtain U.S. assistance during its struggle for independence from Spain in the early nineteenth century.

d. The United States was originally given permanent control over the Canal Zone.

_____ 8. According to Michael Manley, Jamaica's experiment with democratic socialism was designed to:

a. make Jamaica a Soviet satellite.

b. channel more economic benefits to Jamaica's large numbers of poor.

c. convince armed guerrillas there was no longer any need to rebel against the political system.

d. attract and retain powerful foreign investment in Jamaica.

_____ 9. Democratic socialism in Jamaica:

a. helped the most impoverished by creating many new jobs and a flourishing economy.

b. attracted foreign investment to build new industries of food processing and textile manufacturing.

c. reduced Jamaica's vulnerability and dependence on the global economy.

d. was popularly seen as an expression of Jamaican sovereignty.

_____ 10. In the 1970s, many poor Jamaicans: *(Mark all that apply.)*

a. were the primary base for Manley's popularity but later turned against him.

b. were opposed to Manley's decision to stand up to more powerful nations.

c. opposed the bauxite levy because they feared losing jobs if it were implemented.

d. were initially supportive of democratic socialism but also suffered from the economic problems of the 1976–80 period.

_____ 11. Bauxite was the focus of Jamaica's fight for sovereignty because: *(Mark all that apply.)*

a. it was one of the island's most abundant and important resources.

b. most of the profits from bauxite production were going to foreign companies.

c. bauxite had a traditional role in the culture dating back to the "maroon communities."

d. Jamaica didn't want to export the bauxite but wanted to conserve it for future generations.

_____ 12. Edward Seaga was favored over Michael Manley by the United States in the 1980 election for prime minister in Jamaica because:

a. he promised to reduce Jamaica's foreign debt.

b. he represented a return to capitalist values.

c. he promised to ask for U.S. military aid to end Jamaica's social violence.

d. he promised to continue Manley's program of democratic socialism.

_____ 13. When Michael Manley returned to office in 1989:

a. he was more conservative in his political and economic views.

b. he imposed a unilateral bauxite levy of 7.5 percent.

c. he revoked Seaga's policies and campaigned against foreign investment.

d. he sought to reimplement the policies he had developed during his first term in office.

_____ 14. Which of the following represents a current or recent threat to sovereignty in Colombia? (*Mark all that apply.*)

    a. Insurrection by domestic guerrilla movements.
    b. Pressure from the United States to pursue certain domestic policies.
    c. The decision to stop extradition of drug lords.
    d. Illegal narcotics trafficking.

_____ 15. Armed vigilante groups in poor neighborhoods of Medellín, Colombia:

    a. were responsible for the 1989 assassination of presidential candidate Luis Carlos Galán.
    b. have created widespread fear in the communities in which they operate.
    c. are symbolic of the central government's complete loss of authority and public confidence.
    d. have accepted the government's offer of political amnesty if they lay down their weapons.

_____ 16. Which of the following statements are true of the constitutional convention that took place in Colombia in 1990? (*Mark all that apply.*)

    a. It was prematurely ended because of antigovernment violence in the major cities of Bogotá and Medellín.
    b. It led to a new government policy offering protection from extradition for drug traffickers who turned themselves in.
    c. It was viewed by many as a chance for the government to reassert its sovereign authority over its domestic rivals.
    d. It was an opportunity for guerrillas to reassess their opposition to the Colombian government.

_____ 17. In 1991, Colombia reversed its policy on extradition of wanted drug criminals to the United States because:

    a. it agreed that they would be more likely to end up in prison if trials took place in the United States.
    b. the public was calling for a general amnesty of the drug lords and the government finally agreed.
    c. the policy had backfired and the country wanted to regain control over its own internal affairs.
    d. the guerrillas agreed to cooperate with the government in hunting down and capturing drug cartel leaders.

_____ 18. Most Latin Americans have tended to react to U.S. armed intervention in the region:

    a. by viewing U.S. military action as justified to keep Communism out of their countries.
    b. by protesting U.S. lack of respect for Latin American sovereignty.
    c. by seeking military alliances with European countries as protection from future U.S. invasions.
    d. by criticizing Soviet attempts to characterize it as twentieth-century imperialism.

_____ 19. Which of the following could be interpreted as an example of a Latin American effort to assert sovereignty? (*Mark all that apply.*)

    a. Establishment of the principle of nonintervention in the charter of the Organization of American States.
    b. Mexico's establishment of limits on foreign investment in the country.
    c. Brazil's agreement to accept financial assistance from the International Monetary Fund.
    d. Peru's decision to stop making payments on its international debt.

_____ 20. In general, Panamanian reaction to Operation Just Cause:

   a. was strongly negative from the very beginning.
   b. was 100 percent in favor of U.S. intervention to remove a hated dictator.
   c. has been mixed, with some supportive and others opposed to the U.S. action.
   d. was initially negative but has become more positive over time due to large influxes of U.S. aid needed to rebuild.

Identification/Short Answer

Define or describe the following terms, concepts, or persons, or answer the following questions. Answers should be no longer than a few sentences.

21. *La violencia*:

22. According to the program, what are the major threats to sovereignty in Jamaica?

23. Medellín cartel:

24. Organization of American States:

25. What are the major tenets of the Roosevelt Corollary?

ESSAY QUESTIONS

1. Is the defense of sovereignty a problem only for smaller nations? What are some examples of ways in which U.S. sovereignty can be threatened, and what are some possible policy responses?

2. Write a response to the essay by Roque Saenz Peña, in which you construct a defense of the Roosevelt Corollary and later U.S. justifications for intervention in the hemisphere.

3. In his book *The Politics of Change: A Jamaican Testament,* excerpted in the anthology, Michael Manley says, "Our duty [was] wider than to ourselves alone. We were very conscious of a responsibility to the hopes of the Third World in what we did." Explain what Manley means by this statement, and how it reflects on his policies.

ANSWER KEY

Test Bank

Answers indicate sources.

1. d (textbook, study guide)
2. a, c (anthology)
3. d (anthology)
4. a, b, c (anthology)
5. b (textbook, study guide)
6. a, d (textbook, study guide)
7. d (textbook, study guide)
8. b (program, textbook, study guide)
9. d (program)
10. a, d (program)
11. a, b (program, anthology, study guide)
12. b (program, textbook, study guide)
13. a (program, textbook, study guide)
14. a, b, d (program, textbook, study guide)
15. c (program)
16. b, c, d (program, study guide)
17. c (program, study guide)
18. b (anthology, textbook)
19. a, b, d (anthology, study guide)
20. c (anthology, study guide, textbook)
21. Period from 1948 to 1958 of extreme civil violence in Colombia in which about 200,000 people are estimated to have died. Ended in a truce between the Liberal and Conservative parties which formed the basis for power sharing in government. (program, study guide)
22. Foreign monopolization of the bauxite industry; vulnerability to world economic trends; reliance on tourism; lack of self-confidence. (program)
23. Name given to the international drug ring based in Medellín, Colombia, which has amassed a huge fortune, runs its own armies, and went to war against government efforts to eradicate it. (program, textbook)
24. International organization of the nations in the Western Hemisphere, including the United States and Canada, established by a treaty in 1948. The OAS charter states that all signatories will observe the principle of nonintervention in one another's internal affairs. (anthology)
25. The Roosevelt Corollary was an extension of the Monroe Doctrine, issued by President Theodore Roosevelt in 1904, which asserted the United States' role as international policeman and debt-collection agency in the Western Hemisphere. The Roosevelt Corollary was used to justify numerous military actions in Latin America and the Caribbean over the next 40 years. (anthology)

Essay Questions

1. Sovereignty can be threatened in any country, no matter how large or small. Students should demonstrate an understanding of the internal as well as the external threats to sovereignty. Examples in which the United States has felt its sovereignty threatened might be drawn from the Civil War; the Cold War and the McCarthy period; the domestic unrest of the 1960s, including the civil rights and antiwar movements; fears of international investment, especially by the Japanese, in the U.S. economy; gang- and drug-related violence in the major U.S. cities; or the debate on multiculturalism; or the effects of racism and a persistent underclass as exemplified in the 1992 Los Angeles riots. Depending on the examples students select, official and popular responses to the perceived threat should also be discussed.
2. Students should use the Monroe Doctrine, Roosevelt Corollary, and "Defense of the Roosevelt Corollary" from the anthology to argue the U.S. right to intervene in Latin America to protect its own interests. More recent justifications should also include the perceived threat from the Soviet Union and Cuba, and the damaging impact on the United States of international drug trafficking. Students should cite U.S. views that Latin America's military, legal, and judicial systems are unable to defend themselves adequately against these threats, giving the United States an obligation to use its greater power to help.
3. Students should be able to draw upon the text, program, and anthology to discuss what Manley tried to do in Jamaica. Students should show the similarities between Jamaica's situa-

tion and that of other small, weak nations, and link Manley's efforts to the desire of other Third World nations to assert their sovereignty. Students should also show some understanding of the sometimes exaggerated threat to sovereignty that Third World nations tend to perceive in U.S. actions and policies, and their use of inflated rhetoric to com-pensate for the lack of political and economic muscle. In addition, students ought to discuss the common threats to sovereignty felt by all small countries, and especially the feeling among Third World nations that the U.S. poses a threat to their economic sovereignty.

Unit 11

Fire in the Mind:
Revolutions and Revolutionaries

UNIT SUMMARY

Unit 11 examines revolutionary movements in twentieth-century Latin America using the examples of Mexico (1910–17), Cuba (1959), and Nicaragua (1979), as well as contemporary revolutionary processes in El Salvador, Guatemala, and Peru. The factors leading to the growth of revolutionary sentiment, the role of Marxism and other ideologies, the U.S. response, and the effect of the Cold War are discussed in the context of each country's experience.

At the end of the unit, students should grasp the complex nature of revolutions in Latin America. They should understand that revolutions are processes, not one-time events, and that the outcome is not predetermined. They should also recognize that Latin America's successful revolutions were led by diverse, multiclass coalitions whose motivations ranged from Marxist ideology to the desire for a more favorable climate for private sector investment. The impact of the end of the Cold War on existing and future revolutionary movements in the region is an important point for discussion. Finally, students should be able to compare and contrast the contemporary revolutionary movement in Peru with earlier revolutions in the hemisphere, and understand the reasons for the concerns raised by Sendero Luminoso's continued

growth and power, even among many who have supported revolutionary movements elsewhere in the Americas.

LEARNING OBJECTIVES

After completing this unit, students should be able to:

- Name some of the common factors that contributed to revolutionary movements in Mexico, Cuba, Nicaragua, Guatemala, El Salvador, and Peru.

- Recognize that revolutions are not one-time events, but instead are processes that develop over many years and do not have a predetermined course or outcome.

- Understand the role of Marxist ideology in most of these revolutionary movements and its effect on the policies of the revolutionary governments in Cuba and Nicaragua.

- Analyze the nature of revolutionary coalitions in Latin America in the twentieth century and explain the reasons for their difficulties in holding together after taking power.

- Describe the U.S. response to revolutionary movements in Cuba, Nicaragua, and El Salvador.

- List the key features that distinguish Peru's revolutionary movement from others in the region, and discuss how a government led by the Shining Path in Peru could differ from the other revolutionary regimes in the Americas.

- Explain the impact of the end of the Cold War on revolutions and revolutionary movements in Latin America.

OVERVIEW

Many North Americans have the impression that Latin America is a hotbed of revolutionary sentiment. It is true that economic dislocations, social inequality, and authoritarian rule in many Latin American countries have spawned numerous revolutionary movements, but few have actually succeeded in overthrowing the government and taking power. The recent history of Latin America and the Caribbean—where revolutionary movements in Guatemala, Venezuela, and Colombia in the 1960s and in Brazil, Argentina, and Uruguay in the 1970s all met with failure—indicates the difficult odds facing would-be revolutionaries.

"Fire in the Mind: Revolutions and Revolutionaries" examines the roots of revolution in Latin America, the similarities and differences among historical and contemporary revolutionary movements, and the broad changes implemented by twentieth-century revolutionary governments that assumed power in Mexico, Cuba, and Nicaragua. It also looks at the impact revolutionary governments have had beyond their own borders, both elsewhere in the region and in relations with the United States.

The television program, set primarily in El Salvador, looks especially at revolutionaries' motivations and at their changing methods in the wake of the Cold War. The program also considers the outcome of El Salvador's revolutionary process, and examines whether the 1992 peace accords be-

tween the government and the rebels will be able to bring about lasting peace after 12 years of warfare. Finally, the program travels to Peru to gain some insight into the Sendero Luminoso, or Shining Path, guerrilla movement, considering what its growth and possible success might herald for Peru and for other Latin American countries.

There are both new and review reading assignments for the unit. It is important that students review earlier assignments on Mexico, Peru, El Salvador, and Nicaragua from Units 5, 6, 8, and 9 to have a complete understanding of the issues presented in this unit. New material provided in the textbook is particularly focused on Cuba, with some additional information on Peru and Guatemala.

The anthology readings include excerpts from the writings and speeches of revolutionary leaders in a number of different countries, which may serve as a useful point for comparison and discussion. The anthology also covers peace efforts in Central America such as the Esquipulas Plan and the peace negotiations in El Salvador and Guatemala, along with the U.S. analysis of Central American revolutionary threats as outlined in the 1984 report of the National Bipartisan Commission on Central America.

STUDENT READING ASSIGNMENT

Modern Latin America, 3d ed.
In chapter 6, "Peru: Soldiers, Oligarchs, and Indians," pp. 201–3 and 213–20.

In chapter 8, "Cuba: Late Colony, First Socialist State," pp. 254–56 and 263–82.

In chapter 10, "Guatemala: Reaction and Repression," pp. 337–43.

Students should also review *The Mexican Revolution*, pp. 228–33, which was covered in Unit 5; *Nicaragua: From Dynasty to Revolution*, pp. 326–30, and *El Salvador: From Stability to Insurgence*, pp. 332–37, both of which were covered in Unit 8; and the introduction to chapter 6, Peru: Soldiers, Oligarchs, and Indians, pp. 185–87 covered in Unit 6.

Americas: An Anthology, chapter 11, pp. 299–334.

WRITING ASSIGNMENTS/
DISCUSSION QUESTIONS

1. Why has Cuba, a small island nation, had so much influence since 1959 on revolutionary movements elsewhere in Latin America and even outside the region? How has the revolution in Cuba affected U.S. foreign policy? How might the end of the Cold War and the demise of the Eastern bloc affect the course of future U.S.-Cuban relations?

2. Why haven't more revolutions been successful in Latin America, given the extent of poverty and the history of repressive governments in so many countries of the region?

3. How have concerns for human rights affected U.S. policy toward revolutionary movements in Latin America, especially in El Salvador, Guatemala, and Peru?

4. Evaluate the causes of the defeat of the Sandinistas in the February 1990 Nicaraguan election. Did their departure from government mean the end of the Nicaraguan Revolution?

SUGGESTED ACTIVITIES

1. Have students research the debate in the U.S. Congress over the Reagan and Bush administrations' policy in Central America. Using newspaper clippings, the *Congressional Record*, and information from human rights monitoring groups such as Americas Watch or the Washington Office on Latin America, ask students to outline the major points of contention. What enabled or prompted U.S. policy to shift toward support for a negotiated settlement in the late 1980s?

2. In the period following the February 1990 Nicaraguan elections, which resulted in Violeta Chamorro's becoming president, Nicaragua was virtually absent from the major U.S. media. Yet the Nicaraguan revolutionary process continued to unfold. Have students search a variety of media sources for information on Nicaragua during the 1990s, seeking as wide a range of viewpoints as possible. They could prepare a simulated news program or write an article to update the class, including an overview of current events and presentations of the positions of various factions: the Chamorro government, the U.S. State Department, the Sandinistas, the *contras*, and recent actors such as the "re-contras" and "re-compas."

3. Ask students to research Sendero Luminoso. How would they characterize this group? What are the distinctions between Sendero and other revolutionary movements in the Americas? What are some possible outcomes should Sendero come to power in Peru?

RESOURCES

Nonfiction

Arnson, Cynthia J. *Crossroads: Congress, the Reagan Administration, and Central America*. New York: Pantheon, 1989. An account by a former congressional staff member of the struggles between the Congress and the Reagan administration over U.S. policy toward Nicaragua and El Salvador.

Black, George. *Triumph of the People: The Sandinista Revolution in Nicaragua*. Austin: University of Texas Press, 1971. An account and analysis of Sandinista struggle and victory.

Brenner, Anita, and George R. Leighton. *The Wind That Swept Mexico: The History of the Mexican Revolution, 1910–1942*. London: Zed Press, 1981. An illuminating collection of photographs of the Mexican Revolution. Text by Brenner, historical photographs assembled by Leighton.

Cabezas, Omar. *Fire from the Mountain: The Making of a Sandinista*. New York: New American Library, 1985. A personal account by a Sandinista commander and former Nicaraguan student leader who joined the Sandinista guerrillas in the 1970s and discovered that revolution was much more difficult than he had imagined.

Castro, Fidel. *History Will Absolve Me.* New York: Lyle Stuart, 1961. A transcript of Fidel Castro's speech in his own defense at his trial after a 1953 attack on the Cuban army's Moncada barracks. Castro articulated the demands of the revolutionaries. The title is taken from the final phrase of his speech, "Condemn me. History will absolve me."

Cockcroft, James D. *Intellectual Precursors of the Mexican Revolution, 1900–1913.* Austin: University of Texas Press, 1968. Helps explain the origins and justifications of the Mexican Revolution of 1910.

Costain, Pam. "What Ever Happened to Nicaragua?" *Utne Reader*, May/June 1991. The author argues that although Nicaragua was at the center of U.S. foreign policy in the 1980s, attention to the country has dissipated considerably although the country's political and economic problems continue.

Crahan, Margaret E., and Peter H. Smith. "The State of Revolution." In *Americas: New Interpretive Essays*, edited by Alfred Stepan. A study of the consequences and future of revolutionary movements in the Americas, written by two members of the *Americas* academic advisory board as an optional addition to this unit.

Cuban Studies/Estudios Cubanos. Focused on Cuba, this periodical, published annually by the University of Pittsburgh Press, contains some of the best of recent research. Each issue includes a bibliography of current books and articles, and commentary on past issues of the periodical.

Dalton, Roque. *Miguel Mármol.* Translated by Kathleen Ross and Richard Schaaf. Willimantic, Conn.: Curbstone Press, 1987. Thirty thousand peasants and workers were killed in a month-long massacre when General Maximiliano Hernández Martinez attempted to wipe out "subversion" in El Salvador in 1932. One of the founders of El Salvador's Communist Party, Miguel Mármol survived, and continued to lead and organize the Communist Party. Fellow Communist Roque Dalton began this three-week interview about revolutionary advice, history,

and adventure in an effort to clear the Communist Party of blame for the 1932 massacre and to educate future rebels.

Debray, Regis. *Revolution in the Revolution? Armed Struggle and Political Struggle in Latin America.* Westport, Conn.: Greenwood Press, 1980. Primer of the Cuban model of guerrilla revolution, intended to serve as a "how-to" guide for revolutionaries elsewhere in Latin America.

Domínguez, Jorge. *Cuba: Order and Revolution.* Cambridge: Belknap Press, Harvard University Press, 1978. The most detailed study of the Cuban Revolution and its evolution to the end of the 1970s.

Eckstein, Susan, ed. *Power and Popular Protest: Latin American Social Movements.* Berkeley: University of California Press, 1989. A survey of the origins and characteristics of both revolutionary and nonrevolutionary movements in Latin America.

Franqui, Carlos. *Diary of the Cuban Revolution.* New York: Viking, 1980. Documents tracing the origin and rise to power of Fidel Castro's revolutionary movement.

Gould, Jeffrey L. *To Lead as Equals: Rural Protest and Political Consciousness in Chinandega, Nicaragua, 1912–1979.* Chapel Hill: University of North Carolina Press, 1990. Excellent study of how ordinary people reacted to both dictatorship and revolution in Nicaragua.

Guevara, Ernesto Ché. *Handbook for Guerrilla Warfare.* New York: Vintage Books, 1968. Personal views of a leader of the Cuban Revolution on how to organize and lead a successful revolutionary movement.

Gutman, Roy. *Banana Diplomacy: The Making of American Policy in Nicaragua, 1981–1987.* New York: Simon & Schuster, 1988. A journalist's account of the Reagan administration's efforts to topple the Sandinista government in Nicaragua.

Guzman, Abimael. *Interview with Chairman Gonzalo.* Conducted by the editors of El Diario (Lima). Translated by Committee to Support the Revolution in Peru. Berkeley, CA: Committee to Support the Revolution in Peru, 1991. A rare extended interview, from a newspaper controlled by Sendero Luminoso, with the Shining Path's founder and leader, in which he explains his "Gonzalo Thought" and his movement's revolutionary strategy, while responding to the criticisms frequently made of the Shining Path.

Kinzer, Stephen. *Blood of Brother.* New York: Putnam, 1991. A U.S. journalist's view of where the Nicaraguan Revolution went wrong.

Knight, Franklin W. "Cuba." In *The Modern Caribbean*, edited by Franklin W. Knight and Colin A. Palmer. Chapel Hill: University of North Carolina Press, 1989. Examines the politics, economy, and culture in Cuba from the end of Spanish colonialism in 1898 to 1985, covering the acts and influence of the United States at the turn of the century, periods of democracy and repression, and Fidel Castro's revolution.

LaFeber, Walter. *Inevitable Revolutions: The United States in Central America.* New York: Norton, 1983. Covers U.S. intervention in Central America from Thomas Jefferson to Ronald Reagan. Author speculates that the United States destabilized the region by subverting the leaders and institutions that could have brought peaceable change in Central America.

Liss, Sheldon B. *Roots of Revolution: Radical Thought in Cuba.* Lincoln: University of Nebraska Press, 1987. Explores the origins of Cuban revolutionary thinking, from the nineteenth century into the Castro period.

Perez, Louis A., Jr. *Cuba: Between Reform and Revolution.* New York: Oxford University Press, 1988. A very well-written history of Cuba, emphasizing the twentieth century.

Perez, Louis A., Jr. *Cuba and the United States: Ties of Singular Intimacy.* Athens: University of Georgia Press, 1990. Focuses on Cuban history from 1810 to 1899 and on relations between the United States and the island nation.

Smith, Peter H. *Labyrinths of Power: Political Recruitment in Twentieth-Century Mexico.* Princeton:

Princeton University Press, 1979. Examines the backgrounds of the political elite that emerged out of the 1910 Mexican Revolution.

Smith, Wayne A. *The Closest of Enemies: A Personal and Diplomatic Account of U.S.–Cuban Relations Since 1957.* New York: Norton, 1987. Personal account by a U.S. diplomat of U.S.–Cuban relations, from before the 1959 revolution to the present. The author was posted in Cuba at the outset of the revolution and again at the time of the 1980 Mariel exodus.

Wilson Quarterly 12:1 (1988). This issue of the *Wilson Quarterly* focuses on Nicaragua. Selections include a systematic history of the nation by Richard L. Millet, a selection on democracy by Clifford Krauss, and an essay by Henry A. Kissinger on U.S. foreign policy in Nicaragua.

Womack, John, Jr. *Zapata and the Mexican Revolution.* New York: Vintage Books, 1968. An award-winning account of the role of Emiliano Zapata and his peasant movement in the Mexican Revolution.

Wyden, Peter. *Bay of Pigs: The Untold Story.* New York: Simon & Schuster, 1979. The most complete examination of the 1961 CIA-backed invasion of Cuba, which contributed to the Cuban missile crisis.

Fiction and Poetry

Arenas, Renaldo. *The Ill-fated Peregrinations of Fray Servand.* New York: Avon, 1987. Originally titled *Hallucinations* and banned in Cuba, the author's homeland, this comic picaresque novel is about a wandering Catholic priest, part rogue, part revolutionary.

Argueta, Manlio. *Cuzcatlán Where the Southern Sea Beats.* New York: Vintage, 1987. Traces the history of El Salvador, from the 1930s into the early 1980s, through one family's experiences.

Azuela, Mariano. *The Underdogs.* New York: NAL-Dutton, 1963. Translated by E. Munguia, Jr. The most famous novel about the Mexican Revolution; focuses on the rural population.

Cabrera Infante, Guillermo. *Three Trapped Tigers*. New York: Harper & Row, 1971. This sometimes humorous novel depicts Havana's corrupt and lively nightlife in the 1950s, just before Castro's rebellion overthrew the Batista regime.

Cortazar, Julio. *A Manual for Manuel*. New York: Pantheon, 1978. Translated by Gregory Rabassa. Depicts future revolutions as producers of social freedom without the puritannical repressiveness of socialist regimes.

Desnoes, Edmundo. *Memories of Underdevelopment, and Inconsolable Memories*. New Brunswick, N.J.: Rutgers University Press, 1990. Gripping account of the reaction of a member of the bourgeoisie to the Cuban Revolution and the 1962 missile crisis.

Guillen, Nicolás. *The Great Zoo and Other Poems*. New York: Monthly Review Press, 1972. Anthology of poetry by a Cuban revolutionary who emphasizes the contributions of the African heritage of many Cubans.

Lezama Lima, José. *Paradiso* (Paradise). Translated by Gregory Rabassa. New York: Farrar Straus Giroux, 1974. This story of Cuban José Cemí begins at the turn of the century and focuses on José's relationship with his mother after his father's death. She becomes the power behind José's creativity in his search for understanding of his father, love, and the power of the mind.

Sayles, John. *Gusanos*. New York: HarperCollins, 1991. This novel stretches over six decades in the history of a family and Cuba. It describes the corruption in Batista's Cuba as well as the fervor of Cuban exiles for recapturing their country.

Films

Unless otherwise indicated, all films listed are available in VHS video format.

Cuba: In the Shadow of Doubt. 58 minutes, 1987. This color documentary examines some of the successes and failures of the Cuban Revolution. Narrated by Raúl Juliá, the film won a 1987 American Film Festival award. Available for rental ($85, plus $10 shipping) from: Filmakers Library, 124 East 40th Street, New York, NY 10016; (212) 808-4980.

Fire from the Mountain. 58 minutes, 1987. Autobiographical story of Omar Cabezas, as he grew up under the Somoza dictatorship in Nicaragua, which follows him as a student activist, a guerrilla fighter, and a leading government figure. Interviews with Cabezas illuminate the struggle and courage in Nicaragua. The future of the revolution, war with the *contras*, and Nicaragua's relationship with the United States are also considered. Available for rental ($100, plus $10 shipping) from: Icarus Films, 153 Waverly Place, 6th floor, New York, NY 10014; (212) 727-1711.

Havana. 140 minutes, 1990. Set in Cuba under Batista's rule this film has been called a modern *Casablanca* and stars Robert Redford. Available in most video-rental outlets.

A House Divided. 60 minutes, 1983. Part of the *Inside Story* series, which uses the Chamorro family and the Sandinista regime's opposing views to depict conflict in Nicaragua. The story of Nicaragua's civil strife is told through interviews with members of the Chamorro family, Nicaraguan workers, business leaders, and Sandinista Interior Minister Tomás Borge. Available for purchase only ($125, plus $5 shipping) from: *Inside Story*, 330 West 58th Street, Suite 409, New York, NY 10019; (212) 307-6280.

Memories of Underdevelopment. 97 minutes, 1968. (Spanish, with English subtitles.) This film version of the Edmundo Desnoes novel, listed above, is a cinematic masterpiece. Set in the early 1960s, the story focuses on a Europeanized Cuban intellectual too idealistic to leave for Miami but too decadent to fit into the new Cuban society. The first film from postrevolutionary Cuba to be released in the United States. Available for purchase ($125, plus $5 shipping & handling) only from: New Yorker Video, 16 West 61st Street, 11th floor, New York, NY 10023; (212) 247-6110. Also available in some video-rental outlets.

Nicaragua: Campaign '84. 30 minutes, 1984. Assesses the state of press censorship on the 1984 Nicaraguan election. Part of the *Inside Story* series.

Available for purchase only ($70, plus $5 shipping) from: *Inside Story* (see above).

Portrait of Teresa (*Retrato de Teresa*). 103 minutes, 1990. (Spanish, with English subtitles.) A housewife and mother who works in a Cuban textile factory displeases her husband when she gets involved in political and cultural groups. Available in most video-rental outlets.

Salvador. 122 minutes, 1985. Veteran war correspondent is sent in 1980 to cover the effects of civil war on the people in El Salvador. Directed by Oliver Stone. Available in most video-rental outlets.

Uprising. 96 minutes, 1981. (Spanish, with English subtitles.) A recreation of a Nicaraguan urban insurrection, similar to those that overthrew the Somoza regime in 1979. Available for purchase ($69.95, plus $3.50 shipping) only from: Kino International Corporation, 333 West 39th Street, Suite 503, New York, NY 10018; (212) 629-6880.

U.S. Foreign Policy: Projecting U.S. Influence. 30 minutes, 1988. Part of the *Great Decisions in Foreign Policy* series. U.S. policy toward Nicaragua is examined via an analysis of the limits of power and influence, not only for the United States, but for all superpowers. Available for purchase only ($39.95, order #WDBT108) from: PBS Video, 1320 Braddock Place, Alexandria, VA 22134.

Other Resources

Bigelow, Bill, and Jeff Edmundsen, eds. *Inside the Volcano: A Curriculum on Nicaragua.* This curriculum guide is a collection of stories, poems, and interviews organized into 14 chapters which provide insight into the lives of Nicaraguans from a progressive perspective. Available for $12.50 from: Network of Educators' Committees on Central America, 1118 22d Street, N.W., Washington, DC 20037; (202) 429-0137.

TEST BANK

Questions reflect content from the programs, text-book, and anthology.

Multiple Choice

*Mark the letter of the response that **best** answers the question or completes the statement.*

_____ 1. Which of the following statements is true of revolutionary movements in twentieth-century Latin America?

  a. The Cuban Revolution in 1959 was the first successful revolution in the Americas.
  b. They have tended to be led primarily by the urban working class in a revolt against the excesses of capitalism.
  c. Very few revolutionary movements have succeeded overthrowing the state.
  d. Marxist ideology has been unimportant in the development of policies by revolutionary governments.

_____ 2. Which of the following is true of the three most successful revolutions in twentieth-century Latin America?

  a. They took place in large countries with a diversified economic base.
  b. They were led by a Communist vanguard that united the people behind the banner of Marxist ideology.
  c. They brought diverse revolutionary coalitions to power that could not maintain their unity once in government.
  d. They sought significant foreign investment and private sector development as a means of modernizing their countries.

_____ 3. Which of the following statements is true of Mexico's revolution? (*Mark all that apply.*)

  a. It did not begin as a popular peasant uprising but as a struggle by mostly elite groups to end the authoritarian rule of Porfirio Díaz.
  b. It was a quick and relatively bloodless civil conflict that brought little change to the lives of most Mexicans.
  c. It was primarily a struggle between the competing ideologies of capitalism and socialism, and was heavily influenced by the success of the Bolshevik Revolution.
  d. It took place over nearly a decade, and was marked by a succession of changes in the objectives and leadership of the revolutionary movement.

_____ 4. The Plan de Ayala was:

  a. an agreement of the Central American presidents to seek a comprehensive peace for their countries.
  b. the name given to the successful negotiations between the FMLN and the government of El Salvador.
  c. Violeta Chamorro's plan to revitalize democratic institutions in Nicaragua.
  d. the anti-Madero revolutionary appeal issued by Emiliano Zapata demanding land reform.

_____ 5. According to Augusto César Sandino, the biggest threat to an independent Nicaragua in the 1920s was:

  a. Cuban support for revolutionary movements.
  b. the Soviet Union.
  c. the United States.
  d. the corruption of the Somoza dynasty.

_____ 6. The Mexican president who linked the future of the revolution to the loyalty of the rural peasantry by distributing land in *ejidos* was:

  a. Francisco Madero.
  b. Pancho Villa.

c. Lázaro Cárdenas.

d. Porfirio Díaz.

_____ 7. According to the text, the United States opposed Guatemalan president Jacobo Arbenz (1950–54) because: (*Mark all that apply.*)

a. he sought closer ties to Cuba's revolutionary government.

b. his administration was notorious for abuse of human rights.

c. he expropriated lands owned by the United Fruit Company.

d. he was viewed as allowing the Soviets into Central America.

_____ 8. Mexican relations with revolutionary Cuba:

a. were strained to the breaking point by Castro's imposition of socialism.

b. were a means for Mexico to assert its independence from the United States in the area of foreign policy.

c. were initially quite good, but Mexico ultimately succumbed to U.S. pressure to break off relations.

d. got off to a shaky start when Castro launched his first invasion of Cuba from Mexican territory.

_____ 9. In his 1962 speech "The Second Declaration of Havana," Fidel Castro:

a. thanked the United States for its continued high rates of investment in the Cuban economy.

b. held up the Cuban revolution as a model for "liberation" movements elsewhere in Latin America and around the world.

c. set the target of 10 million tons of sugar for the 1970 harvest.

d. apologized to the Cuban people for his inability to bring about economic modernization and industrialization more quickly.

_____ 10. According to the text, the Cuban missile crisis is significant because: (*Mark all that apply.*)

a. Cuba's possession of nuclear missiles proved that the Nuclear Proliferation Treaty had been a failure.

b. it appeared to many that the crisis could lead to nuclear war between the two superpowers.

c. Castro was forced to agree to U.S. terms that prevented Cuba from promoting revolution elsewhere in the region.

d. the crisis resulted in a secret U.S.–Soviet understanding that the United States would not invade Cuba.

_____ 11. Which of the following is true of the Cuban Revolution?

a. It has been a source of inspiration to numerous other revolutionary movements over the past 30 years.

b. Its leaders managed to keep the country out of the Cold War conflict between the United States and the USSR.

c. Its most important success has been in diversifying the Cuban economy.

d. Since 1980, it has followed economic austerity measures required by the IMF.

_____ 12. The Sandinista National Liberation Front: (*Mark all that apply.*)

a. was willing to follow the U.S. lead in developing its foreign policy in exchange for economic assistance.

b. initially took power in Nicaragua as part of a coalition, but soon consolidated its position and dominated the government.

c. pursued a conciliatory line toward the United States because of fears of a U.S.-sponsored invasion.

d. offered moral and material support to rebels in El Salvador.

_____ 13. Which of the following were part of the U.S. response to Nicaragua's revolution? (*Mark all that apply.*)

   a. Initial offers by the Carter administration of substantial U.S. aid.
   b. A cutoff of aid and the imposition of a trade embargo by the Reagan administration.
   c. Official warnings of an outright U.S. invasion if the Sandinistas did not cease support for revolutionaries in El Salvador.
   d. Covert support for an exile army, the *contras*, to topple the Sandinista regime.

_____ 14. The revolutionary process in contemporary Guatemala: (*Mark all that apply.*)

   a. has been marked by high levels of indiscriminate repression and violence directed by the government at the country's indigenous peoples.
   b. can be traced to the lack of possibility for compromise and political reform in the post-Arbenz period.
   c. has been characterized by significant collusion between the revolutionary army and international drug traffickers.
   d. exhibits important similarities in motivation and ideology with the revolutionary movement, Sendero Luminoso.

_____ 15. Guerrillas and government representatives in El Salvador were able to reach a negotiated settlement to the civil war because:

   a. the rebels' military superiority convinced the government that it would be defeated if it chose to fight on.
   b. the United Nations Security Council voted to impose sanctions on the Salvadoran government if it did not agree to UN-brokered peace talks.

   c. FMLN rank and file threatened to rebel against their commanders if they didn't agree to a negotiated settlement.
   d. the changed international climate, the military stalemate, and the war's high toll led both sides to seek a negotiated end to the war.

_____ 16. According to the 1992 peace accords ending the civil war in El Salvador:

   a. foreign aid, including that from the United States, would no longer be accepted.
   b. there would be no further inquiries into human rights abuses committed during the war.
   c. the FMLN would convert to a political party and participate in national elections.
   d. reforms would be confined exclusively to the political sphere.

_____ 17. The leaders of Peru's revolutionary movement, Sendero Luminoso:

   a. have opposed the use of terror tactics against the rural peasantry.
   b. have taken their inspiration from Ché Guevara, Fidel Castro, and other successful revolutionaries in the region.
   c. have rejected affiliation with international drug traffickers in order to court support from the United States.
   d. have sanctioned the use of calculated violence to destroy the Peruvian state.

_____ 18. U.S. concern over political developments in Central America: (*Mark all that apply.*)

   a. can be traced back for at least a century, and includes direct and indirect interventions in Central American affairs.
   b. coincides with the rise of revolutionary movements in the region in the late 1970s.

c. is long-standing but became rein-
vigorated by the struggle against
the perceived Soviet threat during
the Cold War.

d. has been characterized by support
for reformist leaders such as Jacobo Arbenz in Guatemala.

_____ 19. The revolutionary movement in El Salvador differed from those in Cuba and
Nicaragua because:

a. the rebels succeeded in achieving
some of their aims through a negotiated settlement to the war.

b. the government of El Salvador did
not abuse human rights as systematically as did Batista and Somoza.

c. U.S. policy toward the rebels was
much more conciliatory than was
the case in the Cuban and Nicaraguan revolutions.

d. the FMLN was unable to gather
much support from the Salvadoran
people, unlike the movements led
by Castro and the Sandinistas.

_____ 20. Sendero Luminoso is different from
Latin American revolutionary move-
ments studied in this unit because:
(*Mark all that apply.*)

a. it has closely adhered to Maoist
principles despite the discrediting
of international Communism.

b. it has received significant international support from the U.S. and
European governments.

c. it has used terrorist tactics against the
civilian population to enhance its
control and to overthrow the state.

d. it has expressed a willingness to
reach a negotiated settlement with
Peru's military leaders.

Identification/Short Answer

*Define or describe the following terms, concepts, or per-
sons, or answer the following questions. Answers should
be no longer than a few sentences.*

21. Francisco Madero:

22. Bay of Pigs:

23. *Contras*:

24. What was the thesis of the National Bipartisan
Commission on Central America (the Kissinger Commission)?

25. José Napoleon Duarte:

26. Violeta Chamorro:

27. The Platt Amendment:

28. *Ejido*:

29. Esquipulas Plan:

30. Briefly mention some of the factors that drew
Castro and the Soviet Union together:

ESSAY QUESTIONS

1. Compare and contrast the Mexican, Cuban, and Nicaraguan revolutions in terms of causes, characteristics, and accomplishments.

2. Why is Sendero Luminoso considered to be dramatically different from other revolutionary movements in Latin America? How is it similar? What are some of the fears that other Latin American governments and the United States have expressed about the possibility of a Shining Path victory in Peru?

3. Why have revolutions in Latin America tended to share an emphasis on nationalism and anti-imperialism? Why has the use of these ideological rallying cries been so successful? Use the examples of Cuba and Nicaragua in your answer.

ANSWER KEY

Test Bank

Answers indicate sources.
1. c (textbook, study guide)
2. c (textbook, study guide)
3. a, d (anthology, textbook, study guide)
4. d (anthology)
5. c (textbook)
6. c (textbook)
7. c, d (textbook, study guide)
8. b (textbook)
9. b (anthology)
10. b, d (textbook)
11. a (program, textbook, study guide)
12. b, d (program, anthology, textbook, study guide)
13. a, b, d (textbook, study guide)
14. a, b (anthology, textbook)
15. d (program, anthology, textbook, study guide)
16. c (program, study guide)
17. d (program, study guide)
18. a, c (program, anthology, textbook, study guide)
19. a (program, textbook, study guide)
20. a, c (program, study guide)
21. Mexican revolutionary who issued the Plan of San Luis Potosí, calling for General Porfirio Díaz to step down from power. Madero began the Mexican Revolution and was its first elected president, but lost favor with other rebel leaders and was eventually assassinated by former Díaz army officers. (anthology, textbook)
22. Unsuccessful CIA-backed Cuban exile invasion of Cuba on April 17, 1961, organized and financed by the U.S. government. The defeat was an embarrassment for U.S. president John F. Kennedy and helped to consolidate support for Castro both domestically and in the USSR. (textbook, study guide)
23. Nicaraguan slang for counterrevolutionaries, or *contra-revolucionarios*. Term given to the exiles who fought against the Nicaraguan Sandinistas for most of the 1980s, funded by the United States and commanded in part by former Somoza national guard officers. U.S.

administration support for the *contras* led to the Iran-Contra scandal, which rocked the Reagan administration in the mid-1980s. (program, textbook, study guide)
24. The commission, appointed by U.S. president Ronald Reagan and headed by former secretary of state Henry Kissinger, argued that Soviet and Cuban objectives promoting revolutionary struggle and anti–U.S. activity were responsible for much of the turmoil in Central America. Nicaragua was viewed as a stepping stone for increased Soviet influence in the region, with El Salvador the next likely target. (anthology)
25. Founder of the Salvadoran Christian Democratic Party, prevented from taking office as president when the military nullified the 1972 elections. Duarte returned from exile to head a civilian-military junta in 1980, then became the elected president when the Christian Democrats won elections in 1984. Although he remained in office until 1989, Duarte was unable to rein in military abuses of human rights or end the civil war. (program, textbook, study guide)
26. Violeta Barrilós de Chamorro became Nicaragua's president in 1990 when UNO, the anti-Sandinista coalition she headed, won a decisive victory in national elections and took over the government from the Sandinistas. Chamorro is the widow of Pedro Joaquín Chamorro, a journalist who was one of Somoza's most vocal opponents. (program, textbook, study guide)
27. U.S.-sponsored amendment to the Cuban Constitution adopted over Cuban objections after Cuba's independence from Spain in 1898. The amendment gave the United States the right to oversee the Cuban economy, veto international commitments, and intervene in domestic politics, making Cuba a virtual protectorate of the United States. It remained in force until 1934. (textbook, study guide)
28. Communal system of land ownership in Mexico under which organizations or groups of peasant families farm land received from the state. Mexican president Lázaro Cárdenas's distribution of thousands of acres of land in *ejidos* in the late 1930s was an important symbol of the Mexican Revolution. President Salinas (1989–) proposed significant changes to

the *ejido* system in a symbolic break with revolutionary principles. (textbook, study guide)

29. Peace plan agreed to in a meeting of the Central American presidents in Guatemala in 1987. The agreement began a process that led to a cease-fire and national elections in Nicaragua and facilitated government-guerrilla negotiations, with UN assistance, in El Salvador and Guatemala. (anthology, study guide)

30. Among other things, students could mention that Castro was opposed to U.S. economic domination and so turned to other trading partners; that he followed a Marxist line in terms of policy and received significant financial and technical assistance from the USSR; that U.S. hostility to the Cuban Revolution, especially after the Bay of Pigs, led Castro to look for foreign military support and helped to solidify the Cuban-Soviet alliance; and that Cuba's proximity to the United States made it an ideal spot from which the Soviet Union could challenge the United States in its traditional sphere of influence. (anthology, textbook, study guide)

Essay Questions

1. Mexico, Cuba, and Nicaragua vary widely in terms of geography, demography, history, politics, level of economic development, and social composition, all factors that had impact on the course of each country's revolutionary process. Mexico's population and resource base are much larger than those of Cuba and Nicaragua. Cuba and Nicaragua were affected, unlike Mexico, by Cold War superpower rivalries and by the competition between socialism and capitalism. Marxist ideology was much more important in molding the regimes that took power in Cuba and Nicaragua than it was in Mexico.

The three countries, however, have some things in common. They are the most important successful revolutions in twentieth-century Latin America. Each ended a long-term authoritarian regime (that of Porfirio Díaz in Mexico, Fulgencio Batista in Cuba, and the So-

moza dynasty in Nicaragua) whose repressive tactics, corruption, economic mismanagement and refusal to open up the political system led to broad-based opposition. The revolutions in all three countries were led by multiclass coalitions composed of ideologically and socioeconomically diverse groups. After the revolutionaries took power, the coalitions did not hold together, and, in each case, the most cohesive group took over control of the political apparatus.

2. Using information from the study guide and the program, the students should contrast the ideology, agendas, and methods of Sendero Luminoso with those of other revolutionary movements, such as Castro's movement, the Sandinistas, and the FMLN. Unlike most revolutionary groups, Shining Path does not attract its support from a broad, multiclass coalition. Instead, the guerrilla movement relies on the recruitment of alienated sectors, such as *mestizo* students and unemployed youths. Sendero's goal appears to be the complete restructuring of Peruvian society. Its glorification of violence has encouraged comparisons with Pol Pot's Khmer Rouge and raised fears of another Cambodia should it succeed in taking power. Although Sendero's appeal is so linked to Peruvian conditions that its impact in other countries in the region is questionable, unease at the prospect of a Shining Path victory is very great.

3. The appeals to nationalism have carried a lot of weight in countries such as Cuba and Nicaragua because they have had a great deal of difficulty asserting sovereignty throughout their history. Both countries were at various times under U.S. military occupation and were turned into virtual protectorates. The corruption of their authoritarian governments, which were frequently perceived as being tied to and profiting from foreign interests, also enhanced popular feelings that revolution would drive out foreign influence. Finally, the hostility of the United States to the revolutionary governments allowed them to blame "imperialists" for the revolution's internal difficulties, and dampened domestic opposition by equating antirevolutionary sentiment with being unpatriotic.

Unit 12

The Americans:
Latin American and Caribbean
Peoples in the United States

UNIT SUMMARY

Unit 12 considers the growth in numbers and importance of Latin American and Caribbean peoples living in the United States. The unit addresses three sets of issues. First, what are the most important groups that make up communities of Latin American and Caribbean origin in the United States? What characteristics do they share, and in what key ways do they differ from one another? Secondly, what has been the experience of Latin American and Caribbean peoples who have migrated to the United States? How has the different reception accorded the various groups affected their subsequent adjustment to U.S. society? Finally, how has the growth of Latino and non-Hispanic Caribbean communities in the United States affected U.S. politics, culture, and society? How have these communities in turn adapted to and been changed by the realities of their situation in the United States?

An important theme in this unit is the diversity of the peoples commonly grouped together under the generic label *Hispanic*; another is the extent to which the reality of the migrants' situations contrasts with common stereotypes. Students should also become more familiar with the range of immigrant communities from the English- and French-speaking Caribbean, whose numbers and influence are particularly evident in the eastern United States.

LEARNING OBJECTIVES

- After completing this unit, students should be able to:

- List the major groups of Latin American and Caribbean peoples in the United States, their different histories, experiences, economic status, and levels of political activism.

- Understand the variety of factors underlying immigration from Latin America and the Caribbean to the United States, and explain the reasons for the mixed reaction that has greeted immigrants from Latin America and the Caribbean in the 1980s and 1990s.

- Recognize the effect that their reception in the United States has had on the ultimate success and adaptation of various immigrant groups from Latin America and the Caribbean.

- Explain the controversy over the degree to which Latin American and Caribbean peoples should assimilate into North American society or, instead, seek integration while retaining their identities as separate and unique social groups.

- Evaluate the extent to which Latinos in the United States have evolved from being outside the mainstream to becoming aware of and using their economic and political power.

- Indicate some of the important ways in which the growing numbers of Latinos and non-Hispanic Caribbean peoples within the United States are influencing and changing U.S. society, politics, and culture.

OVERVIEW

For close to 500 years the United States has been a nation of immigrants. For nearly as long, an important part of the national self-image has been to be seen as a beacon of hope, a destination of freedom and opportunity for people from many lands. Because close to three-quarters of U.S. citizens today are descended from the European immigrants who arrived in massive numbers during the nineteenth and early twentieth centuries, the growing numbers of Hispanic peoples living in this country are perceived as newcomers, people quite different from other "Americans." Many North Americans might be surprised to learn that in fact Spanish-speaking peoples were the first nonnative settlers of the territory that is now the United States, and that the Hispanic presence antedated the establishment of an English colony in North America by a full century.

Unit 12 explores the diversity, vibrancy, and struggles of Latin American and Caribbean peoples living in the United States. The unit aims to acquaint students with the important contributions that immigrants from Latin America and the Caribbean have already made to this country, the controversies over the degree to which they should or should not "assimilate," and the likely social and political impact of their growing numbers in communities across the United States.

The television program, set in New York, Los Angeles, and Miami, focuses in particular on the three largest Latino groups: Mexican-Americans,

Puerto Ricans, and Cuban-Americans. Differences among the three groups are outlined, along with the extent to which they share certain perspectives and experiences. Readings in the textbook are primarily a review of relevant materials assigned in previous units which set the context for Cuban, Puerto Rican, and Mexican migration to and incorporation into this country. The anthology readings broaden the focus by describing some of the smaller and more recent groups of immigrants from elsewhere in the Americas: Dominicans, Jamaicans, Haitians, Central Americans, and others from virtually every country in the hemisphere.

An important goal of the unit is to tackle prevalent stereotypes about Latin American and Caribbean immigrants and about migration in general. Students should be encouraged to examine their own preconceptions about the issues raised in the unit, and to use the perspective they have gained in this course on the history and contemporary reality of the Americas to enhance their understanding of the experiences of Latino and other Caribbean peoples living in this country. The mixed reaction that greets most migrants is explored from both U.S. and Latino perspectives. Students will also discover how the reception that is accorded particular migrant groups ultimately affects that group's ability to adapt and succeed in their new country.

Finally, students should appreciate the extent to which these issues are still unfolding. The U.S. Hispanic population is growing not only through immigration but also as a result of natural increase. Despite continued high rates of immigration, three-fourths of Mexican-Americans and a quarter of Cuban-Americans are U.S.–born, and nearly half of all Puerto Ricans reside on the U.S. mainland. The U.S. Hispanic population is just beginning to recognize the potential it has to effect change and make its voice heard at all levels of the political system. As Hispanics continue to grow in numbers and become the largest minority group in the country (and the clear majority in several important regions), that power will undoubtedly make itself felt. Furthermore, the more recent growth of communities whose origin is the English- and French-speaking Caribbean is creating some tensions between these groups and U.S.–born Latinos and African-Americans, as well as affecting U.S. policy toward their countries.

Students should complete this unit with a

deeper understanding of the diversity of Americans in the United States, and of the important influence their presence has had in virtually every realm of public life, from music, art, language, and food to public policies on a broad range of domestic and international issues.

STUDENT READING ASSIGNMENT

Modern Latin America, 3d ed.
In chapter 11, *Hispanic Culture within the United States*, pp. 378–81.

Students should also review pp. 221–53, assigned in Unit 5; pp. 254–82, assigned in Unit 11; pp. 301–3, assigned in Unit 9.

Americas: An Anthology, chapter 12, pp. 335–72.

WRITING ASSIGNMENTS/ DISCUSSION QUESTIONS

1. Unit 1, "Introduction and Overview," explored possible stereotypes of Latin American and Caribbean people which students may have held at the outset of the course. Ask students to recall their earlier views, and to consider how those perceptions may also have affected their reaction to the presence of people from Latin America and the Caribbean within this country. Has their study of the region affected those earlier notions? How? To what extent do students believe that racial and ethnic stereotypes are responsible for the fears expressed by many North Americans of an "invasion" from the south?

2. Puerto Rico presents a unique case among all Latin American countries because it is, in fact, part of the United States. Nevertheless, Puerto Ricans' language, culture, and history connect them to the experience of other Latin Americans, and mark them as "different" in the United States. Is it surprising to students that

Puerto Ricans, who are U.S. citizens by birth, have higher unemployment rates, lower educational levels, and lower income than any other single Hispanic group? What are some of the reasons that may account for this disparity?

3. How, if at all, is the increased presence of Hispanics and other peoples from Latin America and the Caribbean within the United States likely to affect U.S.–Latin American relations in the next decade? Consider, for example, the prospects of U.S. relations with Mexico, Cuba, Haiti, the Dominican Republic, El Salvador, and Nicaragua in the context of current events and political and economic developments in those countries.

SUGGESTED ACTIVITIES

1. The program was able to consider only three of the many important areas in the country which have experienced an increase in their Hispanic and other Caribbean populations. Have students research the presence and impact of Latin American and Caribbean peoples, individually or in groups, in your area or in one of the following areas: Washington, D.C.; Chicago, Illinois; the Rio Grande Valley in Texas. Some of the issues they might consider are the nationalities of the recent immigrants, their impact on local job markets, their reception in the United States, levels of political activism, and interaction with other ethnic groups.

2. Take a poll (by mail if necessary) of students' opinions regarding U.S. immigration policy, tally their responses, and distribute results to students. Some possible questions to ask:

▪ Should the U.S. government have immigration quotas?

▪ Should preference be given to those who migrate for political reasons over those who migrate for economic reasons?

- Should the Simpson-Rodino Act be repealed? Should it be strengthened to make it more effective at stopping the cross-border flow of migrants? Can U.S. policy actually control the flow of undocumented immigrant workers to the United States?

3. Organize a class debate on the arguments for and against immigration, using the anthology selection by former Colorado governor Richard Lamm. Students should do additional research to develop counter arguments to those presented in the article. Have students address the question, Is continued immigration, especially from Latin America and the Caribbean, having a positive or negative impact on the United States? Encourage students to consider this question in historical and comparative perspectives.

4. To focus students' attention on the extent of the influence that Latin American and Caribbean culture has on their own lives, ask them to write down everything they encounter during a week which reflects the presence and impact of Latin American and Caribbean groups in the United States. Their notes may range from news items in the press or on television to foods they eat or music they listen to. Have them share their experiences with the class.

RESOURCES

Nonfiction

Bean, Frank D., and Marta Tienda. *The Hispanic Population of the United States.* New York: Russell Sage Foundation, 1987. A masterful demographic analysis of the U.S. Hispanic population, relying principally on data from the 1960, 1970, and 1980 censuses.

Chávez, Leo R. *Shadowed Lives: Undocumented Immigrants in American Society.* Fort Worth, Tex.: Harcourt Brace Jovanovich, 1991. A thoughtful, well-documented ethnography of primarily Mexican undocumented immigrants in the contemporary United States, based on extensive fieldwork in California and Texas.

Deutsch, Sarah. *No Separate Refuge: Culture, Class, and Gender on an Anglo-Hispanic Frontier in the American Southwest, 1880–1940.* New York: Oxford University Press, 1987. A history of Anglo-Hispanic relationships along the U.S.–Mexican border, from the late nineteenth century to the Great Depression and World War II; focus is especially on the role and status of women.

Gómez Quiñones, Juan. *Chicano Politics: Reality and Promise, 1940–1990.* Albuquerque: University of New Mexico Press, 1990. A thorough and up-to-date analysis of the political development of the second-largest ethnic minority in the United States, both before and after the Chicano movement of the 1960s.

Grasmuck, Sherri, and Patricia Pessar. *Between Two Islands: Dominican International Immigration.* Berkeley: University of California Press, 1991. The best available study to date of Dominican migration between the "two islands" of Manhattan and the Dominican Republic. Includes insightful ethnographic materials from fieldwork conducted in the Dominican Republic, as well as more limited survey data collected in New York.

Griswold, Richard del Castillo. *La Familia: Chicano Families in the Urban Southwest, 1846 to the Present.* Notre Dame, Ind.: University of Notre Dame Press, 1984. An important comparative-historical study of Mexican-Americans in San Antonio, Santa Fe, Tucson, and Los Angeles.

Isgro, Francesco. "The New Employment-Based Immigration Selection System." *Migration World* 19:5 (1991): 34–37. A very readable, detailed description of the major changes in U.S. immigration law contained in the Immigration Act of 1990 (which became effective in October 1991).

Jasso, Guillermina, and Mark R. Rosenzweig. *The New Chosen People: Immigrants in the United States.* New York: Russell Sage Foundation, 1990. A detailed study of contemporary immigration to the United States, focusing on the specifics of U.S. law and the development of "chain migration" patterns and networks among immigrant families.

Lamm, Richard D., and Gary Imhoff. *The Immigration Time Bomb: The Fragmenting of America*. New York: Dutton, 1985. Former Colorado governor Richard Lamm's alarmist critique of the impact of new immigration, especially that from Spanish America, in the United States as of the mid-1980s.

Lemann, Nicholas. "The Other Underclass." *The Atlantic*, December 1991, 96–110. A thoughtful journalistic inquiry into the status of the Puerto Rican community on the U.S. mainland today, focusing on New York City.

Levine, Barry B., ed. *The Caribbean Exodus*. New York: Praeger, 1987. An informed anthology of readings on what may be the world's most emigration-prone region: the Caribbean.

López, David E. "Chicano Language Loyalty in an Urban Setting." *Sociology and Social Research* 62 (1978): 267–78. An important and rare three-generational study of English- and Spanish-language use among Mexican-Americans in Los Angeles. The findings strongly undermine arguments claiming that Mexican-Americans do not assimilate linguistically.

Marks, Arnaud F., and Hebe M. C. Vessuri, eds. *White Collar Migrants in the Americas and the Caribbean*. Leiden, Netherlands: Department of Caribbean Studies, Royal Institute of Linguistics and Anthropology, 1983. This collection of essays explores emigration and economic decline, white-collar migrant labor, emigration to Canada, and U.S. businessmen in Mexico.

Massey, Douglas, Rafael Alarcón, Jorge Durand, and Humberto González. *Return to Aztlán: The Social Process of International Migration from Western Mexico*. Berkeley: University of California Press, 1987. An illuminating study of the role of social networks in shaping the process of emigration from Mexico to the United States, and in linking places of origin and of destination.

Meléndez, Edwin, and Clara Rodríguez, eds. "Puerto Rican Poverty and Labor Markets." *Hispanic Journal of Behavioral Sciences* 14 (February 1992). A special issue of this journal devoted entirely to new analyses of the economic situation of Puerto Ricans, focusing primarily on the U.S. mainland.

Montejano, David. *Anglos and Mexicans in the Making of Texas, 1836–1986*. Austin: University of Texas Press, 1987. An original, excellent study of the formation of the Mexican-American community in Texas over a century and a half, focusing on the nature of Anglo responses.

Moore, Joan, and Harry Pachón. *Hispanics in the United States*. Englewood Cliffs, N.J.: Prentice-Hall, 1985. A comprehensive descriptive text on the subject, focusing on the three largest Hispanic groups: Mexicans, Puerto Ricans, and Cubans.

Palmer, Ransford, ed. *In Search of a Better Life: Perspectives on Migration from the Caribbean*. New York: Praeger, 1990. A recent collection of essays illuminating the nature of migration from the Caribbean, focusing on demographic and economic factors.

Pedraza-Bailey, Silvia. *Political and Economic Migrants in America: Cubans and Mexicans*. Austin: University of Texas Press, 1985. A comparative study of the adaptation of Cuban (political) and Mexican (economic) migrants in the United States, relying on demographic and socioeconomic data from the 1960, 1970, and 1980 censuses.

Pérez, Luis A., Jr. *Cuba and the United States: Ties of Singular Intimacy*. Athens: University of Georgia Press, 1990. An excellent introduction to the history of U.S.–Cuba relations, and of the nature of structural linkages forged between the countries since the nineteenth century.

Portes, Alejandro. "From South of the Border: Hispanic Minorities in the United States." In *Immigration Reconsidered: History, Sociology, and Politics*, edited by Virginia Yans-McLaughlin, pp. 160–94. New York: Oxford University Press, 1990. A detailed overview of the economic and political incorporation of Hispanic minorities in the United States, focusing on Mexican-Americans, Puerto Ricans, and Cuban-Americans.

Portes, Alejandro, and Rubén G. Rumbaut. *Immigrant America: A Portrait*. Berkeley: University of California Press, 1990. See especially chapters 4 and 6. A definitive portrait of contemporary immigration to the United States, primarily from Latin America and Asia. The book presents a typology of the new immigrants and chapters on patterns of settlement, economic and political incorporation, psychological consequences, acculturation, English-language acquisition, and the second generation.

Reimers, David M. *Still the Golden Door: The Third World Comes to America*. New York: Columbia University Press, 1985. A leading historian's analysis of the origins of the "new immigration" to the United States from Third World countries in Asia and Latin America.

Rieff, David. *Los Angeles: Capital of the Third World*. New York: Simon & Schuster, 1991. A sketch of the transformation of Los Angeles as a result of massive new immigration primarily from Asia and Latin America.

Rumbaut, Rubén G. "The Americans: Latin American and Caribbean Peoples in the United States." In *Americas: New Interpretive Essays*, edited by Alfred Stepan. New York: Oxford University Press, 1992. An up-to-date detailed review of Latin American and Caribbean groups in the United States today, relying on data from the 1980 and 1990 censuses. Written by a member of the *Americas* academic advisory board as an optional addition to this unit.

Rumbaut, Rubén G. "Passages to America: Perspectives on the New Immigration." In *America at Century's End*, edited by Alan Wolfe, pp. 208–44. Berkeley: University of California Press, 1991. An analysis of the national and class origins of recent immigration to the United States, and of its impact on economic and cultural institutions, with an extended section on the politics of bilingualism and linguistic assimilation.

Sánchez, Joseph P. "Hispanic American Heritage." In *Seeds of Change: A Quincentennial Commemoration*, edited by Herman J. Viola and Carolyn Margolis, pp. 173–185. Washington D.C.: Smithsonian Institution Press, 1991. A richly illustrated companion book to the Smithsonian Institution's "Seeds of Change" exhibition—a quincentennial commemoration of Columbus's "discovery" of the New World and the global forces it set in motion.

Fiction

Alvarez, Julia. *How the García Girls Lost Their Accents*. Chapel Hill, N.C.: Algonquin Books, 1991. This novel of a prominent family that flees the Dominican Republic portrays the intricacies of immigrant family life in the United States, the fracturing effects of assimilation, and the power of culture and language.

García, Cristina. *Dreaming in Cuban*. New York: Knopf, 1992. A story of three generations of Cuban women and their separate responses to Castro's revolution, this is a novel of and by the second generation, the U.S.–born children of Cuban exiles who came to the United States after 1959.

Hijuelos, Oscar. *The Mambo Kings Play Songs of Love*. New York: Farrar Straus Giroux, 1989. Winner of the Pulitzer Prize, this novel of two young Cuban musicians who make their way from Havana to New York in the late 1940s captures the social and cultural context of pre-Castro and pre-Miami Cuban immigration to the Big Apple.

Thomas, Piri, *Down These Mean Streets*. New York: Knopf, 1967. The story of Puerto Ricans in New York. A classic from the late 1960s.

Films

Unless otherwise indicated, all films listed are available in VHS video format.

La Bamba. 108 minutes, 1987. At age 17 with three rock 'n roll hits, Richie Valens died in the fatal plane crash that also killed Buddy Holly and the Big Bopper, changing rock 'n roll forever. Available in most video-rental outlets.

Crossover Dreams. 86 minutes, 1985. Rubén Blades stars as a salsa artist who becomes overconfident and back-stabbing after cutting his first album. Available in most video-rental outlets.

The Lemon Grove Incident. 60 minutes, 1986. Directed by Paul Espinoza. Documentary about a trial regarding Mexican immigrant children in California schools. The case antedated the 1954 *Brown* decision on "separate but equal" by almost two decades. Available for rental ($95 for two days, plus $11 for shipping and handling) from: The Cinema Guild, 1697 Broadway, New York, NY 10019; (212) 246-5522.

Los Mineros. For *The American Experience.* 60 minutes, 1990. An excellent piece on turn-of-the-century Mexican workers recruited to labor in the mines of Arizona and the Southwest. Available for rental ($59.95, plus $8.50 for shipping and handling) from: PBS Video, 4401 Sunset Blvd., Los Angeles, CA 90027; (800) 328-7271.

Milagro Beanfield War. 117 minutes, 1988. Directed by Robert Redford. A comedy/drama about the citizens of rural Milagro Valley, New Mexico who attempt to preserve their way of life against intrusive big money interests. Available in most video-rental outlets.

El Norte. 139 minutes, 1984. Refugees emigrate to the U.S. fleeing horrendous civil war conditions in Guatemala. Available in most video-rental outlets.

The Oxcart. 20 minutes, 1970. (Spanish, with English subtitles.) Based on the play by René Marques, this film follows the journey of a Puerto Rican family from their rural home to the slums of San Juan and, finally, to New York's Spanish Harlem. Available on videocassette for rental ($50) or purchase ($250) from: The Cinema Guild, 1697 Broadway, New York, NY 10019; (212) 246-5522.

Stand and Deliver. 103 minutes, 1988. True story of a math teacher in the Los Angeles public schools who inspires his students to better their standardized test scores. Available in most video-rental outlets.

Uneasy Neighbors. 60 minutes, 1989. Directed by Paul Espinoza. Documentary about undocumented Mexican migrant laborers in a southern California community. Available for rental ($50, plus $7 for shipping and handling) from: University of California Extension Media Center, 2176 Shattuck Avenue, Berkeley, CA 94704; (510) 642-5578.

TEST BANK

Questions reflect content from the programs, text-book, and anthology.

Multiple Choice

Mark the letter of the response that best answers the question or completes the statement.

_____ 1. Spanish-speaking immigrants' ability to retain their identities, language, and culture within the United States is enhanced by: (*Mark all that apply.*)

    a. a number of states' refusal to provide bilingual education.

    b. the concentration of Hispanic groups in particular areas.

    c. the growing political activism of some Hispanics.

    d. the continued influx of migrants from Latin America.

_____ 2. Of the following countries, which has the largest Spanish-speaking population?

    a. Peru

    b. Chile

    c. The United States

    d. Venezuela

_____ 3. What was the major reason for the initial wave of Cuban emigration to the United States?

    a. Cuba's poor domestic economy.

    b. A forced exodus of the "less desirables."

    c. The revolution of 1959.

    d. Castro's agreement to allow the Mariel boatlift.

_____ 4. According to anthology reading 12.4, which of the following is an accurate statement about Caribbean immigrants in New York?

    a. They have completely integrated with U.S.–born African-Americans.

    b. They tend to remain divided by language, culture, and nationality.

    c. In general they have not been confined to low-wage jobs, unlike most Hispanic immigrants.

    d. Despite their high numbers, their presence in New York has remained virtually unnoticed.

_____ 5. One new strategy of the Immigration Reform and Control Act of 1986 (the Simpson-Rodino Act) was to:

    a. build barricades along the U.S.–Mexican border.

    b. deport undocumented immigrants.

    c. increase the presence of the border patrol.

    d. fine employers of undocumented workers.

_____ 6. The success of the Cuban-American community in Miami has been attributed to: (*Mark all that apply.*)

    a. the high number of professional jobs available to new Cuban migrants.

    b. Cubans' official status as political refugees.

    c. a lack of tensions with other population groups in Miami.

    d. the assistance provided by earlier migrants to new arrivals.

_____ 7. Puerto Ricans are different from other Hispanic groups in the United States today because they:

    a. are U.S. citizens by birth.

    b. are the only major group from the Caribbean.

    c. no longer speak Spanish.

    d. dream of returning to their country of origin.

_____ 8. The Puerto Rican community has *primarily* settled in:

a. the Southwest.
b. the Midwest.
c. Florida.
d. the Northeast.

_____ 9. As a rule, new immigrants from Latin America and the Caribbean: (*Mark all that apply.*)

a. are able to find jobs in keeping with their educational status and skills level.
b. gravitate to areas of the country where earlier migrants from their country have established ethnic enclaves.
c. tend to take jobs in low-wage industries or to work in the informal sector.
d. become U.S. citizens as quickly as possible in order to exercise their right to vote.

_____ 10. Chicano political activism:

a. has just gotten under way since the late 1980s.
b. got started in the 1960s but has accelerated more recently.
c. dates back as long as Mexican-Americans have lived in this country.
d. has been especially concerned with foreign policy issues.

_____ 11. The majority of Latinos in this country:

a. are from the poorest sectors of their home countries.
b. are unemployed and dependent on public assistance.
c. are undocumented migrants subject to deportation.
d. are employed, working-class citizens.

_____ 12. Some of the concerns about the impact of migration expressed by former Colorado governor Richard Lamm are that: (*Mark all that apply.*)

a. the strain of assimilating so many new migrants is disrupting social harmony.
b. the concentration of immigrants in low-skill jobs depresses wage levels for U.S. citizens.
c. immigrants from many different countries are uniting into a dangerous political force.
d. immigrant demands for better working conditions are too costly for most U.S. businesses.

_____ 13. About half of New York City's recent immigrants have come from:

a. Brazil.
b. Mexico.
c. the Caribbean.
d. Colombia.

_____ 14. According to political scientist Rodolfo de la Garza, in anthology reading 12.5, Mexican-Americans are unlikely to develop into a lobby for Mexican interests because:

a. they have already been successful at resisting the pressures put on them by the Mexican government.
b. they feel an unrelenting hostility toward Mexico and the Mexican government.
c. after years in the United States, they are most concerned with improving their quality of life within this country.
d. years of exclusion from the U.S. political system have made them politically apathetic.

_____ 15. Bilingual education has been criticized because it: (*Mark all that apply.*)

a. is too costly for many communities to afford.
b. emphasizes the separateness of Hispanics.

c. is giving an unfair advantage to Hispanic children.

d. discourages children from speaking English as soon as possible.

_____ 16. Which of the following statements is true of recent immigrants in southern Florida? (*Mark all that apply.*)

a. The widespread use of Spanish in Miami has facilitated the transition for Central American immigrants.

b. There are wide disparities of class, income level, and education between newer immigrants and Cuban-Americans.

c. There has been very little rivalry between newer immigrants from Haiti and Central America and the Cuban-Americans.

d. The rapid growth of the immigrant population has created tension and competition with the African-American population.

_____ 17. The largest single group of Hispanics in the United States is:

a. Puerto Ricans.

b. Haitians.

c. Mexicans.

d. Cubans.

_____ 18. One of the most important issues for the Cuban-American community has tended to be:

a. fighting housing discrimination.

b. obtaining access to jobs.

c. extending protection for undocumented immigrants.

d. maintaining U.S. pressure on Cuba.

_____ 19. Hispanic influence within the United States:

a. is declining as more and more immigrants learn to speak English.

b. is confined to the geographic areas where most Hispanics live.

c. is especially reflected in U.S. policy toward Mexico.

d. is likely to grow along with the increased number of Hispanics.

_____ 20. Official U.S. policy toward Latin American and Caribbean immigrants has included which of the following? (*Mark all that apply.*)

a. Guest worker programs.

b. Deportation of undocumented immigrants.

c. Unrestricted free entry for all English-speaking Hispanics.

d. Legislation allowing Hispanics to settle only in certain areas.

Identification/Short Answer

Define or describe the following terms, concepts, or persons, or answer the following questions. Answers should be no longer than a few sentences.

21. Gloria Molina:

22. What is the basis for Chicano political scientist Rodolfo de la Garza's statement, "There is no justification for charging that [Mexican-Americans] have been unwilling to integrate into mainstream society"?

23. Why are Mexican-Americans particularly sensitive to the dilemmas of undocumented immigrants?

24. Latino:

25. Name three ways in which the increased presence of Hispanics in the United States has affected government policies at the local, state, or national levels.

ESSAY QUESTIONS

1. The three major Latino groups profiled in the program—Mexican-Americans, Puerto Ricans, and Cuban-Americans—have had quite different experiences as migrants to the United States. Describe the basic characteristics of each group, citing the geographic, economic, historical, and political factors that make them unique. What, if any, characteristics do they share?

2. The 1986 Immigration Reform and Control Act (the Simpson-Rodino Act) mandated stiff penalties for employers who hire "undocumented aliens" while also offering protection from prosecution for immigrants able to prove a lengthy period of residency in the United States. Defend or critique this legislation, identifying and explaining at least three critical elements that support your opinion. How successful would you call this approach?

3. Discuss two widespread popular reactions to Hispanic immigration presented in the anthology, textbook, and study guide: first, that Hispanics have not assimilated adequately into the United States, and, second, that they have "taken over" certain parts of the country. What are these criticisms based on? What are some counterarguments?

ANSWER KEY

Test Bank

Answers indicate sources.
1. b, c, d (program, anthology, textbook)
2. c (textbook)
3. c (program, anthology, textbook)
4. b (anthology)
5. d (anthology, textbook)
6. b, d (program, anthology, study guide)
7. a (program, anthology, textbook, study guide)
8. d (program, anthology, study guide)
9. b, c (program, anthology)
10. b (program, anthology, study guide)
11. d (anthology, study guide)
12. a, b (anthology)
13. c (anthology)
14. c (anthology)
15. a, b, d (anthology, textbook, study guide)
16. a, b, d (program)
17. c (program, anthology, textbook, study guide)
18. d (program, anthology, study guide)
19. d (program, anthology, textbook, study guide)
20. a, b (anthology, textbook, study guide)
21. Los Angeles city councilor, member of the Los Angeles County Board of Supervisors, former member of the California State Assembly. A Mexican-American, Molina is the first woman to be elected to the county board, and the first Hispanic woman to serve in the state assembly and on the Los Angeles City Council. Her accomplishments illustrate the increased political power being wielded by the Mexican-American population of southern California. (anthology)
22. De la Garza argues that Chicanos have been systematically excluded from the U.S. social and political systems, and until recently were prevented from taking advantage of their right to vote. The fact that they continue to live in particular ethnic enclaves and to speak Spanish is not due to any desire on their part to avoid becoming "Americanized," he says. Now that they are participating in the political process, Chicanos are in fact voting at a higher rate than the rest of the population. (anthology)
23. First, because most undocumented or illegal immigrants are from Mexico, although many are from other countries, including non–Latin American countries. Second, because Mexicans have not experienced the protection afforded to Cubans, based on their political status, or to Puerto Ricans, who are U.S. citizens. They have experienced many of the same struggles and fears as the newer immigrants from Central America and are empathetic to their situation. (anthology, textbook)
24. The term is similar to Hispanic; a term used to refer to persons of Latin American origin living in the United States. *Latino* is preferred by some as a more inclusive term for the culturally diverse people of Latin America and the Spanish-speaking Caribbean. (program, anthology, study guide)
25. Answers might include, at the local level, struggles over redistricting to give Hispanics more political leverage, decisions on whether or not to offer bilingual education, state and federal decisions to publish government documents in Spanish or to provide Spanish-speaking personnel in government offices, and national legislative battles over how to control immigration and encourage assimilation. (program, textbook, study guide)

Essay Questions

1. Students should recall that Mexican-Americans have lived in the United States the longest and are especially concentrated in California and the Southwest; that Puerto Ricans are U.S. citizens by birth, more than 40 percent of them live on the U.S. mainland, and they are concentrated in the Northeast; and that most Cuban-Americans came to the United States to escape the Cuban Revolution and are concentrated in the greater Miami area. They should also mention the relative affluence of Cuban-Americans, the 30-year history of political organizing on the part of Chicanos, and the difficulties of unemployment and poverty experienced by Puerto Ricans. Despite significant differences, these three groups all share an increased tendency to view themselves as having certain shared interests, and as having

more in common with one another than with non-Spanish-speaking immigrants. As immigrants, all have had to struggle in low-wage jobs and have faced certain levels of discrimination in housing, education, and employment.

2. It is important that students demonstrate an understanding of the basic provisions of the law and how it fits into both former immigration policy efforts and actual consequences since the law was passed in 1986. They should draw on the materials from the textbook and anthology to support their views.

3. The argument that Hispanics have refused to assimilate stems from the fact that many Hispanics continue to live in particular enclaves, continue to speak Spanish, and have developed a thriving local culture. This view is criticized by others who argue that Hispanics have actually been prevented from assimilating, that they are indeed learning and using English overwhelmingly in the second and third generations (just like other migrants before them), and that they do value the gains that will come from achieving fuller integration. Those who fear a "Hispanicization" of U.S. society and politics point to Hispanics' increased tendency to become politically organized and activist and to their tendency to vote as an ethnic group. Others point to this same fact as proof that Hispanics are becoming more fully integrated into the U.S. system and are seeing themselves as citizens with rights and the power to make their voices heard. Still others emphasize the differences in political behavior among these groups—for example, Mexican-Americans and Puerto Ricans tend to vote Democratic, Cuban-Americans mostly vote Republican—as evidence that the development of a common "Hispanic" political agenda is unlikely.

Unit 13

Course Review

UNIT SUMMARY

The main goal of Unit 13 is to review the material covered in the telecourse, considering how the examples of the various countries to which students have been exposed over the past 12 weeks illustrate the four major themes: first, Latin America and the Caribbean have a distinct historical relationship to the rest of the world; second, this external relationship in combination with domestic policy decisions has created significant internal tensions; third, people of Latin America and the Caribbean have developed many innovative responses to their social and political situation; and fourth, their innovations have had and continue to have an important impact on the rest of the world and the region's relationship to it.

A second goal for the unit is to consider what the future may hold for the Americas: how the region is likely to develop, and what the main issues in Latin America and the Caribbean's relationship with the United States will be. There is no television program for Unit 13.

LEARNING OBJECTIVES

After completing this unit, students should be able to:

- Understand the historical basis for the distinct relationship of Latin America and the Caribbean with the rest of the world.

- Explain the reasons for the region's history of serious and frequent internal tensions.

- Describe some of the innovations developed by Latin American and Caribbean peoples in response to their social and political realities.

- Recognize the parameters within which the relationship of Latin America and the Caribbean to the world order will most likely continue to evolve.

- Use several examples of different countries to illustrate the various themes of the television course.

- Make predictions about the future course of Latin American and Caribbean development.

- Identify some of the most important issues that will continue to characterize the relationship of the countries of Latin America and the Caribbean, individually and as a region, with the United States and with the rest of the world.

OVERVIEW

Unit 13 is a concise review of the issues and examples covered in Units 1–12. The unit materials integrate the themes of the course with the experiences of the different countries, attempting to help students see that the issues of dependency, sovereignty, nationalism, class, ethnicity, and others are not limited to the country examples used in any one unit. By the conclusion of the review, students should be able to see the interconnectedness of the themes and draw upon their knowledge of the region to provide examples from several different countries.

A second goal of the unit is to encourage students to make reasoned projections, both about the future course of political, social, and economic development in Latin America and the Caribbean, and about the likely relationship between the region and the United States. The textbook chapters are especially helpful in this regard, providing a condensed history of U.S.–Latin American relations along with a comparative framework that is helpful for making predictions about the future of the region. Students may need some additional help in understanding the complexity of the comparative analysis provided in the Epilogue (see Writing Assignment 3).

STUDENT READING ASSIGNMENT

Modern Latin America, 3d ed.
Chapter 11, "Latin America, the United States, and the World," pp. 344–81.

Epilogue, "What Future for Latin America," pp. 382–406.

WRITING ASSIGNMENTS/ DISCUSSION QUESTIONS

1. The issue of sovereignty was a particular focus of Unit 10, "Get Up, Stand Up: The Problems of Sovereignty," but it was an underlying issue in nearly all the units of the course. Have the students consider the countries portrayed in each unit and write about or discuss the many dimensions of sovereignty as presented in the course.

2. The June 1992 United Nations Conference on Environment and Development drew worldwide attention to global environmental problems and to the need for the northern and southern parts of our hemisphere to work together to reduce the threats for all. How are the issues discussed at the conference an example of the post–Cold War relationship between Latin America and the United States? Ask students to think of other examples of "transnational" issues that are becoming major aspects of the relationship between the United States and other countries in the Americas.

3. Ask students to compare their understanding of Latin America and the Caribbean at the conclusion of this course with the stereotypes or limited impressions they may have held at the beginning. If they could sum up what they have learned in the course in four key points, what would those be? How has the course affected their perception of people from Latin America and the Caribbean now living in the United States?

SUGGESTED ACTIVITIES

1. Students can investigate the issues of nationalism and sovereignty in Latin America in the 1990s. Have them research and write reports, individually or in groups, on how nationalism and sovereignty have been part of the domestic debate on one of the following issues: structural adjustment policies in Argentina; the

North American Free Trade Agreement in Mexico; the U.S. trial of former Panamanian leader Manuel Antonio Noriega; rain forest destruction in Brazil.

2. The Organization of American States (OAS) was called upon in the early 1990s to adopt a new role, parallel to that being adopted by the United Nations in the post–Cold War era. Have students study the role of the OAS in responding to the 1991 and 1992 coups in Haiti and Peru, and write reports answering the following questions: Was there any conflict between the perspective of the United States and that of other members? How did member nations balance between their own and United States' objectives? Was the organization able to take any concerted action in the two cases? What, if any, was the impact of the OAS? Is the influence of the OAS likely to increase, decrease, or stay about the same during the coming decades? For a more extensive report, the OAS's role in the early nineties can be contrasted with its role in other regional conflicts in the 1970s and 1980s.

3. Have students research and draw up their own diagrams (similar to those on pp. 376–82 in the textbook) to explain political and social coalitions during a particular period in another country studied in the course, such as Nicaragua, Haiti, the Dominican Republic, Panama, Bolivia, or Colombia. How useful is this type of comparative analysis of social and political class coalitions for understanding the history of particular Latin American or Caribbean countries? Are there other factors missing or underemphasized? If so, what are they?

TEST BANK

Questions reflect content from the programs, textbook, and anthology.

Multiple Choice

Mark the letter of the response that ***best*** *answers the question or completes the statement.*

_____ 1. Internal migration as depicted in "Continent on the Move" shows one important effect of:

a. the lack of national sovereignty throughout Latin America and the Caribbean.
b. the high levels of religious diversity in the region.
c. the unequal division of the benefits of economic growth among different groups.
d. the legacy of multicultural societies which remained after the colonial period.

_____ 2. The commemoration of which historical event poses a dilemma for the Aymara people of Bolivia (presented in "Mirrors of the Heart")?

a. Bolivia's independence day.
b. The quincentenary of Columbus's arrival.
c. The date of Bolivia's 1952 revolution.
d. The date Aymara became Bolivian citizens.

_____ 3. Brazilian Cardinal Paulo Evaristo Arns's testimony on torture, presented in the anthology assignment for Unit 4, is an example of: (*Mark all that apply.*)

a. the brutality of bureaucratic-authoritarian regimes imposed in much of Latin America in the 1960s and 1970s.

b. the tactics of radical revolutionary movements in Brazil and elsewhere throughout the region.
c. the activism of important members of the institutional Catholic Church on behalf of human rights.
d. the criticism levied by the Church at the Communist system developed in Cuba after the 1959 revolution.

_____ 4. Only one of the following literary innovations did not originate in the Americas. It is:

a. muralism.
b. noirisme.
c. magic realism.
d. surrealism.

_____ 5. An important objective for Latin American nationalists has been: (*Mark all that apply.*)

a. gaining national control over important natural resources.
b. integrating their countries more thoroughly into the world economy.
c. promoting domestic industrialization.
d. seeking significant foreign investment to provide needed technology.

_____ 6. The Rio Pact was:

a. a 1947 collective defense agreement signed by the United States and most Latin American countries.
b. the 1948 treaty that established the Organization of American States as part of the UN system.
c. the 1848 treaty, negotiated by Brazil, that ended the Mexican-American War.
d. the 1930 trade agreement creating a common market among the Southern Cone nations of Brazil, Chile, and Argentina.

_____ 7. The analysis of Latin American economies developed by ECLA included which of the following points ? (*Mark all that apply.*)

    a. Latin America would develop fastest by focusing on exports of agricultural products and raw materials.

    b. Latin American countries should seek international commodity agreements to protect the prices of their export products.

    c. the international economy worked systematically to the disadvantage of developing country economies such as those in Latin America.

    d. Latin American countries should emphasize attracting assembly plants rather than seek to carry out domestic industrialization.

_____ 8. Which of the following statements are true of the impact of popular culture in the Americas on the rest of the world? (*Mark all that apply.*)

    a. The appeal of Latin music, such as "salsa" and the bossa nova, has been restricted to countries where the majority of the population speaks Spanish.

    b. The early popularity of Latin American and Caribbean dance, best illustrated by the tango and the merengue, has been eclipsed by Western mass culture in the twentieth century.

    c. Young "Nuyoricans" rapping in Spanish illustrate one way in which popular cultures in the Americas have combined into new forms.

    d. Television has had an important role in spreading innovations such as the telenovela across international boundaries.

_____ 9. Which of the following is unlikely to receive much attention in U.S.Latin American relations in the coming decades?

    a. International narcotics trade.

    b. Human rights and political democratization.

    c. Bilateral military alliances.

    d. Debt repayment.

_____ 10. Economically, Latin America during the 1980s was marked by: (*Mark all that apply.*)

    a. adoption of structural adjustment policies required by the International Monetary Fund.

    b. significant economic growth but with unequal distribution of benefits.

    c. general movement toward free market and free trade policies.

    d. high inflation coupled with prolonged recession.

_____ 11. Which of the following is an important consequence of the end of the Cold War for Latin American and Caribbean countries? (*Mark all that apply.*)

    a. There is no longer a comparable superpower to balance U.S. hegemony within the hemisphere.

    b. The discrediting of international Communism has weakened domestic Communist and socialist parties.

    c. The collapse of the Soviet Union prompted the United States to offer a significant influx of aid to promote democratic reforms.

    d. Revolutionary movements can no longer look to the Eastern bloc for material and military aid.

_____ 12. According to the analytic framework presented in the textbook Epilogue, formal or informal alliances in Latin America have virtually never arisen between which two groups?

    a. The foreign sector and the state.

    b. The foreign sector and the rural lower class.

c. The state and the rural upper class.
d. The state and the urban working class.

_____ 13. In Latin America in the 1990s, the combination of population growth, internal migration, and lack of jobs could lead to: (*Mark all that apply.*)

a. a rapid increase in the size of the urban informal sector.
b. an increasing percentage of the population living in rural areas.
c. a drop in the numbers of people seeking to move to the United States.
d. increased pressure on elected civilian governments.

_____ 14. The coups that took place in Haiti in 1991 and Peru in 1992 are both examples of: (*Mark all that apply.*)

a. the continued power of the military even in countries with elected civilian governments.
b. the fact that necessary social and economic reforms can only take place when imposed by authoritarian governments.
c. the ongoing possibilities for revolution in the aftermath of the Cold War.
d. the continued influence of internal tensions on domestic political processes.

_____ 15. Only one of the following domestic issues is unlikely to be of much importance for Latin American and Caribbean countries in the coming decades. It is:

a. socioeconomic inequalities.
b. racial and ethnic tensions.
c. the burden of debt repayment.
d. the appeal of traditional Communist parties.

Identification/Short Answer:

Define or describe the following terms, concepts, or persons, or answer the following questions. Answers should be no longer than a few sentences.

16. Why are the 1980s known as the "lost decade" in Latin America?

17. What was unique about ECLA's analysis of Latin America's economic problems?

18. The Organization of American States:

19. The "popular classes":

20. Name two contemporary examples of internal or external threats to Latin American sovereignty.

21. Multinational corporation:

22. Briefly describe the manner in which Latin America and the Caribbean were integrated into the world economy.

23. How does nationalism continue to exert influence over individuals, communities, and governments in Latin American and Caribbean countries? In your answer, cite two examples from the 1980s or 1990s covered in the programs of the television course.

24. The nations of Latin America and the Caribbean are both diverse and complex, with many significant differences among them. At the same time, there are also important underlying similarities that affect the region's prospects for the future. Using the examples of Mexico, Bolivia, Jamaica, and Brazil, each covered to some degree in this course, describe at least one issue that influences all four countries' future development, and one other issue for each country that is unique to that nation's particular situation.

25. Briefly describe some of the changes that have occurred in the lives of women of Latin American and Caribbean origin now living in the United States.

ESSAY QUESTIONS

1. Using the examples of import-substituting industrialization and the more recent economic policies promoting export-oriented agriculture and manufacturing, discuss how the economic policies pursued by many countries in Latin America and the Caribbean are a reflection of the region's position in a changing global economy.

2. The struggles and conflicts among the many social groups in Latin American and Caribbean nations have been identified in this course as a major contributor to political instability. According to the textbook, the growth of the middle class throughout the region has sometimes been cited by North American observers as a factor that will end the pattern of repeated return to authoritarian government and frequent internal upheaval in the Americas. What is your view? What arguments can you make about the fundamental differences between middle classes in Latin America and in the United States? Is the growth of the middle class likely to produce a solution to the domestic tensions that have characterized the region?

3. Looking back over the 10 programs of the telecourse, describe an example of the innovations developed by Latin American and Caribbean peoples in four of the following areas: urban growth, race relations, cultural contributions, religious beliefs, gender roles, social change, and U.S. popular culture.

4. Imagine you are a State Department adviser charged with advising the U.S. administration on its Latin American policy. What are the major issues you would point to as critical for U.S. interests in the region? What kind of rationale would you construct for U.S. involvement in the Americas? Can you create a policy or set of policies that will both protect U.S. interests and further the development of Latin American and Caribbean nations? Or do you see the goals as mutually exclusive? Explain.

ANSWER KEY

Test Bank

Sources listed may be from this and previous units.
1. c (program, anthology, study guide)
2. b (program)
3. a, c (program, anthology, textbook, study guide)
4. d (anthology, study guide)
5. a, c (anthology, textbook, study guide)
6. a (textbook, study guide)
7. b, c (textbook, study guide)
8. c, d (textbook, study guide)
9. c (textbook, study guide)
10. a, c, d (textbook)
11. a, b, d (textbook)
12. b (textbook)
13. a, d (textbook)
14. a, d (study guide)
15. d (textbook, study guide)
16. The "lost decade" refers to the economic decline during the 1980s which saw an average drop in per capita income of about 10 percent; prolonged recession with slow or negative economic growth in most countries; continuing battles with inflation; tremendous pressure to make domestic sacrifices to repay the foreign debt; and the hardships of structural adjustment policies adopted to qualify for IMF assistance. (textbook, study guide)
17. ECLA was unique because it was the first international agency to address the region's economic situation from a Latin American perspective; almost all the staff were citizens of Latin American countries and the headquarters was in Santiago, Chile. The result was an analysis that perceived a systematic disadvantage for Latin American economies, particularly those relying heavily on the export of primary products, in the workings of the international economy. ECLA's proposals were for Latin American countries to seek international commodity agreements to protect export prices, and for the larger countries to industrialize to gain greater self-sufficiency. (textbook)
18. An inter-American organization established in 1948 to serve as the diplomatic decision-making body of the Western Hemisphere. According to the charter, OAS members are committed to the principles of nonintervention (sought by the Latin American members as protection for national sovereignty) and continental solidarity (sought by the United States as part of its strategy to resist Soviet expansionism), along with economic cooperation, social justice, democracy, and human rights. All independent Latin American and Caribbean nations except Cuba are members, along with the United States and Canada, but throughout most of its history the organization has served primarily to endorse the policies of its most powerful member, the United States. (textbook, study guide)
19. Term used throughout Latin America to refer to the rural and urban lower classes. According to the textbook, the popular classes are those that have been excluded from the benefits of economic growth, and who continue to live in conditions of poverty, hunger, and illiteracy. Many are unemployed or work in the informal sector. In some countries, such as Mexico and Brazil, the popular classes make up 50 percent or more of the country's population. (textbook)
20. Students could cite any event in the 1980s or 1990s that illustrates their understanding of the concept of sovereignty. Examples might be the U.S. invasion of Panama and the subsequent trial of Panamanian leader Manuel Antonio Noriega; the difficulty the Peruvian government is having in trying to eliminate Sendero Luminoso and regain control over significant portions of Peruvian territory even after suspending civil liberties and allocating wide power to the military; the inability of the United States and several Andean country governments to stop production of or international trade in cocaine; or Brazilian perceptions that international pressure to end rain forest destruction is an intrusion into its own domestic affairs. (textbook, study guide)
21. A company with bases of operation in more than one country, limiting its identification with any particular country or political system, although their home offices are generally in the advanced industrial countries. Multinational corporations, or MNCs, typically are both very large and highly mobile, able to take

advantage of low wages, government incentives, trade conditions, or other favorable market conditions in different places around the world. MNCs also tend to be quite influential in developing country economies due to the magnitude of capital and technology they possess. (textbook, study guide)

22. The most important point students should make is that Latin America and the Caribbean, from the colonial period on, developed in response to the economic needs of external powers. The region's economic development was conditioned, first, by a history of dependency on external powers, especially the industrial powers of Western Europe, the United States, and Japan; second, by the focus on export of raw materials (minerals and agricultural products); and third, by the delayed and incomplete nature of industrialization. (textbook, study guide)

23. The theme of nationalism was prominent in most of the programs in the series, providing students with a broad range of choices for illustrating the continuing importance of the issue. Examples they might cite could include the Falklands/Malvinas war ("Garden of Forking Paths"); Mexican concerns over the potential impact of the proposed North American Free Trade Agreement ("Continent on the Move"); sensitivities within the Dominican Republic over the issue of national identity ("Mirrors of the Heart"); the dilemma of regional artists in choosing how to address local or national themes ("Builders of Images"); the appeal to nationalism voiced by many of the region's revolutionary movements ("Fire in the Mind"); or the reaction to U.S. emphasis on fighting the war on drugs ("Get Up, Stand Up"). (program)

24. Look for students to recognize that despite the enormous variation among these countries, they are all affected to at least some degree by certain common factors. Students could cite the fact that all four countries face the need to address persistent domestic socioeconomic inequalities, or that, for each nation, future economic prospects will continue to be tied to developments in the global economy. Individual characteristics cited could be many; students should demonstrate an understanding of the diversity of these four

countries in terms of language, culture, size, resources, colonial legacy, economic and political development, and history of relations with the United States. (program, anthology, textbook, study guide)

25. Students could mention any of several changes depicted in Unit 12's program and anthology selections. For example, they might recall that recent immigrants to this country from Latin America and the Caribbean have usually been relegated to low-paying service sector employment. For women, even those who come to the United States as well-educated professionals, this has frequently meant working as nannies or housemaids, a very difficult adjustment. At the same time, the women profiled in Unit 12 were examples of the impact that life in the United States has had on their role and self-identity. Latin American and Caribbean women have been very active community and political leaders in this country, and have been at the forefront of struggles to improve life in the United States for their families while also retaining a sense of their unique cultural heritage. Some of the women profiled in Unit 12 also spoke of the changes in their relationships with their partners, and of the fact that they turned away from more traditional women's roles to take on leadership positions in their new communities. (program, anthology, study guide)

Essay Questions

1. Students are being asked to make the connection between domestic policy decisions and the manner in which Latin America and the Caribbean were, and continue to be, integrated into the world economy. They should recall from the early units of the course that ISI policies were developed in response to several factors affecting the region's economic development. First, the basis for the region's relationship to the more industrialized nations was the trade of primary products from Latin America and the Caribbean in exchange for manufactured goods and capital from Europe and the United States. Industrialization had occurred to only a very limited degree and was

restricted to particular sectors that had received significant foreign investment. The vulnerabilities of this position were made extremely clear by the Great Depression of the 1930s, which drastically reduced both the markets for Latin American and Caribbean goods and the availability of the manufactured goods they imported. The resulting policy attempted to accelerate the region's industrialization in order to "catch up" to the rest of the world, using government subsidies and protective trade measures to encourage domestic industries. Similarly, the return to liberal economic policies in recent decades, especially the reliance on export-led growth (this time characterized by the export of manufactured and assembled goods in addition to modern agricultural products), is an effort to respond to the restructuring of the world economy as well as to the inefficiency of import-substituting industries and the region's swollen foreign debt. Latin America and the Caribbean continue to be dependent to a large degree on events and decisions made outside the region, and continue to fashion economic policy measures accordingly.

2. Students should recognize that the middle class throughout much of Latin America is significantly different from the middle class in the United States. As explained in the textbook, the middle class in Latin America is smaller and not as old, historically speaking, as the U.S. middle class. It tends to feel caught between the demands of the majority, the lower or "popular" classes, and the monopolization of wealth by the small elite class. The middle class tends to support the democratic process and reform policies as long as it does not feel its own hard-won status deteriorating. However, when economic or political crises threaten to undermine its own position, when the demands of the poor become too radical, or when the political system no longer appears to respond to its concerns, the middle class has frequently thrown its support to military governments. It is for this reason that the growth of the middle class alone cannot be seen as a panacea to end the domestic tensions within Latin American societies.

3. The student's answer should exhibit familiarity with the programs' topics and with the concept

of innovation in the Americas. There are many examples that could potentially be selected by students; the following list is only suggestive, not exhaustive. In the area of urban growth, they could mention the community soup kitchens of Chile ("In Women's Hands") or the self-help housing developments in Mexico City depicted in "Continent on the Move." In the area of race relations, one unique aspect might be the intermingling of races in the region that has produced a wide range of culturally diverse people with a mixed heritage from European, African, and indigenous roots ("Mirrors of the Heart"). For cultural contributions, any of the artists' work discussed in "Builders of Images" or, here in the United States, from "The Americans" would be good examples. In the area of religious beliefs, students could mention the religions practiced in the region that are a blend of African, indigenous, and European influences, or the fact that many in Latin America and the Caribbean tend to practice more than one religion according to their needs ("Miracles Are Not Enough"). "In Women's Hands" and "The Americans" provide many examples of women who have expanded upon traditional concerns with family and community to become active and dynamic community organizers and political leaders. The topic of social change was covered in many units, from internal migration ("Continent on the Move"), to revolutionary movements ("Fire in the Mind"), to efforts by artists, religious institutions, business leaders, popular organizations, and governments themselves to advocate for change. Using their own experiences as well as information from "The Americans," students could discuss the influence of Latin American and Caribbean culture on dance, popular music, food, festivals, cinema, or other area of their choice.

4. There is no one correct answer to the question. Students should demonstrate a thorough understanding of the issues that continue to link the northern and southern parts of the Western Hemisphere. They should be sensitive to the impact that decisions made in Washington will have in the region, and how those policy recommendations will be perceived by Latin American and Caribbean nations. Among the policy measures they might suggest are those

having to do with private investment, economic or military aid, migration policies, drug trafficking, or debt repayment. They could also cite U.S. interest in promoting the North American Free Trade Agreement, or the potential benefits in job creation represented by an increased emphasis on maquiladora-type assembly plants throughout the region. Above all, students should recognize that although U.S. influence remains strong, the United States will be far less likely in the future to be able to make unilateral decisions regarding its actions in the region. Cooperation, negotiation, and compromise are undoubtedly going to become increasingly important in the conduct of U.S. relations in the Americas.